THE ARTICLES OF CONFEDERATION

THE ARTICLES OF CONFEDERATION

AN INTERPRETATION OF THE
SOCIAL-CONSTITUTIONAL HISTORY OF
THE AMERICAN REVOLUTION
1774–1781

*

BY

MERRILL JENSEN

*

THE UNIVERSITY OF WISCONSIN PRESS

Published 1940
The University of Wisconsin Press
Box 1379, Madison, Wisconsin 53701
The University of Wisconsin Press, Ltd.
70 Great Russell Street, London

Printings 1940, 1948, 1959, 1962,
1963, 1966, 1970, 1976

Printed in the United States of America
ISBN 0-299-00204-7; LC 48-1595

Contents

Contents

Author's Foreword

THE PREFACE I wrote ten years ago for the third printing of this book had two purposes. One was to suggest changes I would make if it were not a photographic reproduction of the original edition. The other was to evaluate and answer some of the interpretations offered during the 1950s by a group of historians and political scientists to whom the labels "consensus school" or "new conservatives" were rather loosely and inaccurately applied. Other writers offered critiques as well. One approving essay had the words "flight from determinism" in its title, while a more critical one used the words "homogenizing our history."

The members of the so-called consensus school did not reach a consensus. Some argued that the Revolution was almost entirely ideological in origin, while others insisted that ideology played no part at all. Others argued that democracy did not become an issue in America until well after the Revolution, while some insisted that Americans had achieved a democratic society before 1776 and that the war for independence was fought to maintain it.

The question naturally arises: have any developments during the past decade had an impact on our approaches to history, and to the history of the American Revolution in particular? The answer is that there has been an impact to the degree that the interpretation of the American Revolution now seems to be swinging around full circle to a position similar to the one I took in this book in 1940, a position which was in line with that of the so-called "Progressive" historians whose work was declared outmoded by the consensus group during the 1950s.

The development of demographic studies in depth of local areas ranging from small New England towns to counties in Pennsylvania in the seventeenth and eighteenth centuries tends to support the assumptions of the Progressive historians about the increasing stratification of American society and growing social tensions in the years before the Revolution. Such demographic studies are adding a new dimension to our knowledge and we need many more of them before any final conclusions can be drawn.

The second development in the 1960s was the growth of violence, which made a shambles of the consensus view of the American past, at least in the eyes of people as far apart as the presidential commission on the causes and prevention of violence and the historians of the so-called "new left," who have been receiving considerable attention during the past few years. The new left historians, with their emphasis on the common man and on social discontent and tension, argue that the American Revolution must be "seen from the bottom up." They are thus taking a position somewhat akin to the Progressive historians, although the new left historians, with a few exceptions, have yet to produce research that in depth and soundness matches the fervor with which they argue their position.

In my own research during the past decade I returned to a detailed re-examination of the years 1763–1776, which resulted in the publication in 1968 of *The Founding of a Nation: A History of the American Revolution, 1763–1776*. A goodly portion of that book of more than 700 pages is devoted to a detailed analysis of the material covered so briefly in Chapters II and III of this book. As a result of that work I would change certain emphases and correct some minor details in those two chapters, but the basic conclusions remain the same. Those are that the social, political, and economic discontent that existed in America before 1776 did not disappear with independence, that that discontent continued to have an impact on American politics, and that the debate over the nature and purpose of the central government of the United States was one of the central issues of the age of the American Revolution.

What the future holds in the way of interpretation or reinterpretation of the American Revolution no one knows. It was suggested in a recent review that as a result of my work and the work of some of my students I might be the founder of a "new progressive" school of historical interpretation. The suggestion, while flattering, is appalling, for I am convinced that the pasting of labels on historians or groups of historians does little to help us understand their work, and nothing whatsoever to help us understand the past.

MERRILL JENSEN

Madison, Wisconsin
January 1970

Preface to the First Printing, 1940

THIS BOOK is in no sense a history of the American Revolution, and for that reason much that is familiar and traditional has been omitted. It is an account of the writing and ratification of the first constitution of the United States in terms of the ideas and interests of the men who wrote and ratified it, men who by word and deed showed that they knew precisely what the issues were. It is, furthermore, an effort to consider the Articles of Confederation in their proper relation to the revolutionary movement in the individual colonies, a movement that was unified in the revealing though seldom considered struggles between party and party in the two continental congresses. It is an attempt to describe the Articles of Confederation in terms of the concrete issues that Americans faced in 1776, rather than in terms of the unwarranted assumption that they are important only because their weaknesses made necessary the Constitution of 1787. The latter approach is hallowed by a hundred and fifty years of history-making and history-writing, but it is valueless in making a realistic appraisal of this significant but little-known portion of the history of the United States.

One cannot understand the Articles if one writes of them in terms of their weaknesses, or of the political naïveté of their creators. They can be understood only in relation to the internal revolution in the American states: the individual and group interests, the social cleavages, and the interstate conflicts that existed at the outbreak of the Revolution. Each of these involved problems that had to be reckoned with in creating a central government acceptable to thirteen independent states and the clashing social groups within them.

In the eighteenth century, as in every age, there were men who sought to further their material welfare by shrouding with verbalisms the basic issues involved. But there were also men, equally adept, who kept in clear relief the broad problems involved in such matters as the basis of taxation, the control of Western lands, and the location of ultimate political authority. Subsequent generations have lost sight of the fundamental constitutional issues fought out during the Revolution, and fought out on grounds that were material rather than nonmaterial, internal rather than international. The purpose here has been to relate only that portion of the story which ends with the adoption of the Articles in March, 1781. In a sense it is introductory to an extended history of the period from the ratification of the Articles to the ratification of the Constitution of 1787.

The sources for this study are the obvious sources for eighteenth-century American history. Many of them have been in print for decades. The exception, without which this work could not have been written, is the magnificent collection of letters of the members of the Continental Congress compiled by Dr. Edmund C. Burnett. Because most of the sources are familiar, no bibliography has been appended. The first citation of each work, giving complete bibliographical information, has been included in the index.

The author's debt to the many people who have in one way or another contributed to this study is very great. He wishes to thank especially professors Curtis Nettels, John D. Hicks, and William B. Hesseltine of the University of Wisconsin; Professor Edward McMahon of the University of Washington; James W. Stevens of the University of Washington; and Howard Clodius of Stanford University. Two of his students, James Ferguson and Whitney Bates, have given invaluable assistance in the preparation of the index.

Preface to the Second Printing, 1948

IN THE second printing of a book such as this it is a powerful temptation to review the reviewers. They have questioned very few points of fact, but they have now and then challenged the author's basic points of view. Sometimes this has been done with discrimination, but quite as often without clear understanding of the interpretation, and without due recognition of the limitations, qualifications, and even paradoxes set forth in both text and notes. The preface and first chapter discuss the problems of interpretation that must be faced by any writer who seeks to understand the Articles of Confederation as the product of political and social turmoil before 1776. Despite the stated qualifications, and what was hoped was scholarly caution, some readers have extended the argument far beyond what the text warrants, or have charged the author with interpretations that cannot be derived from the book either directly or indirectly. Therefore it seems well, since this is a photographic reproduction of the original edition, to add here a few words re-emphasizing some of the basic ideas and calling attention anew to some of the qualifications entailed by the necessarily sharp statement of the major theses.

The movement that produced the Declaration of Independence and the first Constitution of the United States was one of vast complexity. British policy was one of its focal points. The other was the conflict within each of the thirteen colonies among various social groups and leaders for the control of those colonies and, once a kind of colonial unity had been achieved, for control of the first and second Continental Congresses. It is this latter, the strife within the individual colonies, rather than British policy that is the central theme of this book. The strife was enormously complicated by personal, local, and sectional factors. Even a more elaborate statement of the many cleavages than has been attempted in this study would leave innumerable questions unanswered, just as it would fail to fit many facts and people into a pattern of the American Revolution as a democratic movement, and the Articles of Confederation as the constitutional product of that movement. The failure to take into account the complexities enumerated has misled some readers into seeing in the book support for or denial of particular economic and political ideas.

Those who bent their efforts, and a considerable amount of history along with them, to prove the constitutionality of the New Deal denied the fact of "state sovereignty" under the Articles of Confederation. They asserted the old doctrine that the union came before the states and was therefore all-powerful: state sovereignty never existed. From this doctrine they deduced that New Deal measures could not be invalidated by the Supreme Court, which turned to "states' rights" notions and a strict interpretation of the Constitution of 1787. In doing so it was obvious that the majority of the Court were motivated by political and economic predilections rather than concern for the true nature of the Constitution. The opponents of the Court, likewise, in their fervor to attain necessary ends, cited many analogies, the falsity of which they did not recognize. To them the argument of states' rights used to defeat national regulation of business enterprise was specious and unfounded in history. What they did not see was that the eighteenth-century counterparts of nineteenth-century vested interests likewise rejected the doctrine of state sovereignty. For them the only escape from a democracy which found expression in unchecked state governments was the creation of a national government which would limit if not destroy the sovereignty of the states. Despite the theorizing of later days, the fact remains that state sovereignty was a grim reality for those who objected to majority rule.

Critics representing the contemporary "left" have seen in the book's emphasis on the class-consciousness of eighteenth-century America support for their particular approach to history. What they disregard is the fact that this class-consciousness derived not from an industrial but from an agrarian-mercantile economy. The vast majority of revolutionary leaders and followers were property-owners or property-minded. This was as true of the artisans, the "mechanics" of the eighteenth century, as it was of the farmers, planters, and merchants. It was the artisan class, not the contemporary capitalists, who sought such measures as protective tariffs. Even the new hero of the left, Thomas Paine, wrote pamphlets for eighteenth-century capitalism, sometimes for pay but as often not.

At the other extreme are those who say or imply that democracy was not an issue in the Revolutionary era. They do not face the fact that some of the Revolutionary leaders who became the folk heroes of later generations were actually opposed to what they believed to be, and what they called, "democracy." Therefore they are unwilling to accept the idea that the Articles of Confederation were an expression of the democratic philosophy of the eighteenth century and that the Constitution of 1787 was the culmination of an anti-democratic crusade.

Those whose concepts of government are based on the assumption that it is a "science," and who think in terms of formal political structures, find it difficult to understand the ideas of men who looked upon government as an instrument for resolving the tensions among social classes, or "interests," which was the term commonly used in the eighteenth century.

There is no better example of this than the confusion that exists about the notion of "separation of powers." In the twentieth century it is somehow equated with the idea of democracy, or at least with "liberty." It is true that it sometimes had the same connotation in the eighteenth century, when the idea was used to combat the power of royal officials. But the opposite was true in Pennsylvania. Its constitution of 1776, providing for a one-house legislature and an executive without veto authority, was regarded at the time as completely democratic. Therefore in Pennsylvania the anti-democratic forces demanded a "separation of powers" as the only defense against an "unchecked democracy." They demanded a two-house legislature and a governor with veto authority. To men such as John Adams and James Madison the purpose of "separation of powers" was to give both "property" and "the people" a voice in government with a check upon one another. Only in this way could society prevent the exploitation which, it was assumed, would result should either side get sole control of the government. Thus, as used in the eighteenth century, the idea of "separation of powers" could be democratic or anti-democratic, or the result of sheer skepticism about the goodness of mankind. Only the immediate context gives meaning to the term.

Similar confusion has arisen over the term "political party." Too often the definitions born of the facts of one period are applied to an earlier segment of history without adequate understanding of the political assumptions of the men who lived at the time. In this study the emphasis that is placed on the continuity of "party strife" is to be understood not as a continuity of formal party organization nor even of a given set of constitutional formulae but as a continuity of social tensions that found expression in political activity.

No social group in the colonies except British officialdom was eliminated by the Revolution. During and after the war, as before, there continued to be division of opinion between farmers and merchants, dissenters and established churchmen, debtors and creditors. In other words, the concept of "party" in this study is the concept so clearly set forth by James Madison in the tenth number of *The Federalist*, the purest distillation of eighteenth-century thinking on such matters. Madison said that "a zeal for different opinions concerning religion, concerning government, and many other points, as well of speculation as of practice; an attachment of different leaders ambitiously contending for pre-eminence and power; or to persons of other descriptions whose fortunes have been interesting to the human passions, have, in turn, divided mankind into parties, inflamed them with mutual animosity, and rendered them much more disposed to vex and oppress each other than to co-operate for their common good. So strong is this propensity of mankind to fall into mutual animosities, that where no substantial occasion presents itself, the most frivolous and fanciful distinctions have been sufficient to kindle their unfriendly passions and excite their most violent conflicts. But the most common and durable source of factions has been the various and unequal distribution of property. Those who hold and those who are without property have ever formed distinct interests in society. Those who are creditors, and those who are debtors, fall under a like discrimination. A landed interest, a manufacturing interest, a mercantile interest, a moneyed interest, with many lesser interests, grow up of necessity in civilised nations, and divide them into different classes, actuated by different sentiments and views. The regulation of these various and interfering interests forms the principal task of modern legislation, and involves the spirit of party and faction in the necessary and ordinary operations of the government."

There are those, of course, who assert that some social groups were so shattered by the war that "class consciousness" vanished for a time. Actually it is dubious if any group in any state was so disrupted. True, a good many merchants became loyalists, and many key figures fled the country, but the war produced a new host of merchants and speculators whose interests were identical with those of the older merchant aristocracy. Furthermore, it is almost axiomatic that the *nouveau riche* are far more "class" conscious than the more sophisticated members of an old established order. The fact is that during and after the Revolution the patriot members of the old aristocracy and its rich new members fought hand in hand to hold their position, or to regain it in states where it had been lost. Even in those states where there seemed to be only a single party after 1776, close examination reveals sharp cleavages based on material interests as well as on essentially psychological factors.

A satisfactory terminology for such social cleavages when expressed in political life is extremely difficult to formulate. In only one state did definite labels exist at the time. Pennsylvania was divided into the "Constitutionalists," who supported the democratic constitution of 1776, and the "Republicans," who sought to undo it and who finally succeeded in 1790. As for the other states, the historian must struggle as best he can to designate those men who led, or who ruled, in the name of the majority, and their opponents who defended the minority and attacked what they called democracy, a word of ancient lineage with which most Americans were familiar. Contemporaries used all sorts of names to describe one another—Whigs, Tories, rabble, "mechanics," men of property, Presbyterian Republicans, and the like. Sometimes, as after the Revolution, both sides used a name such as Tory to describe their opponents in a political fight. The terms used in this study are "conservative" and "radical" and the precise content is carefully defined in note 23 on page 10. Additional definition has been supplied in a supplementary study.[1]

There it is stated: "It is difficult, though necessary, to provide some label for the opposing parties during the Revolution, because readers at once attach to such labels a content derived from their own experience rather than the content which should be derived from the facts of the period for which they are used. Those called conservatives in this study were members of that group who wished to retain British connection, but failing that, and choosing to become revolutionists, wished to retain the political and economic structure of the colonial period unchanged in the new states. The revolutionary group or party (the 'radicals') wanted independence from the beginning of the struggle. Their motives were extremely various. Some wanted power; some

---

[1] "The Idea of a National Government during the American Revolution," in the *Political Science Quarterly* 58:36on (September, 1943).

wanted political and social change in varying degrees; some had special grievances of various kinds. But on the whole one thing is clear: they disagreed with the 'conservatives' on the issue of the nature of the central government to be adopted for the American states. Most of the conservatives saw in a powerful central government the means of maintaining the status quo, and they saw this from the start."

The creation of a central government for the United States during the Revolution involved no new issues of basic importance; it merely intensified old ones and shifted emphases. That is to say, the old social cleavages which had produced political battles in the states long before 1776 became even more marked when the restraining, if often clumsy, hand of the British Empire was removed.

The kind of central government that was to replace British rule was as vital an issue as independence itself and the political line-up much the same. On the whole, those who were "radicals" in internal politics were for a weak central government, the "conservatives" for a strong one. There were exceptions and these are pointed out. An example was the South Carolina aristocracy, which was sharply "states' rights" in 1776 when it feared the "democrats" of New England, but which switched to an equally strong "nationalist" point of view after the war when the "radicals" of the state began to demand a greater share in its government. Another example was the conservative group in Massachusetts, which was not really converted to the idea of a national government until they were frightened by the outbreak of Shays's Rebellion in 1786. However, there was a strong group from the middle states who, from the First Congress on, consistently demanded a strong centralized government. Men like John Jay and James Duane of New York and John Dickinson and Robert Morris of Pennsylvania never weakened in their insistence on such a government until they got one in 1787.

There were some, of course, who shifted from one side to the other, but to assert that because men shifted sides, the sides themselves did not exist is to argue speciously. Throughout the book care has been taken to point out such shifts, and exceptions and contradictions. But when one has admitted all these, the basic fact remains that there were in the United States two sharply divergent bodies of opinion respecting the nature of the central government to be created for the nation— that is, whether it should be a "federal" or a "national" government.

Americans were thoroughly familiar with a central government before the war for independence. The British government vetoed legislation; reviewed judicial decisions; provided armed force to suppress social revolt and, after 1763, to enforce its will upon the separate colonial governments. Most Americans objected to British policies after 1763. The more radical of them soon denied that Parliament had any authority to legislate for them; others insisted that there must be centralized authority somewhere in the Empire. Until 1776 the proponents of centralized authority sought a constitutional definition of it by proposing plans of union for the American colonies. One such plan was produced by the Albany Congress in 1754. Joseph Galloway proposed another in the First Continental Congress. After the Declaration of Independence the thirteen states no longer faced the double problem of allocating power between Britain and the central government of the colonies, and between that government and the local governments.

Hence independence really simplified the problem by reducing the forces to two—the central government and the state governments. The basic problems involved were, first, the division of powers between the central and local governments; second, and fundamental, the location of sovereignty, of ultimate political authority—should it lie with the separate states or with the central government? The problem was as vital for the American states in the eighteenth century as it is for the United States in the twentieth.

On both issues the political leaders of the new nation divided sharply and they remained divided. The "radical" leaders and some of the "conservative" ones as well, had insisted that there was no legislature superior to that of the local colonial legislatures. This group was in control when the Articles of Confederation were written in 1776 and 1777. Quite naturally they wrote a constitution consistent with their beliefs and their professions. Most of them had programs they wanted to carry on within the states. Their motives ranged from the idealistic to the crassly selfish. But once given complete local autonomy in fact, the majority of the voters within a state could, if it so wished, do anything it pleased without fear of executive or judicial veto, and without the intervention of outside armed force such as British governors, judges, and troops had provided.

It was for this reason that the Articles of Confederation were declared to be the constitutional expression of the philosophy of the Declaration of Independence. The new revolutionary constitutions, however carefully they were written where the conservative element remained in control, made democracy possible. Legislatures achieved supremacy; governors and judges were subordinated to them; property qualifications for suffrage were for the first time successfully attacked; there were the beginnings of adequate representation according to population; established churches were on the verge of losing their privileges. Whatever we may think of such matters, or how little we see in them of "democracy" as we understand it, eighteenth-century citizens of the United States thought it was democracy, and some of them violently opposed it. Edmund Randolph in the Convention of 1787 summed up the fears of those who opposed what had happened as a result of the Revolution when he declared that the chief danger arises "from the democratic parts of our constitutions." His statement came at the end of a long campaign by one segment of American society to evade or check those dangers which some of them went so far as to call a "mad democracy." Thus, although some of the creators of the Articles of Confederation wanted only autonomy for their political groups, they unleashed the potentiality of majority rule within the states. It was, perhaps, the potentiality more than the actuality that motivated leaders on both sides in the years after 1776. As Alexander Hamilton remarked in 1780, "A great source of error in disquisitions of this nature, is the judging of events by abstract calculations; which, though geometrically true, are false as they relate to concerns of beings governed more by passion and prejudice, than by an enlightened sense of their interests. A degree of illusion mixes itself in all the affairs of society. The opinion of objects has more influence than their real nature."

Preface to the Third Printing, 1959

SINCE THIS is the second time that a book first published in 1940 is being reproduced by photographic means, and again with no opportunity for revision, the question is: What would I do if I had it to do over again? What changes are called for as a result of further work on the part of myself and other historians?

The main problem, as I see it, is not with the sections on the writing and ratification of the Articles of Confederation, although certain portions might well be expanded and made more explicit. Instead, the central problem is that of the endlessly fascinating, and probably endless, task of interpreting the American Revolution.

So far as this book is concerned, much of the debate centers around the concept of the "internal revolution." I often think, somewhat wryly, that if the chapter labeled "The Internal Revolution" had been called "Discontent within the Colonies, 1763–1774," little attention would have been paid to it. By "Internal Revolution" I meant, and still mean, that there was a great variety of discontent to be found within the American colonies in the years preceding the Declaration of Independence, that its existence had an impact on the revolutionary movement against Great Britain, on the writing of the Articles of Confederation and the first state constitutions, and on American political history after 1776. It seems to me that to underplay, to ignore, or to deny either the existence or the importance of that discontent is to miss much of the history of the period. While I do not pretend that my delineation, as set forth in 1940, is as precise as I would now be able to make it, I still think the broad outlines are valid. The central assumption is that colonial political society was undemocratic, that the war for independence was accompanied by a degree of democritization, and that in part it was the result of demands for political and social change both before and after 1776.

The idea that there was such an "internal revolution" has been challenged in various ways. There has, for instance, been a considerable emphasis recently on the American Revolution as a "conservative revolution" as contrasted with later European revolutions. Of course it was not like them. Americans did not lop off the heads of their enemies. They did not replace one economic system with another. Their political theory defended ancient British practices and constitutional ideals against the supposedly new. In writing their constitutions they retained the structure of government with which they were familiar. But the American Revolution cannot be judged as either "radical" or "conservative" in terms of assumptions derived from other and quite different revolutions, or from abstract notions of what a "real revolution" ought to be like. It was an *American Revolution* which began within the British Empire. It can be understood only in terms of the ideas and institutions inherited from England, and the ideas, institutions, and problems which were an integral part of American colonial society. What was "radical" and what was "conservative" about it can be measured only in terms of that context. More precisely, it can be measured only by comparing American political society after 1776 with American political society before 1776.

Another challenge to the validity of an "internal revolution" interpretation is the assertion that colonial political society was not undemocratic and therefore that there was no "internal revolution." It is argued in the case of Massachusetts, and by implication, of other colonies as well, that property holding was so widespread that virtually every adult male could vote. Therefore, the argument runs, Massachusetts was a "middle-class democracy," it was not ruled by an aristocracy of any kind, there was no "class struggle," and there were no internal disputes that would support an "internal revolution" thesis. The war for independence was to maintain that democracy against British assaults upon it.

It should be said first of all that in offering an "internal revolution" interpretation of the political history of the age neither I nor anyone who has approached it in this way ever argued that the primary issue was the right to vote, although it was certainly one element involved. It is equally false to imply that the "internal revolution" is a "class struggle" interpretation, at least in any latter-day sense of the idea. It must be remembered, however, that eighteenth-century Americans took for granted the existence of social classes in history and in their own society. Furthermore, many of them saw in the revolutionary movement either a potential or an actual "class struggle"—as they understood and defined classes *at that time.*

The basic issue raised by the emphasis on the presumed widespread right to vote in colonial America is the relationship of the suffrage to democratic government. We can agree, I think, that far more adult males had the right to vote in some colonies than older writers believed to be the fact. They were convinced that the colonies were undemocratic because the property qualification kept so many from voting. Oddly enough, those who insist that the suffrage was widespread do not question this basic assumption. They too rest their argument on the theory that the test of democracy is the number of people who can vote, an idea that runs at least as far back as the Jacksonian democrats who believed the quantity of democracy in government was precisely equal to the extent of the suffrage.

Is the assumption valid? Is this all there is to democracy? I doubt it, either in this age or any other, although it is obvious that the franchise is one essential element. The real question that has to be answered for eighteenth-century America relates to the way the governments did in fact function. What was the real structure of power as opposed to the theoretical structure? What men and groups of men actually determined policy and made the crucial decisions? Above all, how responsive were those governments to the will of the voters? If one asks such questions, it seems clear that ultimate power in every colony rested, not in the hands of the majorities of the voters, but in the hands of a very small group of men.

It makes little difference whether one calls them aristocrats, oligarchs, or political bosses, the fact is the same. They represented self-conscious minorities of planters, merchants, and officeholders as opposed to the majorities of the people in each colony whose votes at election time usually had little real influence on fundamental decisions.

The pattern of political reality varied from colony to colony all the way from self-governing Connecticut and Rhode Island to a proprietary colony like Maryland, but there are some remarkable basic similarities in the structure of real political power. The similarities are clearest in the royal colonies where the political aristocracies worked with or gave orders to the royal governors while at the same time their position depended on the authority which those governors derived from the British Crown. Ultimate power in these colonies hinged upon the appointive power of the governors who exercised it only with the advice and consent of their councils, which were also the upper houses of the legislatures. The councils, nominated by the governors and appointed by the Crown, were almost invariably, as a matter of British policy, named from among the wealthiest and most influential families. Not only, therefore, did a few families in each colony control the upper houses, they controlled also the supreme courts, the county courts, sheriffs, justices of the peace, militia officers, and minor officials, for the holders of all such offices were appointed by the governor with the advice and consent of his council.

This hierarchical power structure based on the governor's power of appointment reached down to the conduct of the most minute local affairs. It made itself felt too in elections to the lower houses of legislatures and it was only in these elections that the ordinary colonial voter had a chance to influence the functioning of the government over him. Any candid examination of such elections reveals that through patronage, pressure, and example, the political leaders of each colony usually had their way. They nominated relatives, political allies, and protégés, and it was rare indeed in an age of oral voting that the nominees were defeated after the leaders made their wishes known. They had also an inestimable advantage, forever denied to politicians of later days: they were "gentlemen," at least in their own opinion, and the ordinary American in the eighteenth century, however democratic the spirit of the times or the extent of the suffrage, usually followed the lead of his "betters," whatever he might think of them privately.

One of the most sweeping political results of the American Revolution was the wiping out of this hierarchical political structure based on the appointive power of the governors. As an inescapable consequence of the replacement of governments deriving their authority from royal charters by governments deriving their authority from the people, the governors, upper houses of legislatures, and supreme courts, and other offices, became subject, directly or indirectly, to the will of the voters.

Furthermore, the political and social prestige of the "gentlemen" declined during the Revolution. The endless attacks by the popular leaders on the political aristocracies before 1776 had an incalculable impact; and the doctrine of equality set forth in the Declaration of Independence was gladly seized upon by many Americans. Great were the laments that "gentlemen" were not treated with the respect to which they had long been accustomed and which they demanded. Some decades were to pass before the process was complete, but it continued inexorably to the point where "gentlemen" found it necessary to obscure their origins or their pretensions if they wished to further their political careers.

It matters little whether one calls the political and social process "internal revolution" or "political and social change"; change there was. For the first time in a century and a half, as a result of the break with Britain, the top levels of state governments became subject to the direct influence of voting majorities, and it was a great stride toward the democratization of American political life.

The stride was not taken without vigorous and sometimes violent political battles among Americans. There are those who would argue that agreements among Americans of the Revolutionary generation were more important than their disagreements; that the important thing was their fundamental agreement on principles, not their partisan warfare about principles; that American unity was more significant than American disunity.

I think that the last to agree with such an approach would be the leaders of the Revolution themselves. They took party politics for granted, they gloried in partisan warfare, and they used methods as invariably deplored but as invariably used by practitioners of the art of politics in every age. The best answers I know to those who would soften the edges of partisan animosity during the Revolution were given by two of its conspicuous leaders, one in 1762 and one in 1817. James Otis was blunt and unromantic in a pamphlet of 1762 defending the conduct of the Massachusetts House of Representatives. In the Preface he declared that "the world ever has been and will be pretty equally divided between those two great parties, vulgarly called the winners and the losers; or to speak more precisely, between those who are discontented that they have no power, and those who never think they can have enough."

Many years later, John Adams, who had survived endless political battles, quoted this Preface to a man who was writing a biography of James Otis. He called it frank, candid, and manly. By 1817 the trigger-tempered ex-president was more than a little irked with the historians of his time who were beginning to romanticize the Revolution and to forget the mighty political battles that took place. He didn't believe that a "true history" of the Revolution could ever be written, and he said as much to the many would-be historians who constantly appealed to him as a "source." "There is," wrote he, "an overweening fondness for representing this country as a scene of liberty, equality, fraternity, union, harmony, and benevolence. But let not your sons or mine deceive themselves. This country, like all others, has been a theater of parties and feuds for near two hundred years." He was writing about Massachusetts but what he said was equally true of most other states as well.

The leaders of the American Revolution were partisan leaders in politics, and on the practical side, they were amazingly skillful. In fact, I would venture that America has not seen their equal to this day. But this is not what raises them above the level of other political generations. What does were their political goals and their political ideas and their capacity for stating those goals and ideas in profound language. Not only were they practical men and political realists, they were students of political theory and of history. They were strong-minded men and it was natural that they should differ with one another as to what political goals were best for the new nation they founded. It is in those differences and the great debates and party warfare that followed upon them that lies the greatness and significance of the American Revolution in America.

Given such arguments and ideas concerning the American Revolution, and I have mentioned but a few, what changes would I make if revision were possible? As I see it, one of the major problems has been and remains that of terminology or descriptive labels to describe various groups of men and their political ideas and actions. Generations of scholars have used the terms "radical" and "conservative" in discussions of the Revolution. The problem is not so much the terms, if carefully defined, but that we tend to ignore the definitions and read our own conceptions of what is radical and conservative back into the eighteenth century. One trouble too is that one is always faced with men who switched from side to side in the course of political debates, or whose reputations changed with changing issues. For example, John Dickinson was consistent enough; yet in 1767 he was regarded as a "radical" for denying the authority of Parliament, while in 1776 he was the "conservative" leader of the opposition to independence.

I still think that "conservative" is the best way to describe the political aristocracies of the colonies. They had achieved colonial self-government; they wished to rule the colonies without British interference; and most of them probably wanted to stay within the British Empire. But after 1763 the British did insist upon interfering and the ruling groups were caught in a politically impossible situation. Most of them sincerely opposed British policies but at the same time their positions ultimately depended on British authority. Therefore they had to offer at least the appearance of public support of policies they privately deplored or they might lose their posts as councillors, judges, and what not. It was this dilemma of the old political leaders of the colonies that gave their political opponents, the "new men" as they were so often called, the opportunity to become the patriotic leaders of American opposition to Britain. As such they defended American rights and liberties, denounced British policies, and damned the old leaders, often falsely, as tools of Britain and enemies of America.

Originally I labeled these "new men" radicals. Today I think I would use the term "popular leaders," for the name was often used at the time and it avoids, in part at least, the reading of present-day connotations into the use of "radical" to describe eighteenth-century politicians. The name "popular leaders" was used at the time because such men appealed to "the people," or in the name of "the people," to support their double-edged attack on British policies and on the colonial aristocracies. Persistently they smeared the latter with the charge that they were aiders and abettors of British policies, and at times, with the charge that they had actually devised them.

But there is one fundamental qualification I would make as to the role of these "radical" or "popular leaders" in the purely internal affairs of the colonies. Further study has convinced me that while these leaders appealed to "the people," few if any men such as Samuel Adams, Patrick Henry, and Christopher Gadsden had any interest in or program for "internal" reform in answer to the demands of the people they led, either before or after independence. But the discontent and the demands for change remained a constant fact and independence offered the opportunity for attempting to bring changes about. As a result, even newer "new men" rose to lead the demand for political and social reforms, and some of the prewar popular leaders found that they had to follow if they wished to remain as leaders. Some seized the opportunity, while others revealed the truth of Thomas Hutchinson's remark that they were merely "outs" who wanted "in."

The most important addition that could be made to this book would be a detailed discussion of the political thought of the times. By this I do not mean the kind of political theory centering around the problems of the relationship between Britain and the colonies, for this has been done many times. I mean the political writing concerning the creation of new governments in America. This is an area little studied despite the wealth of material at hand.

One of the most significant areas of eighteenth-century political thought is that relating to the psychological impact of the possession of power upon the holders of political office. Why did the Articles of Confederation limit membership in Congress to no more than three years in any six? Why was the power and tenure of office of so many state governors so sharply restricted? Why the insistence upon annual elections? Newspapers in 1775 and 1776 abound with essays insisting that there must be annual elections, rotation in office, and constitutional restrictions on the holders of political office. Behind these essays lay the writings of such Englishmen as James Burgh, whose *Political Disquisitions* was published in Philadelphia in 1775 and was widely bought by revolutionary leaders. Another source was Thomas Gordon's and William Trenchard's *Cato's Letters*, a fourth edition of which was published in London in 1748. Americans learned from such works that men in power naturally lusted for more power and that restraints must be put on officeholders or the liberties of the people would inevitably suffer. Writings like these gave Americans a theoretical foundation for what they believed they had learned from practical experience. Ever since 1763 they had had dinned into their ears the dangers to liberty from such multiple officeholders as Thomas Hutchinson and his equivalents in other colonies. It is little wonder then that the men who wrote the Articles of Confederation and the first state constitutions placed so many restraints upon the political power of officeholders and so carefully proclaimed the rights of individuals against the power of government in the bills of rights attached to so many state constitutions.

A second important area of political thought, seriously neglected by most writers on the period, is the debate over the merits of democracy, or "popular government," which took place so vigorously in newspapers and pamphlets in 1775 and 1776. Some Americans were for democracy, some were against it, and both sides appealed to the history of the past to prove the rightness of their arguments. Like men before and since then, they found that "history proved" that what they believed in was right and justified their programs of action for the future. An extended analysis of this debate in relation to the writing of the constitutions of the time would, I think, support my original contention that the Articles of Confederation were the constitutional expression of the philosophy of the Declaration of Independence.

Finally, it would be well if verbal revisions were possible to qualify or to amplify ideas that were put too simply or baldly. I called attention originally to the complexities and to the exceptions that one must always be aware of. The more I study the American Revolution, the more I realize how necessary such awareness is. Conceivably one could write a book on the Revolution with one line of generalization at the top of each page, with the rest of the page consisting of footnotes pointing to the exceptions, qualifications, and contradictions. It might be history, but I doubt it.

THE REVOLUTIONARY BACKGROUND

I

The Problem of Interpretation

THE ARTICLES of Confederation have been assigned one of the most inglorious roles in American history. They have been treated as the product of ignorance and inexperience and the parent of chaos; hence the necessity for a new constitution in 1787 to save the country from ruin. In so interpreting the first constitution of the United States and the history of the country during its existence, historians have accepted a tradition established by the Federalist Party. They have not stopped to consider that the Federalist Party was organized to destroy a constitution embodying ideals of self-government and economic practice that were naturally abhorrent to those elements in American society of which that party was the political expression. The Federalist Party, as none knew better than John Adams, was the party of "the education, the talents, the virtues, and the property of the country." [1] As such it had no faith in the democracy made possible by the Articles of Confederation.

In the Convention of 1787 Edmund Randolph pointed out that the framers of the Confederation were wise and great men, but that "human rights were the chief knowledge of the time." Since then, he said, "our chief danger arises from the democratic parts of our constitutions. It is a maxim which I hold incontrovertible, that the powers of government exercised by the people swallows up the other branches. None of the constitutions have provided sufficient checks against the democracy. The feeble Senate of Virginia is a phantom. Maryland has a more powerful senate, but the late distractions in that State, have discovered that is not powerful enough. The check established in the constitution of New

[1] John Adams to Benjamin Stoddert, March 31, 1801, in *The Works of John Adams*, edited by Charles F. Adams (10 vols., Boston, 1850–56), 9:582. See also Charles A. Beard, *An Economic Interpretation of the Constitution of the United States* (New York, 1925), *passim*. Corroboration is likewise to be found in so conservative a work as Albert Beveridge's *The Life of John Marshall* (4 vols., Boston, 1916), 1:312–313.

York and Massachusetts is yet a stronger barrier against democracy, but they all seem insufficient." [2]

Alexander Hamilton was in profound agreement, and his views are equally illuminating of the character and purpose of the Federalist Party. "All communities," he said in the convention, "divide themselves into the few and the many. The first are the rich and well-born, the other the mass of the people"; if the rich and the well-born are given a permanent share in the government, they will ever after oppose any change in its form. He had only contempt for the popular belief that the voice of the people was the voice of God. The people, he said, seldom judge rightly.[3] In *The Federalist* he took the position that government had been instituted to provide "constraint" because "the passions of men will not conform to the dictates of reason and justice." [4]

John Jay did not elaborate his beliefs to the same extent as did his fellow Federalists, but contented himself with his favorite maxim that "the people who own the country ought to govern it." [5]

Men who believed thus undertook to convince their countrymen of the inadequacies of the Articles of Confederation. They pictured the Confederation period as one of chaos, born solely of the existing form of government. Many contemporaries were so convinced, and posterity has seldom questioned their partisan interpretation. The Federalist papers were only one portion of the propaganda [6] for the Constitution of 1787 which later historians

[2] Max Farrand, ed., *The Records of the Federal Convention of 1787* (3 vols., New Haven, 1911), 1:26–27. Madison's essay No. 10 in *The Federalist* is further proof that the founding fathers were consciously at work to destroy what they recognized as democracy and its evils. In that essay Madison demonstrates the advantages of a republic over a democracy.

[3] Farrand, *Records of the Federal Convention*, 1:299.

[4] *The Federalist*, No. 15.

[5] Frank Monaghan, *John Jay* (New York, 1935), 323.

[6] The development of Federalist propaganda may be traced in the contemporary press. Items with a tinge of special pleading began to appear before the convention met, continued during its deliberations, and burst forth in full strength once the Constitution was presented to the electorate. A few examples will suffice. On May 16, 1787, the *Pennsylvania Gazette* pictured Congress as the object of derision in Europe. On May 23 it stated that it was unanimously agreed that a strong executive power should be lodged somewhere, and predicted chaos unless something were done.

While the Convention was in session, a serious effort was made to prepare the public to accept its work without question. Two lines of argument much have accepted not as propaganda but as the true history of this so-called "Critical Period."[7] Thus the "great office" of the Confederation, as it has been portrayed, was to demonstrate the need for a more perfect union. The American people, having progressed slowly through disaster and trial, had made "great discoveries," which led the way to the Constitution. Faced with the decay of public virtue, the conflict of sectional interests, the almost total dissolution of the bonds that held society together, and the threat of anarchy, they had come to realize the futility of federal union and the necessity of national power.[8] Even the historians who have seen the Revolution as a "social movement" have not tied that movement to the political history of the times.[9] A recent essay in American constitutional history adds nothing to the old interpretation; on the contrary, it lays new emphasis upon the weakness and inadequacy of the Articles of Confederation.[10]

used were (1) that the members of the convention were the wisest and best men in the country, and their deliberations should therefore be accepted without question; and (2) that if their deliberations were not accepted, chaos would ensue. Opponents of the Convention were said to be inspired only by ulterior motives. See the *Pennsylvania Gazette*, July 25, August 8, 15, 1787. On August 29 the *Pennsylvania Gazette* stated in a manner since made familiar by use in political campaigns that "the pulse of industry, ingenuity and enterprise, in every art and occupation of man" stand still awaiting the results of the Convention. On September 5 the *Gazette* stated that every state had its Shays who was trying to do what Shays had done. On September 12 there were predictions of future horrors to be suffered if the yet unseen constitution was not adopted. Such propaganda did not fool all the people. A brilliant answer to it was that of "Brutus Junior" in the *New York Journal and Weekly Register*, November 8, 1787.

[7] The acceptance of Federalist propaganda as fact has not always been the consequence of ignorance. Randolph G. Adams states frankly that "too often has the 'propaganda' of one generation become the classic of the next. . . . So the work of ratifying our Federal Constitution produced a work of propaganda which is a classic. *The Federalist* is itself the frankest, the baldest and boldest propaganda ever penned — but what of it?" *Selected Political Essays of James Wilson*, edited by Randolph G. Adams (New York, 1930), 24.

[8] George Ticknor Curtis, *Constitutional History of the United States from Their Declaration of Independence to the Close of Their Civil War* (2 vols., New York, 1889, 1896), 1:84–85, 102.

[9] J. Franklin Jameson, *The American Revolution Considered as a Social Movement* (Princeton, 1926), 111–112.

[10] Andrew C. McLaughlin, *A Constitutional History of the United States* (New York, 1935), 137. "Almost everything points in only one direction — toward the need of a competent central government and the necessity of finding a system of union which could maintain itself . . . The whole story is one of gradually increasing ineptitude; of a central government which could less

Such analyses differ only in phraseology from the sentiments expressed in the Convention of 1787, the more measured indictment in *The Federalist,* and the violent attacks in contemporary newspapers.[11]

To approach the Articles of Confederation from the point of view of the difficulties and tribulations that followed the Revolution, real as these were, is to miss largely their true significance. Logically they can be approached only from the point of view of the social-political turmoil out of which came the Revolution and the independence of the colonies. With such a perspective the problems involved in their formulation and the ends sought by their adoption appear in a quite different light from that cast on them by hindsight and a too facile and willing acceptance of Federalist propaganda as historical fact.

The American Revolution was far more than a war between the colonies and Great Britain; it was also a struggle between

and less function as it was supposed to function; of a general system which was creaking in every joint and beginning to hobble at every step. The men who came to Philadelphia in the spring of 1787 had learned the lessons taught by the failings of the Confederation."

Professor McLaughlin's views of the Articles of Confederation have not always been so unfavorable. In *The Foundations of American Constitutionalism* (New York, 1932), 147–148, he says that the Articles were "by no means a failure" and that in the distribution of power they "on the whole approached perfection." In an earlier work, *The Confederation and the Constitution* (New York, 1905), 49, he states that the Articles "were in many respects models of what articles of confederation ought to be" and that their "inadequacy arose from the fact that a mere confederacy of sovereign states was not adapted to the social, political, and industrial needs of the time." Professor McLaughlin here recognizes that the fundamental difference between the Articles of Confederation and the Constitution was not one of degree, nor of apportionment of power, but of *kind.*

[11] The study of the British Empire has led to an attempt to approach the Articles of Confederation from the point of view of the problems of the empire. Such study has led historians to see in the American Revolution and the constitutional problems growing out of it little more than a reflection of the disputes between the colonies and Great Britain. This point of view has been best stated by Professor McLaughlin, who says that "the contents of the document are distinctly the products of imperial history, and they constitute (1) the first quasi-legal formulation of imperial existence." He then adds that they were "the immediate preparation for the ultimate real and full formulation in the Constitution." "The Background of American Federalism," in the *American Political Science Review,* 12:239 (May, 1918).

Charles M. Andrews holds that primarily the American Revolution was a political and constitutional movement and only secondarily a financial, commercial, or social movement; that at bottom the fundamental issue was the those who enjoyed political privileges and those who did not. Yet the conclusions which may be drawn from the history of social conflict within the colonies and applied to such matters of mutual concern as the writing of a common constitution are seldom drawn and applied. Ordinarily the Revolution is treated as the end of one age and the beginning of another; a new country was born; political parties sprang into being; political leaders, full of wisdom learned during the Revolution, sought to save the new nation from the results of ignorance and inexperience. So runs the story.[12]

But the story is true only in an external sense. The basic social forces in colonial life were not eliminated by the Declaration of Independence. There was no break in the underlying conflict between party and party representing fundamental divisions in American society. Those divisions had their roots in the very foundation of the colonies, and by the middle of the eighteenth century there had arisen broad social groupings based on economic and political conditions. More and more, wealth and political power were concentrated along the coast, in the hands of planters in the South and of merchants in the North. There were exceptions, of course, but by and large the colonial governments were in the hands of the economic upper classes. Exceedingly conscious of its local rights, the ruling aristocracy was willing to use democratic arguments to defeat the centralizing policies of Great Britain, but it had no intention of widening the base of political power within the colonies to accord with the conclusions which could be, and were, drawn from those arguments.[13] On the con-

political independence of the colonies; that in the last analysis the conflict lay between the British Parliament and the colonial assemblies. "The American Revolution: An Interpretation," in the *American Historical Review*, 31:230 (January, 1926).

[12] The classic statement of this point of view is John Fiske's *The Critical Period of American History* (Boston, 1888). A more recent statement of the same general thesis from essentially the same point of view is to be found in McLaughlin, *Constitutional History of the United States*, ch. 13, "The Tribulations of the Confederate Period: The Chief Problem of the Time."

[13] Charles H. Lincoln, *The Revolutionary Movement in Pennsylvania, 1760–1776* (Philadelphia, 1901); Carl Becker, *The History of Political Parties in the Province of New York, 1760–1776* (Madison, 1909); Arthur M. Schlesinger, *The Colonial Merchants and the American Revolution, 1763–1776* (New York, 1918). Other studies in which the course of the internal revolution has been treated are James T. Adams, *Revolutionary New England, 1691–1776* (Boston, 1923); Edith A. Bailey, *Influences toward Radicalism in Connecticut,*

trary, it had kept itself in power through the use of a number of political weapons. As wealth accumulated and concentrated along the coast, as the frontier moved westward and became debtor and alien in character, and as the propertyless element in the colonial towns grew larger, the owners of property demanded "a political interpretation of their favored position" [14] — that is, political supremacy — as a protection against the economic programs of debtor agrarians and the town poor. Encouraged by the British government, they gradually secured the political safeguards they demanded — property qualifications for participation in government and representation disproportionate to their numbers. The imposition of property qualifications for the suffrage and of even higher qualifications for office [15] effectively quelled the political ambitions of the greater part of the town population, and the denial of proportional representation to the newly settled areas prevented the growing West from capturing control of colonial governments.[16] Laws of entail and primogeniture insured the economic basis of colonial society, so much so that Thomas Jefferson believed that their abolition in Virginia would annul the privileges of an "aristocracy of wealth." [17]

But the economic-political aristocracy which Jefferson hoped to abolish had not always been characteristic of the American colonies. In early Virginia and Maryland every free man, whether

1754–1775 (*Smith College Studies in History*, vol. 5, no. 4, Northampton, 1920); Hamilton J. Eckenrode, *The Revolution in Virginia* (New York, 1916); Isaac S. Harrell, *Loyalism in Virginia* (Philadelphia, 1926); Henry M. Wagstaff, "State Rights and Political Parties in North Carolina, 1776–1861," in *Johns Hopkins University Studies in Historical and Political Science*, 24:9–31 (Baltimore, 1906); Richard F. Upton, *Revolutionary New Hampshire* (Hanover, 1936).

[14] Albert E. McKinley, *The Suffrage Franchise in the Thirteen English Colonies in America* (Philadelphia, 1905), 485.

[15] *Ibid., passim;* Frank H. Miller, "Legal Qualifications for Office in America, 1619–1899," in the *Annual Report of the American Historical Association*, 1899, 1:90–105.

[16] See Adams, *Revolutionary New England*, 161–163; Harry A. Cushing, *History of Transition from Provincial to Commonwealth Government in Massachusetts* (New York, 1896), 20–24; Lincoln, *Revolutionary Movement in Pennsylvania*, ch. 3, "The Pennsylvania Assembly under the Colonial Government"; Upton, *Revolutionary New Hampshire*, 26–29; William A. Schaper, "Sectionalism and Representation in South Carolina," in American Historical Association, *Annual Report*, 1900, 1:44–58.

[17] *The Writings of Thomas Jefferson*, edited by Paul L. Ford (10 vols., New York, 1892–99), 1:49. See also Richard B. Morris, *Studies in the History of*

holding property or not, could vote.[18] The first serious attempt to impose a property qualification for the suffrage came with the Restoration and it met with bitter opposition. One of the significant acts of Bacon's Assembly in 1676 was the abolition of the property qualification imposed by the Berkeley regime.[19] But the victory of the poorer elements was short-lived at best, and in Virginia, as elsewhere in the colonies by the end of the seventeenth century, the property qualification was an integral part of the political system. During the eighteenth century the tendency was in the direction of ever higher qualifications,[20] and colonial assemblies continued to refuse adequate representation to the expanding West. By the middle of the century a small minority of the colonial population wielded economic and political powers which could not be taken from them by any legal means. This political oligarchy was able to ignore most of the popular demands, and when smoldering discontent did occasionally flare up in a violent outburst, it was forcibly suppressed.[21] Thus democracy was decreasingly a characteristic of constitutional development in the American colonies.

Opposition to the oligarchical rule of the planters and merchants came from the agrarian and proletarian elements which formed the vast majority of the colonial population. Probably most of them were politically inert, but from their ranks nevertheless came some of the effective leadership and much of the support for revolutionary activity after 1763. In the towns the poorer people, although a small part of the colonial population, far outnumbered the large property-owners. Most of them — laborers, artisans, and small tradesmen — were dependent on the wealthy

American Law, with Special Reference to the Seventeenth and Eighteenth Centuries (New York, 1930), ch. 2, "Colonial Laws Governing the Distribution and Alienation of Land"; and Clarence R. Kern, "Influence of Primogeniture and Entail in the Development of Virginia," in University of Chicago, *Abstracts of Theses, Humanistic Series,* 5:289-292.

[18] McKinley, *Suffrage Franchise,* 27-29, 48-54.

[19] *Ibid.,* 30-33; William E. Dodd, "The Emergence of the First Social Order in the United States," in the *American Historical Review,* 40:217-231 (January, 1935).

[20] McKinley, *Suffrage Franchise, passim,* especially pp. 478-481.

[21] The most notable outbursts were Bacon's Rebellion in Virginia, the Regulator Movement in North and South Carolina, and the Land Bank controversy in Massachusetts. The latter did not bring on violence, but the elements were the same as later, when violent conflict actually took place. See John C. Miller, *Sam Adams* (Boston, 1936), 9-15.

merchants, who ruled them economically and socially. Agrarian discontent, too, was the product of local developments: of exploitation by land speculators, "taxation without representation," and the denial of political privileges, economic benefits, and military assistance. The farmer's desire for internal revolution had already been violently expressed in Bacon's Rebellion and in the Regulator Movement, events widely separated in time but similar in cause and consequence.[22]

To a large extent, then, the party of colonial radicalism [23] was composed of the masses in the towns and on the frontier. In Charleston, Philadelphia, New York, and Boston the radical parties were the foundation of the revolutionary movement in their towns and colonies.[24] It was they who provided the organization for uniting the dispersed farming population, which had not the means of organizing, but which was more than ready to act and which became the bulwark of the Revolution once it had started.

[22] Max Farrand, "The West and the Principles of the Revolution," in the *Yale Review*, 17:46–47, 51–52 (May, 1908); John S. Bassett, "The Regulators of North Carolina, 1765–1771," in American Historical Association, *Annual Report*, 1894, pp. 141–212.

[23] The terms "radical" and "conservative" in this discussion are not synonymous with "revolutionist" and "loyalist." That they are not interchangeable is obvious from the easily demonstrable fact that there were in internal colonial politics radicals who became loyalists, and conservatives who became revolutionists.

The interpretation of the Revolution is too often confused by the insistence that all revolutionists were radicals. Probably most radicals were revolutionists, but a large number of revolutionists were not radicals. The conservatives were those who — whether they desired independence or not — wanted to maintain the aristocratic order in the American colonies and states. The radicals were those who wanted changes in the existing order, changes which can be best described as democratic, though the term is necessarily relative.

By and large the majority of the colonial aristocracy was opposed to independence. This attitude was due partly to training, partly to self-interest, and partly — increasingly after 1774 — to the fear that independence would result in an internal revolution. The radicals, on the other hand, shifted from mere opposition to British measures to a demand for independence as they came to realize that only independence would make possible the internal revolution which radicalism in the colonies had come more and more to demand.

[24] On the towns as leaders in the Revolution see Lincoln, *Revolutionary Movement in Pennsylvania*; Becker, *Political Parties in New York*; David D. Wallace, *The Life of Henry Laurens* (New York, 1915); Ralph V. Harlow, *Samuel Adams, Promoter of the American Revolution* (New York, 1923); and John C. Miller, "The Massachusetts Convention of 1768," in the *New England Quarterly*, 7:445–474 (September, 1934).

Located at the center of things, the town radicals were able to seize upon issues as they arose and to spread propaganda by means of circular letters, committees of correspondence, and provincial congresses. They brought to a focus forces that would otherwise have spent themselves in sporadic outbursts easily suppressed by the established order.

Colonial radicalism did not become effective until after the French and Indian War. Then, fostered by economic depression [25] and aided by the bungling policy of Great Britain and the desire of the local governing classes for independence within the empire, it became united in an effort to throw off its local and international bonds. The discontented were given an opportunity to express their discontent when the British government began to enforce restrictions upon the colonies after 1763. The colonial merchants used popular demonstrations to give point to their more orderly protests against such measures as the Stamp Act, and it was only a step from such riots, incited and controlled by the merchants, to the organization of radical parties bent on the redress of local grievances which were of far more concern to the masses than the more remote and less obvious effects of British policy. Furthermore, there arose, in each of the colonies, leaders of more than ordinary ability, men who were able to create issues when none were furnished by Great Britain, and who seized on British acts as heaven-sent opportunities to attack the local aristocracy — too strongly entrenched to be overthrown on purely local issues — under the guise of a patriotic defense of American liberties. Thus, used as tools at first, the masses were soon united under capable leadership in what became as much a war against the colonial aristocracy as a war for independence.

The American Revolution thus marks the ascendancy of the radicals of the colonies, for the first time effectively united. True, this radical ascendancy was of brief duration, but while it lasted an attempt was made to write democratic ideals and theories of government into the laws and constitutions of the American states. Fulfillment was not complete, for the past was strong and in some

[25] Adams, *Revolutionary New England*, 252–255, 262–263, 298–299, 351; Charles M. Andrews, "The Boston Merchants and the Non-importation Movement," in the *Transactions of the Colonial Society of Massachusetts*, 19:181–192 (1916–17); Schlesinger, *Colonial Merchants*, 56–64.

states the conservatives retained their power and even strength-ened it.[26] And once independence was won, the conservatives soon united in undoing, so far as they could, such political and eco-nomic democracy as had resulted from the war. Nevertheless it is significant that the attempt at democratization was made and that it was born of colonial conditions. The participation of the radi-cals in the creation of a common government is all-important, for they as well as the conservatives believed that a centralized gov-ernment was essential to the maintenance of conservative rule. Naturally the radicals who exercised so much power in 1776 re-fused to set up in the Articles of Confederation a government which would guarantee the position of the conservative interests they sought to remove from power.[27]

The conservatives gradually became aware that internal revo-lution might be the result of continued disputes between them-selves and Great Britain, but they were not agreed on the meas-ures necessary to retain both "home rule" and the power to "rule at home." Some of them, like Joseph Galloway, sought to tighten the bonds between the colonies and the mother country and thus to consolidate the power and bulwark the position of the colonial

[26] E. Wilder Spaulding, *New York in the Critical Period, 1783–1789* (New York, 1932), ch. 5, "Politics." The conservatives in New York wrote the new state constitution. The city laborers and mechanics were disfranchised by freehold and leasehold requirements for the suffrage. "Freeman" status in New York and Albany was made more difficult to attain, with the result that in 1790 there were only 93 freehold voters in New York City, whereas in 1769 there had been 602 "freemen" voters. See McKinley, *Suffrage Franchise,* 217–218. However, the radicals captured the machinery of government and controlled the state until 1788. The Massachusetts constitution of 1780 was more conservative than the colonial charter. See James T. Adams, *New Eng-land in the Republic* (Boston, 1926), 90–91, 142–143. The power of the past is well described in John B. McMaster, *The Acquisition of Political, Social, and Industrial Rights of Man in America* (Cleveland, 1903), 14.

[27] See Robert L. Schuyler, *The Constitution of the United States: An Historical Survey of Its Formation* (New York, 1923), 26–27. The belief in the "nationality" of the states was an equally strong force against centraliza-tion. A state was a nation in the minds of its citizenry. Many of the conserva-tives, especially in the Southern states, shared this conviction during the Revolution. But in the South, as in the Middle states, when democracy threat-ened the home rule of the conservatives, they soon transcended their localism and became "nationalists." See William E. Dodd, *Statesmen of the Old South* (New York, 1911), 42; Wagstaff, "State Rights and Political Parties in North Carolina," in *Johns Hopkins University Studies in Historical and Political Science,* 24:14–15; Ulrich B. Phillips, "The South Carolina Federalists," in *American Historical Review,* 14:541–542 (April, 1909).

aristocracy. Other conservatives, like John Dickinson, denied that Parliament had any authority over the colonies and cared little for a close tie with the mother country; what they demanded was a status that was in effect home rule within the British Empire. Complete independence was to be avoided if possible, for it was fraught with the danger of social revolution within the colonies. As these men became aware that conservative rule had as much or more to fear from the people of the colonies as from British restrictions, they sought more and more for reconciliation with the mother country, in spite of her obvious intention to enforce her laws by means of arms. But they made the fatal yet unavoidable error of uniting with the radicals in meeting force with force. They made themselves believe that it was neither traitorous nor illegal to resist with arms the British measures they disliked.[28]

When independence could no longer be delayed, the conservatives were forced to choose between England and the United States. Some became "Tories," or "Loyalists." Others, the victims of circumstances partly of their own creation, fearfully and reluctantly became revolutionists. But in so doing they did not throw away their ideals of government. They were too cool, too well versed in checkmating radicalism and in administering governments in their own interest, to be misled by the democratic propaganda of the radicals. Not even John Adams, one of the few conservatives who worked for independence, was willing to stomach the ideas of Tom Paine when it came to the task of forming governments within the American colonies.[29]

The continued presence of groups of conservatives in all the states, weakened though they were by the Revolution, is of profound importance in the constitutional history of the United States. They appeared in strength in the first Continental Congress. In it their ideas and desires were expressed. They were still powerful at the beginning of the second Continental Congress, but gradually their hold was weakened by the growing revolu-

---

[28] See the "Second Petition to the King," July, 1775, the work of the conservatives in the second Continental Congress, in the *Journals of the Continental Congress, 1774–1789* (Library of Congress edition, 34 vols., Washington, 1904–37), 2:158–162; James Wilson, "An Address Delivered in the Convention of the Province of Pennsylvania Held at Philadelphia in January, 1775," in *Selected Political Essays*, 96.

[29] John Adams, Autobiography, in *Works*, 2:507–508.

tionary movement in the various states. They were strong enough, however, to obstruct the radical program during 1775 and to delay a declaration of independence in 1776 until long after the radicals believed that independence was an accomplished fact. In the bitter controversies which occurred the conservatives stated their ideas of government. In its simplest form their objection to independence was that it involved internal revolution. When forced to accept independence, they demanded the creation of a central government which would be a bulwark against internal revolution, which would aid the merchant classes, which would control Western lands, which would, in short, be a "national" government. In this they were opposed by the radicals, who created a "federal" government in the Articles of Confederation and who resisted the efforts of the conservatives to shape the character of those Articles while they were in process of writing and ratification.

It is against such a background of internal conflict that the Articles of Confederation must be considered. Naturally any statement of the issues or principles of the Revolution, however broad the terminology, is likely to be misleading, for, as John Adams wrote, "the principles of the American Revolution may be said to have been as various as the thirteen states that went through it, and in some sense almost as diversified as the individuals who acted in it." [30] There are inconsistencies and contradictions that cannot be forced into a logical pattern. Generalizations must therefore be understood as statements of tendencies and of presumed predominance rather than as unexceptionable statements of fact.[31] Thus when the Revolution is interpreted in the following pages as predominantly an internal revolution carried on by the masses of the people against the local aristocracy, it is not without recognition of the fact that there were aristocratic revolutionists and proletarian loyalists; that probably the majority of the people were more or less indifferent to what was taking place; and that British policy after 1763 drove many conservatives into a war for independence.

[30] John Adams to Mercy Warren, Quincy, July 20, 1807, in the *Massachusetts Historical Collections*, 5th series, 4:338 (Boston, 1878).
[31] See Crane Brinton, *The Anatomy of Revolution* (New York, 1938), ch. 1, especially p. 20.

Any interpretation of the American Revolution is subject to such qualifications, discomforting as it is to those who want complexities reduced to simple formulas. Any collection of facts must, however, be grouped around a theme, and particularly is this true of a movement having so many aspects as the American Revolution. Such grouping is unavoidable if one seeks to understand how the course of events, how the course of social revolution within the several states, often played a far more important role in determining political attitudes than did the more remote dangers of British policy.

In spite of the paradoxes involved one may still maintain that the Revolution was essentially, though relatively, a democratic movement within the thirteen American colonies, and that its significance for the political and constitutional history of the United States lay in its tendency to elevate the political and economic status of the majority of the people. The Articles of Confederation were the constitutional expression of this movement and the embodiment in governmental form of the philosophy of the Declaration of Independence.

II

The Internal Revolution

THE ARTICLES of Confederation were written by men many of whom rose to leadership as a result of the tempestuous local political battles fought in the years before the Revolution. Most of these new leaders gained power because they voiced the animosities and thus won the support of the discontented — the masses in the towns and the farmers of the backcountry —, who in most of the states won the right to express themselves politically, or were able to force concessions where the conservative element remained in control of the new governments created.

When it came to the formation of a common government for all the states, the radicals were guided by experience and by certain political ideas. Experience had taught them to dislike the colonial governing classes and to fear the concentration of wealth and political power. Their political philosophy taught that governments exercising power over wide areas were inherently undemocratic in action. This distrust of the concentration and centralization of unchecked political authority was deepened by the fact that most of the revolutionary leaders were essentially local leaders whom necessity had forced into an international movement for independence but who continued to be guided and controlled by the exigencies of local politics. It is necessary, therefore, to turn to the revolutionary history of the individual colonies for an explanation of the many exceptions one must make to any generalizations regarding the revolutionary movement as a whole and the constitution it produced.

* * *

Pennsylvania offers the clearest illustration of some of the basic issues upon which the course of the American Revolution turned. In no other colony were the racial-political-economic lines so sharply drawn, nowhere was the ruling class so opposed to change or to concession, and nowhere was the political revolution so complete in 1776.

As the colony had grown in wealth and population, political control had been retained by the three old counties of Philadelphia, Bucks, and Chester, and the city of Philadelphia. By the middle of the century an oligarchy of Quaker merchants and lawyers was dictating most of the policies of government. Their instrument was the colonial assembly, control of which they retained by denying representation to the ever-growing west. Even when new counties were created, they were made so vast in extent and were allotted so few representatives in the Assembly that the rule of the east was never endangered. In the east itself the masses were prevented from threatening oligarchical rule by suffrage laws which excluded all but a small minority of the population. The right to vote was contingent upon the possession of fifty pounds in personal property or a freehold. Neither was easy to secure, at least in the east. In Philadelphia in 1775 only 335 of 3,452 taxable males had estates large enough to give them the vote.[1]

Opposition to the oligarchy was centered in the Susquehanna Valley and in the city of Philadelphia. The Susquehanna Valley, peopled largely by Scotch-Irish and Germans, was separated from the east by geography, by economic interest, by race, and by religion. Its natural market was the city of Baltimore, which very early improved roads to attract the trade of its northern neighbors, while the Pennsylvania Assembly refused to build roads or in any way to tie the west to the east.[2]

Aside from racial and religious animosities, the grievances of the west against the east were very specific. It carried a burden of taxation without adequate representation, which in 1771, when an excise tax on hard liquor was instituted, was opposed in a manner prophetic of the later Whiskey Rebellion. The Presbyterian Scotch-Irish were driven to desperation by the refusal of the Quaker Assembly to aid them in their ever-continuing war with

[1] Lincoln, *Revolutionary Movement in Pennsylvania*, ch. 3; J. Paul Selsam, *The Pennsylvania Constitution of 1776* (Philadelphia, 1936), ch. 1; McKinley, *Suffrage Franchise*, pp. 290, note 2, 291–292.

[2] Lincoln, *Revolutionary Movement in Pennsylvania*, ch. 2, "The Influence of German and Irish Immigration," and ch. 4, "The Growth of the Revolution in the West."

the Indians. The Proclamation line of 1763, which threatened to dispossess many westerners of lands already settled, was blamed on the Quakers. The pacifism of the Quaker merchants enraged frontiersmen, who suspected them of being moved more by a desire to maintain the fur trade than by humanitarian concern over the fate of the Indians.[3]

The western farmer could meet the eastern merchant on terms of approximate equality only if he could secure adequate representation in the Assembly. This too was the demand of the populace of Philadelphia, where government was in the hands of the same wealthy class as controlled the colony. The sources of urban discontent were even more immediate than those of the west. All through the century the merchants had tried by various means to overthrow the system of markets and auctions in order to get a monopoly of the retail trade. Finally, in 1771, they devised a scheme which led to the most startling outburst of popular feeling that occurred before the Revolution. They agreed among themselves to buy from none but vendue masters who would agree to sell in large quantities. It was obvious that to continue in business the vendue masters would have to meet the demands of the big merchants. It was equally obvious that the poor could not afford to buy in large quantities and would thus be forced to buy from the merchants, who had long shown a disposition to take a more than "reasonable" profit in fixing retail prices. The merchants likewise tried to check the activity of wandering peddlers. Fishing rights in the navigable rivers were restricted, a measure which the poor felt to be aimed directly at them. In the face of such events it was natural that the lawyer-agents of the merchants should be bitterly attacked by the masses of the population.[4]

The attempt of the Quaker element in the east to convert Pennsylvania from a proprietary into a crown colony was fought bitterly by the Presbyterians in both east and west. Though they had none too great a love for the Penn family, they knew full well that the creation of a crown colony would place them entirely at the mercy of the oligarchy. In this struggle John Dickinson led the proprietary party, which had the support of the west. Franklin, who, oddly enough, has since acquired a reputation as a democrat, was the agent of the oligarchy in England. A future

[3] *Ibid.*, 49–51, 72–74, 78, 104–113.   [4] *Ibid.*, 44–45, 81–96.

loyalist, Joseph Galloway, led its forces in the Pennsylvania Assembly.[5]

British policy was at once the occasion and the excuse for action in Pennsylvania. As in the other colonies, the propertied classes were strongly opposed to any acts of Parliament infringing upon their local independence or interfering with the profits of trade. But the arguments they advanced in support of their rights were a double-edged weapon that cut in favor of the unrepresented classes as well as colonial self-government. By 1775 the oligarchy began to realize that it was caught between the hammer and the anvil.[6] This became increasingly clear as a revolutionary organization was developed wherein the old restrictions on the franchise and county representation no longer held. The creation of a provincial congress gave the west a dominance in the colony [7] and deprived the three old counties of the hold they had had over the majority of the others. Yet the old Assembly continued to meet and to refuse concessions that would have weakened the radical program and enabled the Assembly to assume the leadership itself.[8] By thus refusing either to lead or to guide, the conservative party was thrown from power in June, 1776.[9] The radical party, temporarily unhampered, was able to write the most democratic constitution any American state has ever had.[10]

The conservatives, led by James Wilson, Robert Morris, John Dickinson, and others, opposed the new order so bitterly that they very nearly wrecked the government of the state and did in

[5] *Ibid.*, 100–103.

[6] *Ibid.*, 14–15. "Not until the eastern leaders realized that American independence meant the recognition of new forces within the colony, did the counties of Philadelphia, Chester and Bucks refuse to support the revolutionary movement."

[7] Edward Channing, *A History of the United States* (6 vols., New York, 1905–1925), vol. 3, p. 197, note 1. In 1775 the east had twenty-six members in the Assembly; the eight western counties, thirteen. Under the constitution of 1776 the situation was reversed; the east had twenty-four representatives and the west forty-eight.

[8] Selsam, *Pennsylvania Constitution of 1776*, chs. 3–4.

[9] The substitution of the provisional revolutionary government for the old colonial government is discussed in James E. Gibson, "The Pennsylvania Provincial Conference of 1776," in the *Pennsylvania Magazine of History and Biography*, 58:312–341 (October, 1934).

[10] Lincoln, *Revolutionary Movement in Pennsylvania*, ch. 13, "The Fall of the Quaker Government"; Selsam, *Pennsylvania Constitution of 1776, passim.*

fact render it largely ineffective in fighting the Revolution. The unicameral legislature, which they had considered satisfactory so long as it had been in their own control, they now criticized as the worst of all possible forms of government. Their proposal of a system of "checks and balances" as the remedy for all political ills was a thin disguise for their desire to regain control of the state. By 1779 they had made some political gains, but since they were a minority their control of a democratic government was bound to be precarious. Recognizing this to be so, they turned more and more to "nationalism" in the hope of gaining power and protection in another political sphere. They became more and more insistent upon the creation of a "national" government. Their program involved strengthening the Articles of Confederation, but when this failed they participated in a conservative political revolution which ignored the legal methods of constitutional change and created a government in harmony with conservative ideas and experiences.[11]

*   *   *

The same division between east and west existed in Maryland, but there the planters, more ardent in their opposition to Great Britain than the merchants of the North and more willing to make concessions, were able to maintain their customary control. The equality of representation awarded to the counties forestalled some of the discontent that arose in Pennsylvania.[12] There were, however, enough instances of democratic propaganda[13] and of violence on the part of the masses[14] to alarm those in power. Maryland therefore united with Pennsylvania in opposing independence as her planters came to fear that democratic rule might

[11] Selsam, *Pennsylvania Constitution of 1776*, ch. 4, "The Battle over the Constitution and the Organization of the Government"; Charles J. Stillé, *The Life and Times of John Dickinson* (Philadelphia, 1891), 205–209; Burton A. Konkle, *Benjamin Chew, 1722–1810* (Philadelphia, 1932), 201–203; W. Roy Smith, "Sectionalism in Pennsylvania during the Revolution," in the *Political Science Quarterly*, 24:208–235 (June, 1909); Burton A. Konkle, *James Wilson and the Constitution* ([Philadelphia], 1907), 17–19, 21.

[12] Lincoln, *Revolutionary Movement in Pennsylvania*, 171.

[13] Letter of January 28, 1775, from "A Merchant at Annapolis" to "His Friend in Philadelphia," in Peter Force, ed., *American Archives* (4th and 5th series, 9 vols., Washington, 1837–53), 4th series, 1:1194.

[14] The burning of the *Peggy Stewart* is an example. Schlesinger, *Colonial Merchants*, 389–392. After that event a "Gentleman" in Bladensburg wrote

be the result of separation.[15] As late as May 15, 1776, the Maryland convention instructed its delegation in Congress to oppose any declaration of independence and reiterated its belief in the desirability of the British connection.[16]

The fears of the aristocracy proved groundless. The Maryland constitution of 1776 was one of the most conservative of the period. The senate became a refuge for wealth and an effective brake upon radicalism, for its members had to possess one thousand pounds' worth of property, and they were chosen by an electoral college.[17] This continuance in power of the wealthy aristocracy had an important effect on the Articles of Confederation, inasmuch as it enabled the great men who had been land speculators to exercise political influence in the bitter controversy over the disposition of the Western lands.

* * *

Virginia, like the other colonies, had come to be dominated by an aristocracy, in this case an aristocracy of wealthy planters in the tidewater area, who regarded themselves as Englishmen and were as jealous of their local rights as Englishmen everywhere are said to be.[18] They ran the colony for their own particular benefit, they embezzled public funds,[19] and they used their control of the legislature to further their speculative schemes in Virginia's vast western territory. They were members of the established church and looked askance upon and even persecuted dissenting sects.[20]

West of the tidewater lay an area, much like that of western Pennsylvania, which during the first half of the century had been settled by Scotch-Irish and Germans. The grievances of this re-

his brother in Glasgow, on November 1, 1774, that "the common sort seem to think they may now commit any outrage they please; some of them told the Merchants yesterday, that if they would not sell them Goods, they would soon find a way to help themselves." Force, *American Archives*, 4th series, 1:953.

[15] Channing, *United States*, 3:196.

[16] Force, *American Archives*, 4th series, 6:463.

[17] Allan Nevins, *The American States during and after the Revolution, 1775–1789* (New York, 1924), 157–158. See Hamilton's approving comments on the Maryland senate in *The Federalist*, No. 63.

[18] Eckenrode, *Revolution in Virginia*, 3–10.

[19] Burton J. Hendrick, *The Lees of Virginia* (Boston, 1935), 105.

[20] William Wirt Henry, *Patrick Henry: Life, Correspondence, and Speeches* (3 vols., New York, 1891), 1:117–119.

gion were many. Its people were taxed for the support of a church they hated.[21] They were largely unrepresented in the colonial legislature, for the Virginia aristocracy was as slow as the Pennsylvania oligarchy to admit new people to power.[22] They resented the pre-emption of vast areas of land by men who had no intention of settling upon it, but were holding it merely for speculative purposes.[23]

The rise of this region to power was personified in Patrick Henry, who came to the House of Burgesses as the mouthpiece of "that poor region which stretches from Hanover Courthouse to Fredericksburg — the New Light Presbyterian, Baptist, and Quaker country." [24] Two others, Richard Henry Lee [25] and Thomas Jefferson,[26] who was eventually to replace Henry as the leader of Virginia democracy, joined with him in the attack upon the tidewater. Under Henry's leadership the dissenters were united against the established church and the planters themselves. A western county sent Henry to the House of Burgesses, where he soon won attention by his opposition to the Stamp Act.[27] Shortly afterward he and Richard Henry Lee exposed the peculations of John Robinson, speaker of the Burgesses, treasurer of the colony, and leader of the aristocracy.[28] This exposé won, for Richard Henry Lee at least, the undying enmity of the first families of

[21] Hamilton J. Eckenrode, *Separation of Church and State in Virginia* (Richmond, 1910), ch. 3, "The Dissenters." The Presbyterians had opened the way for the freedom of religion in Virginia, but by the time of the Revolution they had been accepted and had become fairly conservative. The Baptists, working largely in the tidewater and Piedmont areas, were the real disturbers of the established order and were treated accordingly.

[22] Thomas Jefferson, in his *Notes on the State of Virginia* (London, 1787), 192–193, shows the heavy weighting in favor of the tidewater which existed even under the constitution of 1776, a weighting that continued until the Civil War.

[23] Charles H. Ambler, *Sectionalism in Virginia from 1776 to 1861* (Chicago, 1910), 21–23. The settlers in western Virginia, like their fellows in Pennsylvania, saw in the Proclamation of 1763, Dunmore's War, and the Quebec Act the design of the tidewater to deprive them of homes and to subject them to the wrath of the Indians.

[24] William E. Dodd, "Patrick Henry," in the *Dictionary of American Biography* (20 vols., New York, 1928–36), 8:555.

[25] Hendrick, *Lees of Virginia*, 19–105. The support of a member of the influential Lee family gave the radical cause great strength.

[26] Dodd, *Statesmen of the Old South*, 1–24.

[27] Dodd, "Patrick Henry," in the *Dictionary of American Biography*, 8:555.

[28] Eckenrode, *Revolution in Virginia*, 16–17.

Virginia who had been party to the transactions of Speaker Robinson.[29]

From 1766 to 1773 Henry was an important influence in the Assembly.[30] In 1773 he was instrumental, with Lee and Jefferson, in establishing a committee of correspondence for Virginia, and thus was begun that intercolonial union which was so necessary to the achievement of radical aims.[31]

The attitude of the conservative party toward the final break with England, like that of conservatives elsewhere in the South, was somewhat different from that of the conservatives in the colonies where wealth was based on trade. Some of the Virginia land speculators, particularly those connected with the Ohio Company, were disturbed by the policy of limitation inaugurated in the Proclamation of 1763 and by the boundary line policy which followed in its wake. The encouragement given the Vandalia project by the British government was a hard blow to the Ohio Company group.[32] There was also the matter of debts owed by Virginia planters to British merchants. Granted that the evidence is necessarily circumstantial rather than conclusive, it would seem that the planters were aware of the benefits to be derived

[29] John Adams, Autobiography, in *Works*, 3:31–32.

[30] Dodd, "Patrick Henry," in the *Dictionary of American Biography*, 8:555.

[31] Henry, *Patrick Henry*, 1:159–162; Eckenrode, *Revolution in Virginia*, 32–33.

[32] Clarence W. Alvord, "Virginia and the West: An Interpretation," in the *Mississippi Valley Historical Review*, 3:25 (June, 1916): ". . . the interests of Virginia were directly injured. Land speculation in the west had been for years the most important interest of Virginia's public men and it is not strange, therefore, that this imperial encroachment upon Virginia's charter rights, this curtailment of the ambition of her citizens, drove the latter almost unanimously into the party of the American revolutionists. To them the very existence of their colony seemed at stake." Harrell supports this view. See his *Loyalism in Virginia*, ch. 1. Thomas P. Abernethy, in his *Western Lands and the American Revolution* (New York, 1937), 161, disputes the view that Britain's policy toward the West drove the Virginia planters into the Revolution, although he admits that there was a strong current of opposition in Virginia to the Vandalia scheme (p. 55). Elsewhere (pp. 72–73) he indicates that the tidewater magnates, whose chief interest was in the Loyal Company, seem to have had some understanding with the Vandalia group. But the speculators connected with the Ohio Company had no such understanding and they did object to the Vandalia scheme. Possibly it is not without significance that three leading revolutionary leaders in Virginia — George Washington, George Mason, and Richard Henry Lee — were intimately connected with the Ohio Company.

from separation, if one may judge by the alacrity with which those who were most heavily involved proposed the nonpayment of debts in 1774, and the unusual means they evolved of discharging those debts once the Revolution had begun.[33] Moreover, there was the constant factor of the sturdy independence which the planters had always maintained in their political relations with Great Britain. The attack on Massachusetts seemed to them a prelude to further attacks on the other colonies, and they saw themselves as Englishmen fighting for the rights of Englishmen.[34]

Whatever the motivation, when the time for decision came, enough of Virginia's old ruling class took the road to revolution to temper the force of radicalism. These planters became active patriots, but "with regrets." They hoped that the Revolution would stop short at independence and would not touch the framework of colonial law and society; that the colonial constitution and the colonial church would be continued in the new state. The radicals, on the other hand, hoped to establish a more democratic government.[35] The destruction of the established church, the abolition of entail and primogeniture, the easing of laws for the manumission of slaves, these are weighty evidence of the profound changes wrought by the rise of radicalism in Virginia.[36] Such encroachment on the established order alarmed the men who had prevented a drastic change in government during the writing of

[33] Harrell, *Loyalism in Virginia*, 27–28, 80–81. A law of October, 1777, provided that debts due British subjects from the citizens of Virginia could be discharged by the payment of depreciated Virginia currency into the state loan office. The first families and leading citizens took advantage of the opportunity to pay sterling debts in this fashion.

[34] Eckenrode (*Revolution in Virginia*, 38–40) denies the economic motivation and maintains that the Revolution in Virginia and the South generally was political in origin. Abernethy (*Western Lands*, 161) disputes the idea that debts owed to British merchants were a factor in the planters' attitude toward Great Britain. His reasoning on the debt question does not invalidate the facts set forth in Harrell's *Loyalism in Virginia*, which is not cited in his bibliography. See Force, *American Archives*, 4th series, 5:798–799, for the address "To the Inhabitants of Virginia," April 6, 1776, signed by "A Planter," which combines both points of view.

[35] Eckenrode, *Revolution in Virginia*, 161. Abernethy is in substantial agreement with Eckenrode. See his *Western Lands*, 161.

[36] The radicals were by no means satisfied with their achievements. Jefferson's proposed constitution of 1776 was more democratic than the one adopted. He continued to attack the conservative position after the Revolution as he had before. See Dice R. Anderson, "Jefferson and the Virginia Constitution," in the *American Historical Review*, 21:750–754 (July, 1916).

the constitution of 1776. Hence they too, like the merchants of Pennsylvania, turned to nationalism to protect them against the threats of the dissatisfied democracy of the frontier.[37]

* * *

The situation in North Carolina resembled that in Virginia in some obvious ways, but in more ways it was very different. There was the same division between tidewater and upland, and the same social and economic distinctions. As in Virginia, the great planters of the tidewater united with the merchants and professional classes of the small towns in a society similar to that of Williamsburg. The upland area was a region of small farmers — English, Scotch-Irish, and German — whose produce found an outlet through Virginia and South Carolina.[38]

The administration of the colony was so firmly in the hands of the royal governor that local self-government was practically non-existent, especially in the western counties, where sheriffs and court officials were the governor's appointees. This made possible a system of corruption and extortion unequalled in the other twelve colonies. Placemen were sent out to gather taxes. If the farmer had no ready money, as was usually the case, his property was sold, and he could redeem it only by paying extortionate fees to crooked sheriffs and court officials.[39] Demands for political reforms, bolstered by the refusal to pay taxes and by intimidation of the courts, had procured nothing but false promises. After a number of sporadic uprisings the discontent of the west culminated in the Regulator Movement, which lasted from 1768 until the battle of Alamance in May, 1771. The farmers' resort to arms

[37] Dodd, *Statesmen of the Old South*, 42.

[38] Delbert H. Gilpatrick, *Jeffersonian Democracy in North Carolina, 1789–1816* (*Columbia University Studies in History, Economics, and Public Law*, no. 344, New York, 1931), 12–19.

[39] Bassett, "Regulators of North Carolina," in American Historical Association, *Report*, 1894, pp. 144–155. See "An Address to the People of Granville County by George Sims," June 6, 1765, in the *American Historical Review*, 21:324–332 (July, 1916). The address indicates that the west was concerned with neither the form of government nor the laws, but "with the malpractices of the Officers of our County Court, and the abuses which we suffer by those empowered to manage our public affairs." Specifically, the grievances were the extortionate and illegal fees of lawyers and clerks of courts, the inability to secure honest representation in the Assembly, and the sale of lands and goods for a small portion of their value by officials who bought them with public money.

culminated in their pathetic defeat by the governor and the tide-water aristocracy.[40]

The failure of the Regulator Movement resulted in a situation that was the reverse of that in Virginia. In North Carolina many of the discontented frontiersmen were Loyalists, for the reason that it was their bitterest enemies, those who had helped to put down the Regulators, who led the opposition against British policy in 1774 and 1775.[41] Nevertheless western discontent remained, to become a powerful basis of radical political action within the state once independence was achieved. More than a fourth of the sections of the North Carolina constitution of 1776 dealt with and embodied reforms that had been demanded by the Regulators.[42]

Of all the thirteen colonies North Carolina had the most unpleasant relations with Great Britain. In 1754 the King in Council repealed twenty-six of its most important laws, thereby virtually demolishing the legal basis of the representative system, election customs, church organization, and land laws. The intention behind this move was to make the governmental system rest on the royal prerogative as embodied in instructions to the governors.[43] The question of indebtedness to British merchants was also a source of irritation and is said to have been especially important in North Carolina.[44]

Notwithstanding such irritations and grievances, the North Carolina conservatives were not eager for independence. Many of them were natives of the British Isles and were in close touch with friends and relatives there.[45] Above all, they deplored the "unhappy, the *impolitic*, and inhuman violences of the people" of the North, and the "most illegal and unconstitutional conduct" which by 1775 had taken the place of argument and orderly protest.[46] Joseph Hewes complained that "in these times, when every

[40] Bassett, "Regulators of North Carolina," in American Historical Association, *Report*, 1894, pp. 159–212.

[41] *Ibid.*, 209–210. Thomas Person was the only Regulator to play an important part in the radical party.

[42] Farrand, "The West and the Principles of the Revolution," in the *Yale Review*, 17:51–52.

[43] McKinley, *Suffrage Franchise*, 106–107.

[44] Schlesinger, *Colonial Merchants*, 359.

[45] Gilpatrick, *Jeffersonian Democracy in North Carolina*, 21–22.

[46] Archibald Neilson to James Iredell, New Bern, February 4, 1775, in Griffith J. McRee, *Life and Correspondence of James Iredell* (2 vols., New York, 1857, 1858), 1:233.

mechanic is employed in learning to kill Englishmen, it is impossible to get anything done right."[47] In June, 1776, James Iredell wrote a pamphlet in which he urged that a just and constitutional connection with Britain, "in spite of every provocation, would be the happier for America, for a considerable time to come, than *absolute independence.*"[48] This "Creed of a Rioter," written after the turmoil incident to the election of a congress to write a constitution for the new state, is an excellent example of the fear, disgust, and hatred aroused in the conservatives by the methods and ideas of the radicals.[49]

The conservatives accepted independence when forced to it, the vote for independence being unanimous. But the two parties split immediately and hopelessly on the question of what kind of government was to be created. As in the other states, the conservatives wanted to retain the old system of government, including a restricted suffrage and an independent judiciary. The radicals wanted a break with the past and a government more responsive to the will of the people. The constitution finally drafted was in many ways a victory for the radicals; for while it was undemocratic according to later standards, it actually worked as a democracy responsive to the wishes of backcountry farmers who wanted cheap land and paper money. Yet all too often this new democracy was manipulated by land speculators whose support of "the people" was a mask to hide their theft of the public domain.[50]

[47] Joseph Hewes to James Iredell, Philadelphia, March 26, 1776, *ibid.*, 1:274.

[48] *Ibid.*, 1:322. The pamphlet is printed on pages 283–323. It was not printed at the time, but was discreetly passed from hand to hand among the conservatives.

[49] *Ibid.*, 1:335–336.

[50] Gilpatrick, *Jeffersonian Democracy in North Carolina*, 22–26; *The Colonial Records of North Carolina*, edited by William L. Saunders (10 vols., Raleigh, 1886–90), 10:504–512, 1003–1013. Thomas P. Abernethy writes in his *From Frontier to Plantation in Tennessee* (Chapel Hill, 1932), 34, that "the leaders of the west who essayed to give voice to the will of the people were often uneducated and more often unscrupulous. In return for votes they frequently offered something which had the face of liberty but the body of corruption. They exploited Democracy in the name of the people and took their pay in public lands." On the other side, one evidence of the new trend was the temporary abolition of the poll tax, one of the worst abuses of the royal regime, and the substitution of a tax on real and personal property levied according to value. The poll tax was revived in 1779. Abernethy, *Frontier to Plantation*, 37, 39.

The numerical strength of the radical party lay among the small farmers, but its leadership came from a strange variety of men: dishonest land speculators like the Blounts; fiery democrats like Dr. Thomas Burke, a recent immigrant from Ireland; great planters like Willie Jones, one of the largest slaveholders in the state; and unique characters like Timothy Bloodworth the blacksmith. Such diversity of leadership resulted in many a shift in internal policy as the wheel of political fortune turned, but most of the radicals believed in the independence of the state and in the slightest of connections with the other states. Thomas Burke was to play a vital role in determining the federal character of the Articles of Confederation; yet he and the other radical leaders ignored them once they had been adopted. The conservatives, on the other hand, like those in Pennsylvania and Virginia, saw in the creation of a national government a possible escape from the unpleasant fact of majority rule within the state. When they gained control of the state, as they did after ten years of radical rule, they united with fellow conservatives from other states in overturning the Articles of Confederation.[51]

* * *

The situation in South Carolina had features in common with both the plantation and the mercantile colonies. The greatest fortunes were made in trade, but they were given social expression in the great plantation and in plantation life, for the merchants were also planters. Charleston was the center of the colony. Here the great trader-planters lived part of the time, and here also was a population of "mechanics," who formed the backbone of the radical party as they did in the towns to the north.[52] As was often the case in the other colonies, the mechanics were led by men from another class. The chief radical leader in South Carolina was a merchant, Christopher Gadsden.

The uplands had been settled almost entirely after the middle

[51] Gilpatrick, *Jeffersonian Democracy in North Carolina*, 21; James G. de R. Hamilton, "Willie Jones," in the *Dictionary of American Biography*, 10: 210–211 (New York, 1933); Wagstaff, "State Rights and Political Parties in North Carolina," in *Johns Hopkins University Studies in Historical and Political Science*, 24:14, 15. See also Wagstaff's *Federalism in North Carolina* (*James Sprunt Historical Publications*, vol. 9, no. 2, Chapel Hill, 1910), 1–8.
[52] Wallace, *Henry Laurens*, 44, 124, 151–154.

of the century by Scotch-Irish and Germans from North Carolina, Virginia, and Pennsylvania. For many years this area had little connection with the coastal region, although by 1776 the population outnumbered that of the dominant tidewater.[53] Frequent petitions for representation in the government of the colony had gone unheeded. The Regulator Movement which swept North Carolina had its origins among the discontented backwoodsmen of South Carolina. The west was first recognized by the tidewater politicians when they began organized opposition to Great Britain in 1774, but they so limited the participation of the west in the movement that it could do no more than voice its discontent. Thus, politically, the backcountry, which was so important in the colonies to the north, had little influence on the political situation in the colony before the Revolution.[54]

The sense of independence so keenly felt by all the colonies had come to be very strong in South Carolina. Many of its leading men were lawyers trained in England, and they had a profound appreciation of what they conceived to be the "rights of Englishmen," especially the right of self-government. The wealthy merchants and planters were ardently opposed to British policy, but they deplored the violence that attended the arrival of the stamps and the tea.[55] Almost to a man, the South Carolina merchants opposed the Revolution.[56] When independence was proclaimed in Charleston, Henry Laurens, who was in mourning for the death of a son, declared: "In truth, I wept that day as I had done for the melancholy catastrophe which caused me to put on black clothes — the death of a son, and felt much more pain."[57] The conservatives retained control of the state, however, and the constitution adopted in 1778 was in no sense radical, although men like John Rutledge thought so.[58]

[53] Schaper, "Sectionalism and Representation in South Carolina," in American Historical Association, *Report*, 1900, pp. 249–250, 277.

[54] *Ibid.*, 347–348.

[55] Wallace, *Henry Laurens*, 116–117, 159–174.

[56] Edward McCrady, *The History of South Carolina in the Revolution* (2 vols., New York, 1901), vol. 1 (1775–1780), 171–172.

[57] Letters of Laurens, February, 1778, in Wallace, *Henry Laurens*, 224–225.

[58] Nevins, *American States, 1775–1789*, 173–175; Robert L. Meriwether, "Christopher Gadsden," in the *Dictionary of American Biography*, 7:82 (New York, 1931). Gadsden was able to secure the disestablishment of the church and the popular election of senators. The conservatives then removed Gads-

The conservatives had kept such firm control of the state that they saw no advantage in surrendering power to a central government. At the time the Articles of Confederation were written the conservative party of South Carolina was distinguished by the intensity of its belief in the independence of the state, and this was its position until after the Revolution, when the radicals first threatened to get out of hand. Then, faced with the possibility of radical rule, and realizing that a political alliance with conservatives from other states would be a safeguard if the radicals should capture the state government, they gave up "state rights" for "nationalism" without hesitation. South Carolina planters and merchants not only favored a remodeling of the central government in the interests of conservatism, but for a number of years thereafter favored the exercise of broad powers under the Constitution of 1787.[59]

* * *

In New York the history of the outbreak of the American Revolution is in large measure the history of the conflict between a conservative party composed of wealthy landowners and merchants, and a radical party composed of artisans, mechanics, small shopkeepers, and the unfranchised generally in the city of New York. The farmers played little part in the preliminaries of the Revolution, largely because agriculture was dominated by the great landed families. The aristocracy had long used democratic arguments in its struggles with royal governors, and a certain amount of democratization of politics had resulted in the city, largely as a result of strife between family political machines. By 1763 a beginning had been made in the nomination of candidates for office and the formulation of political platforms to entice the support of the voters.[60]

The actual organization of radical and conservative parties came with the Stamp Act. Since mere approval of a Stamp Act Congress was hardly effective opposition, the merchants and landowners encouraged popular demonstrations to indicate the solidarity of

den from a place of influence by elevating him to the vice-presidency of the state.

[59] Phillips, "The South Carolina Federalists," in the *American Historical Review*, 14:541–542.

[60] Becker, *Political Parties in New York*, 14–19.

colonial opposition when the stamps arrived from England. Mobs are seldom governed by considerations of restraint and decorum, and the New York mob was no exception. It threatened violence and brought about the storage of the stamps in the fort. Then one night "the people" broke loose. They threw bricks at the fort, hung the lieutenant-governor in effigy, burned the governor's chariot, sacked the house of an officer, and wound up the evening with a raid on the houses of prostitution. Such diverse and enthusiastic activity on the part of the submerged nine-tenths was duly alarming to men of property. They united with certain ship captains — for sailors had played a large part in the night's activity — in restoring the peace and subduing the mob.[61]

The conservative reaction and the formation of two distinct parties dates from this riot of November 2, 1765. "A little rioting was well enough, so long as it was directed to the one end of bringing the English government to terms. But when the destruction of property began to be relished for its own sake by those who had no property, and the cry of liberty came loudest from those who were without political privilege, it was time to call a halt. These men might not cease shouting when purely British restrictions were removed. The ruling classes were in fact beginning to see that 'liberty and no taxation' was an argument that might be used against themselves as well as against the home government."[62]

The merchants, preferring legal means of resistance to British measures, adopted nonimportation agreements. This course of action was eminently unsatisfactory to the radicals, who regarded the discontinuance of business as tacit recognition of the validity of the law. They organized a party which they called the Sons of Liberty and tried to force the resumption of trade without the use of stamps, though less successfully than their more ably led brethren in Massachusetts. With the repeal of the Stamp Act their greatest excuse for agitation was eliminated.[63] This flurry of popular feeling had the effect of alienating some of the conservatives from the radical party. Though the merchants as a whole con-

---

[61] *Ibid.*, ch. 2, "The Stamp Act: Radicals and Conservatives."

[62] *Ibid.*, 31–32.

[63] *Ibid.*, 36–39, 40–41, 43–51; Virginia D. Harrington, *The New York Merchant on the Eve of the Revolution* (New York, 1935), 327.

tinued to favor radical methods of resistance, party lines were now broadly drawn between rich and poor.[64]

The internal strife engendered by the Stamp Act had no sooner subsided than the passage of the act quartering troops in the colonies and the Townshend Acts again raised the problem of resistance. As elsewhere in the colonies, all factions were agreed that there should be opposition, but not until the summer of 1768 did New York adopt a nonimportation agreement. There followed two years of increasing animosity between the factions. For if nonimportation was strictly enforced, it gave a monopoly to local merchants, who had overstocked their shelves before the agreement went into effect; if not strictly enforced, it offered a golden opportunity to smugglers. In any case, the poorer classes suffered more than the merchants, for nonimportation increased the prevailing business stagnation and unemployment, and it resulted in higher prices, which benefited the merchants at the expense of the people who were hardest hit. The Sons of Liberty revived and led the mobs in rioting and hanging effigies, while the property-owners soon swung to the support of the British government and voted supplies for the British troops in New York, an act bitterly attacked by the radicals as a sacrifice of the liberties of America.[65]

When the Townshend Acts were partially repealed in 1770, the men of property, moved by an increasing distaste for the popular movement, decided to modify the nonimportation agreement by making it apply only to the articles taxed. The radicals opposed any modification whatsoever, asserting that they would brand with public infamy "the miscreants who, while the odious Power of Taxation by Parliamentary authority, is in one single instance exercised, even dare to speak to the least infraction of the nonimportation agreement." But the merchants won a victory for their program by making a house-to-house canvass and the radicals were thereby discredited.[66]

From 1770 on, the division between the two groups was clear. The advantage lay with the radicals, who stood for the principle of absolute nonintercourse, which could easily be urged as the

[64] Becker, *Political Parties in New York*, 50–52.

[65] *Ibid.*, ch. 3; Schlesinger, *Colonial Merchants*, 115.

[66] Becker, *Political Parties in New York*, 83–93; Schlesinger, *Colonial Merchants*, 186–190, 217–218, 222–227.

only patriotic measure, based, as it seemed to be, entirely on principle. The merchants, on the other hand, were obviously actuated by self-interest and not by principle when they advocated the nonimportation of only those articles taxed.[67]

Nevertheless, until the passage of the Tea Act peace and conservative control prevailed in New York as in most of the colonies. All factions objected to that measure, but it was actually a boon to the radicals, who for three years had been without a specific issue. They revived the Sons of Liberty as an association sworn to brand as enemies all importers of tea and their abettors. The conservatives, thoroughly alarmed, tried unsuccessfully to discover if force would be used to prevent the landing of the tea. The first tea ship was stopped at Sandy Hook, but when Captain Chambers came to port — first denying that he had tea and then admitting that he had — the people did not wait for the "Mohawks," who were ready, but went aboard and dumped the tea into the harbor.[68] This destruction of property aroused all the old conservative fear of violence and resentment over the intrusion of the masses into political affairs.

With the passage of the Intolerable Acts the old issue of absolute versus modified importation was revived, and also the question whether the unfranchised should take part in the election of the extra-legal committees which were formed. The conservatives began to realize that they must join in the illegal movement if they were to direct the policy of the colony. The result was that the New York merchants were able to play a far more important role than those in most of the other northern towns. Recognizing that the activity of the Sons of Liberty was backed by wide popular support, the conservatives determined to capture the organization.[69] Through clever political strategy they secured the election of a policy-forming committee dominated by themselves, in a meeting in which Gouverneur Morris beheld his "fellow citizens very accurately counting all their chickens, not only before any of them were hatched, but before above one half of the eggs were laid. In short they fairly contended about the future of our Gov-

[67] Becker, *Political Parties in New York*, 93–94.
[68] *Ibid.*, 103–109; Schlesinger, *Colonial Merchants*, 291–294.
[69] Becker, *Political Parties in New York*, 110–111; "Extract of a Letter to a Gentleman in Scotland," New York, June, 1774, in Force, *American Archives*, 4th series, 1:302; Lieut.-Gov. Colden to Lord Dartmouth, *ibid.*, 342.

ernment, whether it should be founded upon aristocratic or democratic principles." [70] But the committee was soon faced with a far more practical problem. At its first meeting on May 23, 1774, it considered a letter from Boston demanding that New York join with Boston in absolute nonintercourse with England. The New York merchants were in a dilemma. They were firmly opposed to nonintercourse, but they knew that if they failed to support Boston they would lose control of the radical movement, so high did popular feeling run. On the other hand, if they agreed to absolute nonintercourse, they would lose all they had gained in their long struggle with the radical party in New York. Their only hope lay in a delay; therefore they wrote to the Boston radicals that absolute nonintercourse was a general problem which only a congress of all the colonies could settle. [71]

The call for a continental congress was a way out for the New York conservatives, who hoped to defeat radicalism by putting up to a body which presumably the conservatives would control the question of how British measures should be thwarted. They had no idea that the radicals would dominate the first Continental Congress, adopt complete nonintercourse, and transform mere opposition into the beginnings of a movement for independence. [72]

Many men were wise after the first Continental Congress, but in the months preceding it only a few foresaw the danger to the established order. One of these was Gouverneur Morris, who saw, possibly before any other of the conservative class, that it was the British connection that kept the wealthy in control, and that they could not remain in power forever unless they could keep the mob in ignorance. This they could not do, he wrote, for "the mob begins to think and reason. Poor reptiles! it is with them a vernal morning; they are struggling to cast off their winter's slough, they bask in the sunshine, and ere noon they will bite." The gentry feared this, he said, but he predicted that the committee appointed would deceive the people once more and again forfeit a share of their confidence. If this is kept up, "farewell aristocracy. I see, and I see with fear and trembling that if the

[70] Gouverneur Morris to Mr. ——— Penn, New York, May 30, 1774, in Force, *American Archives*, 4th series, 1:342.

[71] *Ibid.*, 297–298.

[72] Becker, *Political Parties in New York*, ch. 5, "The Election of Delegates to the First Continental Congress."

disputes with *Great Britain* continue, we shall be under the worst of all possible dominions; we shall be under the domination of a riotous mob. It is to the interest of all men, therefore, to seek for reunion with the parent state." [73]

Thus Morris saw in 1774 what others were not to see until 1775 and even 1776: that the British connection was the guarantee of the existing order. And, like many another, he preferred the existing order, even with irritating British legislation, to the possibility of an internal social revolution. As it turned out, the conservatives in New York were clever enough to keep control of the revolutionary organization and to prevent the overturn that occurred in Pennsylvania.[74] They opposed independence as ardently as did the Pennsylvania conservatives, but they kept control of the revolutionary organization long enough to write a conservative constitution for the new state.[75] Then they lost power to the small farmers united behind the leadership of George Clinton. When the Revolution was over, they engaged, like the conservatives in other states, in undoing the Articles of Confederation.

* * *

Most of the characteristics of the internal revolution were present in New England in an intensified form. Here, more than anywhere else, there was skilful leadership by politicians in the coastal towns, a sharp division between rich and poor, and great violence of mob action and of oral and written expression. Here the clash between radical and conservative groups came to a head much earlier than elsewhere, partly because of the relatively more democratic organization of local politics. While possibly a smaller proportion of the citizens possessed the colonial franchise than in the other colonies,[76] the town meetings were an arena in which

---

[73] Morris to Penn, in Force, *American Archives*, 4th series, 1:342–343.

[74] Becker, *Political Parties in New York*, ch. 11, "Independence and the New State Government."

[75] Spaulding, *New York in the Critical Period*, 84–101.

[76] McKinley, *Suffrage Franchise*, 487; Adams, *Revolutionary New England*, 161. Adams says that a large part of the rural population did not possess the colonial franchise and that "practically not a single workman, laborer, fisherman, sailor, mechanic or small tradesman had a vote, except in purely local affairs, and even for them the franchise was by no means as wide as it is frequently stated to have been." Lawrence H. Gipson, in his *Jared Ingersoll* (New Haven, 1920), 19, says that there were 115 freemen in New Haven in 1703, and that in 1784 only 215 of 600 adult males were freemen.

they could air their grievances and bring pressure to bear on delegates to the colonial legislatures.[77] Another cause of the intensity and early outbreak of strife was probably the small area within which the life of New England was confined. There was little room for territorial expansion and hence scant opportunity for distance to blunt the sharp edges of social animosity.

As in the other colonies, a wealthy ruling class had grown ever stronger,[78] until by the eighteenth century the conflict between radical and conservative parties was an extremely bitter one: between farmers who demanded paper money and protection from land-grabbers, and merchants and British officials who fought inflation and sought to exploit the land and its inhabitants.[79]

One of the most obvious causes of discontent in New England was the gradual change in the land system. Unlike the Southern colonies, New England had no easily accessible western land claims. Not only were migrations within her bounds definitely limited, but the opportunity for free land was gradually eliminated. In the seventeenth century communities wishing to move to the frontier had received land grants without purchase price and had divided them among themselves. During the eighteenth century, however, the western lands were being purchased as an investment for the increased wealth along the coast, at the same time that rising land values in the east were forcing many to seek wider opportunities for themselves and their children. Responding to the influence of men of wealth, colonial legislatures granted to wealthy speculators the lands which had once gone only to actual settlers. The speculators in turn sold lots to settlers, retaining some for themselves, which naturally rose in value as the settlers improved their own lands.[80]

[77] Adams, *Revolutionary New England*, 108.

[78] *Ibid.*, 253. "Wealth was increasing, but with even more rapidity it was concentrating. . . . This growing disparity of wealth between the few and the many, increased the feeling between the poor and the rich which we have already noted as steadily developing throughout the century." Ann Hulton wrote, "All the Luxury & Elegance that is in this Province is confined to Boston, & twenty Miles round, if you travel further it is necessary to carry your Provisions with you." Ann Hulton, *Letters of a Loyalist Lady* (Cambridge, Massachusetts, 1927), 45.

[79] Adams, *Revolutionary New England*, 108–109.

[80] *Ibid.*, 88–89, 143, 202–203, 259–264; Lois K. Matthews, *The Expansion of New England* (Boston, 1909), ch. 4; Roy Akagi, *The Town Proprietors of the New England Colonies* (Philadelphia, 1924), *passim*.

A practiced hand at this game of speculation was Benning Wentworth, governor of New Hampshire. In 1740 he had been a bankrupt merchant. When he became governor, he acquired the power to dispose of the colony's public lands. In two decades he granted more than two hundred townships, reserving for himself in each township a choice lot of five hundred acres and extracting from the grantees fees in accordance with their means. This procedure, which amounted virtually to selling lands to the highest bidder, was viewed with disgust by the actual inhabitants, who were thus exploited for the benefit of moneyed people both within and without the colony. By 1760 Wentworth was the richest man in New Hampshire and had his family well placed in important public offices.[81]

Such speculation in New England townships had an antidemocratic effect, for the original grantees usually reserved all political rights to themselves and refused to give the actual settlers any part in township government. In many instances the majority of the proprietors were absentee owners who refused to bear their share of taxation. An extreme example was the town of Maidstone, Vermont, all of whose proprietors remained in Connecticut, whence they conducted the affairs of the town without consulting the inhabitants. The inevitable result of such exploitation by the money-lending and investing classes was widespread discontent among the agricultural population.[82]

Another aspect of the struggle between rich and poor in New England was the bitter controversy over the question of paper currency. In so far as the assemblies reflected the will of the people, they were for paper money, while the governors and councils, as the representatives of wealth, were opposed to it. The most striking instance was the controversy in Massachusetts, where a "land bank" was started for the purpose of issuing paper money secured by land. The merchants immediately started a counter scheme,

[81] Lawrence S. Mayo, *John Wentworth* (Cambridge, Massachusetts, 1921), 21–22. Upton shows, in his *Revolutionary New Hampshire*, ch. 1, that conditions in New Hampshire were similar to those elsewhere in the colonies. Portsmouth, the home of the ruling commercial oligarchy, controlled the colony. Inadequate representation in the legislature was the chief means of maintaining that control.

[82] Adams, *Revolutionary New England*, 263–264; Akagi, *Town Proprietors of New England, passim.*

the "Silver Bank," to issue notes based on silver and to receive only those notes redeemable in silver or gold. The Massachusetts council favored the latter scheme, the Assembly the former. The preliminary attacks on the land bank failed and it began operations. An appeal was made to Parliament, which responded by making the Bubble Act of 1720 apply to the colonial situation.[83]

This futile attempt of the debtors to find a solution of their problem is significant from two points of view. In the first place, it showed the people and their leaders the essential identity of interest between the local aristocracy and the British government.[84] Secondly, it illustrates the inconsistency between profession and deed on the part of the conservatives. They were loud in their defense of law and order so long as they were in command of the situation, but the moment they lost control they employed means that were of dubious honesty, if not actually illegal, in order to regain it.[85]

Social and economic discontent found expression in religious as well as financial radicalism. The churches continued to defend the established order, but with less and less justification as the basis of New England society shifted gradually from a religious to an economic foundation. The "Great Awakening" was influential largely among the masses of the people. It was opposed by the aristocracy, who saw in it only another aspect of the movement whose expressed aims were to them unintelligible and whose manifestations they deemed worthy only of summary suppression.[86]

Aside from these general influences, certain local factors in each colony contributed to political upheaval. In Connecticut radicalism was largely agrarian. Politically and economically the state was divided between east and west. New Haven, in western Connecticut, was the commercial center of the colony and the seat of

[83] Andrew M. Davis, *Currency and Banking in the Province of the Massachusetts Bay* (2 vols., New York, 1900, 1901), 1:406–412; 2:130–235. The issue is not entirely clear, since some of the Boston leaders of the opposition to the colonial oligarchy were leading stockholders in the land bank. Sam Adams' father was one of the heavy investors and his property was later subject to confiscation as the affairs of the bank were liquidated.

[84] Adams, *Revolutionary New England*, 95–96.

[85] *Ibid.*, 157–158.

[86] John C. Miller, "Religion, Finance, and Democracy in Massachusetts," in the *New England Quarterly*, 6:29–58 (March, 1933).

conservatism. Eastern Connecticut, a region of small farms, was the center of radicalism. There the available land had been taken up early, and an outlet for the surplus population was needed. The result was the evolution of speculative land schemes, the most important being the Susquehanna Company, which tried to settle the Wyoming Valley in Pennsylvania on the uncertain basis of Connecticut's charter claims.[87] Disputes with Pennsylvania followed, during the course of which Pennsylvania appealed to the British government and succeeded in obtaining an order forbidding Connecticut to settle in the Wyoming Valley. The conservative party in Connecticut was more than willing to yield to the wishes of Pennsylvania and the British government, since its members had no stake in the land company. Because it was in control of the government of the colony at the time, it denied all connection between the colony and the land scheme and thus added bitterness to discontent in the hearts of politicians and farmers.

After 1763 the colony was divided in its attitude toward British policy. Furthermore, it was becoming plain that the radical party was now in large part identical with the thwarted Susquehanna Company. In 1765 Governor Fitch was one of the chief supporters of the Stamp Act, while Eliphalet Dyer, a leader of the company, was one of its chief opponents.[88] The situation was lucidly described by a contemporary, who said that the Sons of Liberty in the colony were the offspring of "several factions which have subsisted in this Colony, originating with the New London Society, — thence metamorphisd into the Faction for paper Emissions on Loan, thence into the N. Light, into the Susquehannah and Delaware Factions, — into 'Orthodoxy' now into Stamp Duty opponents."[89]

The next year the radical party won the elections. From this time until the outbreak of the Revolution the government of Connecticut was manned by members of the Susquehanna Company and was consistently opposed to all restrictive measures of the British government. The ousted conservatives went so far as

[87] Bailey, *Influences toward Radicalism in Connecticut*, chs. 1, 2; Gipson, *Ingersoll*, ch. 11; Adams, *Revolutionary New England*, 204–216.

[88] Bailey, *Influences toward Radicalism in Connecticut*, chs. 2–5.

[89] Quoted in Gipson, *Ingersoll*, 157.

to hold a convention in 1774, in a futile attempt to break the hold of the company on the government of the state.[90] It is significant that when the time came for the break with England, only one prominent member of the company opposed it,[91] whereas western Connecticut was the heart of loyalism.[92]

* * *

In Rhode Island, which, like the other Northern and Middle colonies, was a battleground for conservative merchants and radical farmers,[93] radicalism won victories earlier than in the other colonies. In 1755 it elected Stephen Hopkins, candidate of the agrarian north, governor of the colony and moved the capital to Providence, the rising competitor of Newport. There followed a struggle between the two sections that was almost smothered in the personal struggle between the rival candidates for the governorship, Stephen Hopkins and Samuel Ward. It was a struggle marked by vilification, corruption, and slander, and was terminated, so far as personalities were concerned, by the withdrawal of both from the race in 1768.[94] The two politicians became friends, but the two sections remained enemies. When the break with England came, Newport and the Narragansett country remained loyal,[95] whereas the agrarian north, which was in control of the government, declared Rhode Island's independence of Britain two months before the radical party was able to achieve that end in the Continental Congress.[96] Throughout the revolutionary period the Rhode Islanders were staunch defenders of democracy and state sovereignty.

[90] Bailey, *Influences toward Radicalism in Connecticut*, ch. 4.

[91] *Ibid.*, 247.

[92] *Ibid.*, 241–243, 246; George A. Gilbert holds that loyalism in Connecticut was the result of religious fears and jealousies. "The Connecticut Loyalists," in the *American Historical Review*, 4:273–291 (January, 1899).

[93] William E. Foster, *Stephen Hopkins, a Rhode Island Statesman* (Providence, 1884), 6–7, 16. Foster says that at first the contest was one between the South and North, "or of social inequality, (the merchants and planters of Newport and the Narragansett Country, against the farmers and mechanics of the country towns)."

[94] *Ibid.*, 8, 17–18, 24–33.

[95] Irving B. Richman, *Rhode Island: A Study in Separatism* (New York, 1905), 203–215.

[96] *Records of the Colony of Rhode Island and Providence Plantations in New England*, edited by John R. Bartlett (10 vols., Providence, 1856–65), 7:522–523, May 4, 1776.

The significance of leadership, of the political struggle between radicals and conservatives, and of the effects of British measures after 1763 are best illustrated by the political history of Massachusetts Bay. The colony was united in its opposition to British measures from 1763 until the outbreak of the war, but that it was a superficial unity is revealed upon closer analysis of the forces and the individuals at work. The merchants sincerely opposed any restriction on business and were willing to be loyal subjects of the empire whenever such restrictions should be removed. But they were faced with a radical movement centering in the town of Boston, a movement led by clever politicians whose motives were a mixture of desire for office, animosity toward the aristocracy, and a belief in independence of Great Britain. Whenever the merchants sought their cooperation against British measures, the radicals gave it gladly but used the opportunity to further their own campaign against the merchants. This fundamental cleavage between the merchants and the radical town population became ever wider, until in the end the merchants became the most ardent defenders of the British connection as the only alternative, so they believed, to their own destruction.

The lines of internal controversy were more and more sharply drawn after the passage of the Sugar Act, which revealed that the several groups in the colony did not see eye to eye when it came to modes of opposition.[97] After the passage of the Stamp Act in 1765, mob violence was directed against the aristocracy, much as in New York. Wine cellars were raided. Houses were sacked, notably that of the wealthy conservative leader, Thomas Hutchinson, the chief enemy of such radical leaders as James Otis and Sam Adams. Governor Bernard was convinced that the radical leaders of Boston were more powerful than the colonial government.[98]

In the General Court the radicals attempted to force through a resolution that business should proceed as usual despite the Stamp Act, whereupon Governor Bernard ended the session. The

[97] Andrews, "The Boston Merchants and the Non-importation Movement," in Colonial Society of Massachusetts, *Transactions*, 1916–17, pp. 168, 171, 180; Harlow, *Adams*, 30–36; Channing, *United States*, 3:4–5; Adams, *Revolutionary New England*, 304–305.

[98] *Ibid.*, 318–324; Harlow, *Adams*, 51; James K. Hosmer, *The Life of Thomas Hutchinson* (Boston, 1896), ch. 4, "The Stamp Act Tumults."

merchants then took a hand and entered into a voluntary non-importation agreement. This was approved by the radicals, but they still desired a positive nullification of the Stamp Act. It had gone into effect on November 1, and business was at a standstill. Using the Boston town meeting as a tool, they were able to bluff the customs commissioners into issuing qualified clearance papers. So successful were they in this move that by January, 1766, Thomas Hutchinson reported that the courts of common law, the Admiralty Court, and the Customs House were proceeding as if the Stamp Act had never been passed.[99]

This practical nullification of an act of Parliament was followed by other radical victories during the next few years. The radical organization in Boston was complete, with the Caucus Club as its executive body and Sam Adams as its guiding genius. It had the support of some of the merchants, notably John Hancock and John Rowe. The Caucus Club controlled the Boston members of the General Court and through them, in large measure, the colony as well. In addition the radicals had a "mob," a well-organized group of men under the direction of the shoemaker Mackintosh and two captains, which could be called into immediate and effective action whenever verbal appeals and ordinary political procedure proved inadequate to further the curiously contradictory aims of the radical leaders.[1]

In 1766 the radicals secured control of both the House and the Council. Thomas Hutchinson and his friends were ousted from the Council, which thenceforth acted more nearly in conformity with the wishes of the radical-controlled House.[2] But almost immediately the power of the radicals was threatened. The portion of the Townshend Acts[3] providing that colonial governors and judges be paid out of the proceeds from customs duties rather than from legislative grants threatened to remove from the legislature at a single stroke one of its most potent means of control over the executive and the judiciary. It was a threat to local

[99] Schlesinger, *Colonial Merchants*, 80–81; Andrews, "The Boston Merchants and the Non-importation Movement," in Colonial Society of Massachusetts, *Transactions*, 1916–17, pp. 196–201; Harlow, *Adams*, 53–60.

[1] Hosmer, *Hutchinson*, 103–104, 117–148; Harlow, *Adams*, 68–70.

[2] John Adams, Diary, June 26, 28, in *Works*, 2:194–196; Harlow, *Adams*, 72–77; Hosmer, *Hutchinson*, 117–118.

[3] 1 George III, ch. 46.

independence which radicals and conservatives alike could unite in opposing, but it was an especially bitter pill for the Massachusetts radicals who had so recently acquired power.

Opposition to the Townshend Acts was a foregone conclusion, but what form it should take at once became the subject of dispute. The radicals proposed nonconsumption of English goods. The merchants, recognizing that they as well as the English would be affected by such a policy, considered it almost as bad as the economic features of the Townshend Act themselves.[4] A writer in the merchants' newspaper, the Boston *Evening Post*, asserted that the nonconsumption policy was being advocated chiefly by "persons who have no property to lose, therefore subject to no danger on that account, and whose only hopes of living are founded in anarchy and confusion."[5] Nevertheless the radicals were able to induce the General Court to approve their policy. They also sent requests for approval to the other colonial legislatures.[6]

The merchants then came forward with a proposal to import only necessaries for a year if the other trading towns would cooperate in such a measure. Since Philadelphia would not do so, the proposal was dropped for the time being.[7] But when news was received of the impending arrival of British troops, the question of nonimportation was revived,[8] this time, apparently, under the leadership of James Otis and Sam Adams rather than the merchants. On August 1, 1768, an unconditional agreement was made to suspend the importation of all except necessaries during 1769. Two-thirds of the signers seem to have been shopkeepers rather than importers, and the importers who did sign were declared to have prepared themselves for the contingency by stocking their shelves with goods.[9]

[4] Schlesinger, *Colonial Merchants*, 106–111; Andrews, "The Boston Merchants and the Non-importation Movement," in Colonial Society of Massachusetts, *Transactions*, 1916–17, pp. 201–203; Harlow, *Adams*, 100–102.

[5] October 12, 1767; quoted in Harlow, *Adams*, 102.

[6] Adams, *Writings*, 1:184–188; Harlow, *Adams*, 106–107.

[7] Andrews, "The Boston Merchants and the Non-importation Movement," in Colonial Society of Massachusetts, *Transactions*, 1916–17, pp. 201–202; Schlesinger, *Colonial Merchants*, 113–120.

[8] Harlow, *Adams*, 115–116; Schlesinger, *Colonial Merchants*, 120–121.

[9] Harlow, *Adams*, 116–117; Andrews, "The Boston Merchants and the Non-importation Movement," in Colonial Society of Massachusetts, *Transactions*,

Another demonstration of the growing radical power was the colonial "convention" which convened after Governor Bernard refused to summon the General Court to deal with the impending arrival of British troops. Although it accomplished little, largely because the backcountry delegates were conservatives who refused to be led by the Boston radicals, it had one positive effect: it convinced the Boston leaders that the backcountry must be converted to the cause.[10] Accordingly they set about manufacturing the popular support they needed. Every possible occasion, such as the anniversary of the repeal of the Stamp Act, was used to further this end. Meetings were held at which radical ideas were expounded. "Otis and Adams," wrote John Adams, who had just dined with 350 Sons of Liberty, "are politic in promoting these festivals; for they tinge the minds of the people; they impregnate them with the sentiments of liberty; they render the people fond of their leaders in the cause, and averse and bitter against all opposers." [11] Newspapers were supplied with dignified arguments for those less susceptible to the influence of convivial gatherings.[12]

The radicals increased their strength steadily until the summer of 1770, though it was still centered largely in the area near Boston. At the same time ever-increasing mob violence created more and more fear among the conservatives.[13] Ann Hulton wrote that "most of the better sort of People" were "sensible of the great want of a reform, or alteration in the Constitution of Government here, for certainly the Tyranny of the Multitude is the most Arbitrary & oppressive; there's no justice to be obtain'd in any case, & many Persons awed by the people, are obliged to court Popularity for their own Security." Much more mischief would have been done "had not the Troops, arrived seasonably for our Protection, as well as that of every person of property." But very few of the people who associated with British officials would concede the

1916–17, pp. 204–206, 224–230; Schlesinger, *Colonial Merchants*, 120–121. Professor Andrews believes that the control of the nonimportation movement did not pass out of the merchants' hands until 1770. *Op. cit.*, 234–235.

[10] Miller, "The Massachusetts Convention of 1768," in the *New England Quarterly*, 7:445–474.

[11] John Adams, Diary, August 14, 1769, in *Works*, 2:218.

[12] Harlow, *Adams*, 141–142.

[13] Adams, *Revolutionary New England*, 366–367.

right of taxation to the British Parliament.[14] Mrs. Henry Barnes of Marlborough wrote that "these dareing Sons of Libberty are now at the tip top of their Power and to transact anything contrary to their Sentiments or even to speak disrespectfully of the well disposed, is a Crime equal to high Treason." She took comfort, however, in a conviction that they would "not be much longer imposed upon with a Cry of Libberty when they see Private property is only sought after."[15]

The radicals had achieved practical independence within the empire, as no one realized more clearly than their opponents. In 1769 Governor Bernard was recalled. The customs commissioners were driven out and returned only under the protection of troops.[16] Mrs. Barnes wrote that "the Merchants in Boston are now intirely out of the question in all debates at their Town Meeting which is caried on by a mob of the lowest sort of people" headed by some persons "that I never before heard off."[17] The merchants were determined to resume business once the Townshend Acts had been repealed. Like the conservatives generally, they had no desire to see a continuance of mob rule. There was a violent quarrel over relaxation of the nonimportation agreement. New York and Philadelphia merchants gave up nonimportation gladly, but "tho' 90 out of a 100 of the Merc^ts & traders here, want to do the same, yet they are terrified to submit to [the] Tyranny of that Power they at first set up, & are going to reship their British Goods."[18] Nevertheless the merchants persisted, and by September they were openly repudiating the leadership of Adams. Even so radical a merchant as John Rowe was alienated.[19] The conserva-

[14] Ann Hulton to Mrs. Adam Lightbody, Boston, April 10, 1769, in *Letters*, 18–19.

[15] To Mrs. Elizabeth Smith, November 20, 1769, among the Letters of Mrs. Henry Barnes of Marlborough, Mass., 1768–1784, in the Library of Congress, Division of Manuscripts.

[16] Ann Hulton to Mrs. Adam Lightbody, April 10, 1769, in *Letters*, 18–19.

[17] To Mrs. Elizabeth Smith, July 6, 1770, among the Letters of Mrs. Henry Barnes in the Library of Congress. She bewailed the fact that those who had formerly been non-voters were taking part in the town meetings.

[18] Ann Hulton to Mrs. Adam Lightbody, July 27, 1778, in *Letters*, 26; Schlesinger, *Colonial Merchants*, 232–233. See also Mrs. Barnes to Mrs. Smith, July 6 and 13, 1770, among the Letters of Mrs. Henry Barnes in the Library of Congress.

[19] *Letters and Diaries of John Rowe, Boston Merchant, 1759–1762, 1764–1779*, edited by Anne R. Cunningham (Boston, 1903), 201, 204–205; Adams,

tives won the elections in the fall of 1770 and kept control of the colony until 1773. Since there was no issue over which the radicals could stir up excitement, the party itself split up. John Hancock, John Adams, and Benjamin Church all deserted the leadership of Sam Adams. Hancock came out openly against him and very nearly defeated him in the elections of 1772, promising meanwhile never to be led astray by Adams again.[20]

Sam Adams continued his propagandizing, however, ringing the changes on the subject of British tyranny. The radicals seized upon anything that might be inflated into an excuse for direct action. The populace was told that the British customs commissioners had unlimited power to tax, including the power to tax land for the purpose of bringing over bishops.[21] Adams wrote a series of articles designed to whip up anti-Catholic feeling, declaring "that what we have above everything else to fear, is POPERY."[22] After the Boston massacre orators declaimed of "our beauteous virgins exposed to all the insolence of unbridled passion — our virtuous wives, endeared to us by every tender tie, falling a sacrifice to worse than brutal violence, and perhaps, like the famed Lucretia, distracted with anguish and despair, ending their wretched lives by their own hands."[23] In 1772 the radicals made a futile effort to inflate into an issue the payment of royal salaries to colonial judges.[24]

In spite of repeated defeats, the radicals set about to create an organization that meant ultimate victory for their cause. In this the Boston town meeting took the lead, and by the summer of 1773 committees of correspondence had been established in virtually every town in the colony.[25] More than any other, it was Sam Adams who really kept the spirit of radicalism alive, or at least vocal, in Massachusetts, and more and more he was forced to de-

Revolutionary New England, 379–380; Samuel Adams to Peter Timothy, November 21, 1770, in *Writings*, 2:65.

[20] Adams, *Revolutionary New England*, 379–380; Harlow, *Adams*, 163–168.

[21] Ann Hulton to Mrs. Adam Lightbody, Boston, June 30, 1768, in *Letters*, 13; Adams, *Revolutionary New England*, 378–379.

[22] Adams, *Writings*, 1:210. See also pages 202–212.

[23] Hezekiah Niles, ed., *Principles and Acts of the Revolution in America* (Philadelphia, 1876), 22.

[24] Ann Hulton to Mrs. Adam Lightbody, November 21, 1772, in *Letters*, 55; Adams, *Revolutionary New England*, 382.

[25] Schlesinger, *Colonial Merchants*, 255–260; Hosmer, *Hutchinson*, ch. 10, "The Committee of Correspondence"; Harlow, *Adams*, 191–202.

pend upon the "mechanics" for support.[26] He engaged in long dissertations, the conclusions of which were that Parliament had no authority over the colonies, since it had never been given to Parliament by the colonists;[27] that the authority of the General Court was supreme and unlimited; and that true liberty existed only if people were governed by laws made with their consent.[28]

By the summer of 1773 the radical organization in Massachusetts was complete, and the beginnings of an intercolonial organization had been made. The Virginia Assembly initiated this movement under pressure from its radical members and established a committee of correspondence to communicate with similar committees in other colonies.[29] The Boston radicals were delighted. The town meeting instructed the Boston members of the General Court that since the British government viewed the colonial assemblies with contempt, a redress of grievances was to be demanded and, furthermore, that it had "most sanguine expectations that a *union* of *Councils* among *Colonies* will fix . . . our rights on such a solid basis, as may intimidate our implacable enemies from any further attempts to invade them." [30]

But effective propaganda and an efficient organization were not enough to arouse the colony to support the radicals: an effective issue was also necessary. This was provided by the East India Act of 1773. The news that tea ships were being sent in accordance with its provisions reached Boston in September. In October the provincial committee of correspondence met and anticipated events a good deal by deciding to correspond with the other colonies as to what should be done in case of war. Hutchinson stated that the radicals talked openly of an intercolonial congress for the purpose of bringing the dispute to a crisis.[31]

By November the radicals had decided that the tea should not

---

[26] Adams, *Revolutionary New England*, 382; Schlesinger, *Colonial Merchants*, 254–255.

[27] Adams, *Writings*, 2:256–264.

[28] "American Solon," in the *Boston Gazette*, January 27, 1772, cited in Harlow, *Adams*, 178–179.

[29] Henry, *Patrick Henry*, 1:159–160; Edward D. Collins, "Committees of Correspondence of the American Revolution," in American Historical Association, *Annual Report*, 1901, 1:249–255. The occasion for this move was the establishment of a court of inquiry to investigate the burning of the *Gaspee* in Rhode Island.

[30] Quoted in Harlow, *Adams*, 202.   [31] *Ibid.*, 209–212.

be landed.[32] The consignees were asked to resign, and when they refused to do so, were treated with extraordinary violence, which did not end with the "Tea Party," a fact indicative of more than animosity toward the Tea Act.[33] Then the Boston town meeting adopted a series of resolutions written by Sam Adams declaring that the Tea Act had been passed without the consent of the people; that it nullified colonial assemblies and hence introduced arbitrary government and slavery; that the shipment of tea under its provisions was a violent attack on the liberties of America; and that since the merchants generally were opposed to it, the just expectation of the inhabitants of the town was that none of them would import tea until it was repealed. As late as October 28, however, the *Massachusetts Spy* complained that the merchants had taken no part in the opposition.[34]

It was true that the merchants were decidedly cautious. They had had too much experience with radical leadership to fall easily into another trap. Indeed, one of the most ardent supporters of the radicals among the merchants, John Rowe, had practically deserted the cause. He deeply regretted his appointment to the steering committee of "the Body," a mass meeting of the populace of Boston and the surrounding towns which conducted affairs after the last town meeting of the year.[35]

The consignees proposed a compromise: that the tea be landed and stored under the guard of a committee of the town until word could be had from England as to its disposal. The radicals, determined to force a crisis, refused to accede to this plan, ostensibly because it would involve the payment of the tax, which they called a "tribute." Governor Hutchinson refused to issue clearance papers so that the tea might be returned. The radicals now deliberately took a last defiant step and dumped the tea into Boston harbor.[36]

[32] Adams, *Revolutionary New England*, 389–390; Schlesinger, *Colonial Merchants*, 284–285.

[33] Ann Hulton to Mrs. Adam Lightbody, Boston, November 25, 1773, and January 31, 1774, in *Letters*, 64–65, 69–71.

[34] Harlow, *Adams*, 214–215, 217.

[35] John Rowe, *Letters and Diaries*, 256, November 30, 1773. He wrote that he was chosen a "Committee Man much against my will but I dare not say a word."

[36] Schlesinger, *Colonial Merchants*, 281–290; Arthur M. Schlesinger, "The Uprising against the East India Company," in the *Political Science Quarterly*,

The British government took drastic steps and passed what are known as the "Intolerable Acts." The radicals, delighted with the success of their "Tea Party," asserted that the Port Bill was the best thing that could have happened to America; that it would unite the colonies against Britain; that much was to be expected from the general congress which was to be held in the fall; that a rebellion might be expected "which will answer our purpose, & we shall become intirely free & Independant." They pictured the sad fate of the colonies if they submitted now. "Our Lands will be taxd — Popery introduced & we shall be Slaves for ever." [37]

At a town meeting held in Boston on May 13, 1774, Sam Adams was appointed to appeal to the other colonial governments for help.[38] In his letter he proposed the essence of the Association which was later adopted by the Continental Congress: the termination of import and export trade until the Port Bill should be repealed.[39] The Boston merchants were not enthusiastic, but they agreed to suspend commercial dealings with the empire if the merchants in other towns would pledge themselves to do likewise.[40] The merchants of Philadelphia and New York refused to do so, for they looked upon the Port Bill as a just, though severe, punishment for the destruction of property, a matter about which they were particularly sensitive.[41]

The Boston merchants then withdrew their promise to suspend commercial relations with Britain.[42] In the meantime they had been as busy as the radicals, for they had secured the signatures of most of the prominent merchants in Boston to an address to Governor Hutchinson lamenting his departure, disclaiming responsibility for the damage done at the "Tea Party," and expressing their willingness to pay their share of the damage.[43] On June 2, while they were in meeting, the merchants received the news

---

32:60–69 (March, 1917); Adams, *Revolutionary New England*, 389–392; Harlow, *Adams*, 215–221.

[37] Ann Hulton to Mrs. Adam Lightbody, July 8, 1774, in *Letters*, 75.

[38] Schlesinger, *Colonial Merchants*, 313.

[39] Adams, *Writings*, 3:107–109.

[40] Schlesinger, *Colonial Merchants*, 315–316.

[41] Philadelphia Committee of Correspondence to the Boston Committee, May 21, 1774, in Force, *American Archives*, 4th series, 1:341–342.

[42] Schlesinger, *Colonial Merchants*, 318.

[43] Force, *American Archives*, 4th series, 1:361–362. The news of the preparation of this petition had reached other ears. A protest against it, dated

of the act of Parliament changing the charter of the colony. John Rowe probably expressed their sentiments when he wrote in his diary that this would result in many evils and sour the minds of most of the inhabitants of the province. "I am afraid of the consequences that this Act will produce," he wrote. "I wish for Harmony & Peace between Great Britain Our Mother Country & the Colonies — but the Time is far off." [44] Nevertheless the merchants continued their meetings and finally, on June 8, presented to General Gage, Hutchinson's successor as governor, an address in which they again offered to pay their share of the damage done and deplored the violence. They asked Gage to recommend the opening of the port as soon as the provisions of the Port Bill had been complied with. [45]

The merchants' eagerness to make amends by paying for the destroyed tea was born of their fear that unless the port was opened civil war would result. But, as one of them wrote, "those who have govern'd the town for years past and were in a great measure the authors of all our evils, by their injudicious conduct are grown more obstinate than ever, and seem determin'd to bring total destruction upon us." [46]

Before the merchants had withdrawn their promise to cooperate in nonimportation, the Boston town meeting had ordered

May 24 (*ibid.*, 362–363), states that the address was handed around in secret, and that since it was suspected of being intended as a justification of the administration of Governor Hutchinson, "we hereby utterly disclaim said Address, and disavow a measure so clandestinely conducted, and so injurious in its tendency." It is significant that this protest, headed "Protest of the Merchants and Traders of Boston," had no signatures, whereas the names of the best-known merchants were signed to the address to Governor Hutchinson. The radical strategy is obvious. See also Schlesinger, *Colonial Merchants*, 316–317.

[44] John Rowe, *Letters and Diaries*, 273–274.

[45] Force, *American Archives*, 4th series, 1:398–399; John Rowe, *Letters and Diaries*, 274.

[46] John Andrews to William Barrell, Boston, June 12, 1774, in the *Proceedings of the Massachusetts Historical Society*, 1864–65 (1st series, vol. 8), 329. Ann Hulton summed up the dilemma of the aristocracy when she wrote that "The People of Property of best sense & Characters feel the Tyrrany of the Leaders, & forsee the Consequences of their proceedings, would gladly extricate themselves from the difficulties, & distress they are involv'd by makeing their peace with G: Britain, & speedily submiting to the Conditions & penalties required." The cause of their attachment, she likewise saw, was the result rather of interest than of principle. To Mrs. Adam Lightbody, July 8, 1774, in *Letters*, 73–74.

the formulation of a nonconsumption agreement.[47] When the merchants finally withdrew, the so-called Solemn League and Covenant was drawn up as a direct attack upon them. "The next plan is in opposition to the Merch[ts]," wrote Ann Hulton, "& which if it spreads must be attended wth the ruin of most of 'em here 'tis a Solemn League & Covenant, not to use any British Manufactures, till the Port is opend, & the New Acts repeald. This is a deep & diabolical scheme, & some people are taken into the Snare." [48] Faced with what they considered to be ruin, the merchants made a last desperate effort to moderate the program of the radicals. At a town meeting on June 27 "a number of the better sort of people attended with a design to make a push to pay for the tea, and annihilate the Committee of Correspondence, but they were outvoted by a great majority of the lower class." [49]

The town meeting then listened to the reading of the letters of the committee of correspondence since the receipt of the Port Bill. When the merchants moved that the committee be censured and disbanded, Sam Adams left the moderator's chair to defend his group. The meeting was so large that it was forced to adjourn to Old South Church, where the issue was so hotly debated that a vote was postponed until the next day, when the motion to censure the committee was negatived by "a vast majority" and a motion of approval was passed by an equally decisive vote.[50] Sam Adams had done his work well. The merchants were overpowered "by Numbers, & the Arts, Machinations of the Leader, who Governs absolutly, the Minds & the Passions of the People." [51]

The badly beaten merchants drew up a final protest against the proceedings of the committee of correspondence, against the Solemn League and Covenant, and against the town meeting. The Solemn League and Covenant, they charged, was "a base, wicked, and illegal measure, calculated to distress and ruin many merchants, shop keepers, and others, in this metropolis, and affect the whole commercial interest of this Province"; that it would "intro-

[47] Harlow, *Adams*, 226–227. This was on May 30, 1774.
[48] Ann Hulton to Mrs. Adam Lightbody, July 8, 1774, in *Letters*, 74.
[49] Governor Gage to the Earl of Dartmouth, July 5, 1774, in Force, *American Archives*, 4th series, 1:514.
[50] John Rowe, *Letters and Diaries*, 276–277, June 27–28; Force, *American Archives*, 4th series, 1:489–490.
[51] Ann Hulton to Mrs. Adam Lightbody, July 8, 1774, in *Letters*, 74.

duce almost every species of evil that we have not yet felt, and cannot serve any good purpose." The committee of correspondence, they said, had enunciated principles to which the merchants could not suscribe and which involved them in further difficulties. And finally, they protested, the letters sent to New York and Philadelphia had "falsely, maliciously, and scandalously, vilified and abused the characters of many of us, only for dissenting from them in opinion; a right which we shall claim so long as we hold any claim to freedom or liberty." [52]

It was a despairing statement of a point of view that now had no chance of consideration. A continental congress had already been agreed upon, and the Massachusetts General Court had elected its delegates while the secretary of the colony had stood outside the locked door — the key of which was in the pocket of Sam Adams — reading Governor Gage's proclamation of dissolution. [53]

In the years that followed, the Massachusetts leaders showed little interest in alleviating the discontent that gave them much of their power. They controlled the provincial congresses which governed the state until 1780, when they wrote a constitution more conservative than the old charter. They held most of the important offices after its adoption and most of them supported the Constitution of 1787. It seems that the radicalism of such men as Sam Adams, John Adams, and James Bowdoin extended only to independence. Furthermore, the revolutionary movement centered in the eastern part of the state, where the merchant class was only temporarily weakened by the Loyalist exodus. Thus they remained an effective force in the politics of the state, supporting the constitution of 1780 and providing the funds to put down agrarian revolt in 1786–87.

* * *

The calling of the first Continental Congress wrought a fundamental change in the growing revolutionary movement. No longer were the scattered revolutionary forces, feeding upon the vacillations of British policy and the exigencies of local politics, the center of the movement. When Congress outlined general policies which achieved the status of law as a result of popular

[52] Force, *American Archives*, 4th series, 1:490–491, June 29.
[53] Harlow, *Adams*, 232.

support, it took the lead in the Revolution, although its effectiveness as a revolutionary organization was determined ultimately by the political character of the state organizations sending delegates to it. As the local radical parties gained power and sent radicals to Congress, it changed its policies. The history of those changing policies is the history of the outbreak of the American Revolution.

III

Independence and Internal Revolution
1774–1776

THE FIRST CONTINENTAL CONGRESS

THE IDEA of a continental congress was not a new one, for the Albany and the Stamp Act congresses had been convened to consider problems common to all the colonies. And ever since the Stamp Act Congress the radical parties had grown steadily in the realization that an intercolonial union was necessary to the achievement of their various aims.[1]

Ironically enough, the actual call for the first Continental Congress grew out of the dilemma with which the New York conservatives were faced when the Boston committee of correspondence proposed absolute nonintercourse until the repeal of the Port Bill. If they accepted the proposal they would identify themselves with the program of the New York radicals and thus lose all the gains they had made in a long struggle; if they rejected it and advocated their own policy of modified nonimportation, they would lose whatever influence they had with the radicals. Only by seeming to do that which they had no intention of doing could they remain in control. Hence they suggested to the Boston radicals the very thing the latter had long desired, a congress of all the colonies.[2] They justified this means of escape from their dilemma on the ground that the cause was general and affected the whole continent. A congress of deputies should be called without delay to pass "some unanimous resolutions formed in this fatal emergency, not only respecting your deplorable circumstances, but for the security of our common rights." In the light of these sentiments, wrote the committee, it would be "premature

[1] Richard Frothingham, *The Rise of the Republic of the United States* (10th ed., Boston, 1910), 189–192, 207–208, 241–244, 262–264; Harlow, *Adams*, 191–202; Samuel Adams to Arthur Lee, Boston, September 27, 1771, and April 9, 1773, in *Writings*, 2:234; 3:18–19.

[2] Becker, *Political Parties in New York*, 117–118.

to pronounce any judgment" on the question of nonintercourse.[3] In taking this course the New York leaders undoubtedly felt that the congress would be controlled by the conservatives. Certainly they would not have suggested it had they foreseen what was to happen.

With the calling of the congress the question of what policy should be adopted toward Great Britain was transferred from thirteen separate political entities to a central body delegated to handle it.[4] Fundamentally there was no ground for compromise between Great Britain and the radical party in the colonies. By word and deed the radicals had denied that Parliament had power to legislate for them. The British position, as stated by Lord Dartmouth in a letter to Joseph Reed, was that "the Supreme Legislature of the whole British Empire has laid a duty (no matter for the present whether it has or has not the right so to do, it is sufficient that we conceive it has). . . . The question then is whether these laws are to be submitted to? If the people of America say no, they say in effect that they will no longer be a part of the British Empire."[5] With the radicals denying that Great Britain had any authority whatever, and Great Britain claiming unlimited authority, there was little hope for the conservative home-rule party in the colonies, should the proponents of the two extreme views be in power at the same time. That conjunction came with the meeting of the first Continental Congress.

The delegates who converged on Philadelphia in the autumn of 1774 were the product of twelve rigorous schools of practical and theoretical politics. The internal affairs of their respective colonies and the external relations of those colonies with Great

---

[3] Letter to the Boston Committee of Correspondence, May 23, 1774, in *The Correspondence and Public Papers of John Jay,* edited by Henry P. Johnston (4 vols., New York, 1890), 1:13–15. The committee which drafted the letter was composed of Isaac Low, James Duane, John Jay, and Alexander McDougall, three conservatives and one radical.

[4] Becker, *Political Parties in New York,* 142. "In sending delegates to a general congress, the two factions in New York virtually agreed to throw the burden of formulating a policy of resistance upon a power outside the colony; consciously or unconsciously they thereby greatly increased the difficulty of ever again having a policy of their own." What was true of New York was true of all the colonies.

[5] July 11, 1774, in William B. Reed, *Life and Correspondence of Joseph Reed* (2 vols., Philadelphia, 1847), 1:73.

Britain had brought forth some remarkable theoretical disquisitions and inspired some extraordinary political strategy. On the whole, colonial politicians had displayed as much ingenuity and agility in the one field as in the other.

In their relations with one another the colonies had developed attitudes that can best be described by the term "nationalistic." In spite of social, racial, and economic affinities and the cohesive force of the British connection, they had become practically independent political entities. Each delegate thought of his own colony as his country, as an independent nation in its dealings with England and with its neighbors, with whom relations were often as not unfriendly. It is this simple fact that is too often overlooked. Instead of lamenting the absence of "national feeling," one must recognize that it was there in an intense form, but in the form that is illustrated by the attitude of John Adams when he wrote of Massachusetts Bay as "our country." [6]

Essentially, then, the delegates to the first Continental Congress came as the ambassadors of twelve distinct nations (or of certain groups within those nations), and most of them came voluntarily as a result of certain forces at work within the colonies and of a common external force: the threatening power of Great Britain, which was taking the form of increasingly forceful attacks upon colonial liberties. Of course the colonies were not thirteen independent entities in all their relations with one another. The shifting kaleidoscope of political and economic interests and beliefs constantly brought about new alignments. Broadly speaking, the New England colonies had interests in common which differentiated them from the others. The same was true of the Middle colonies, whose attitude toward independence was so different for a time from that of New England. The Southern colonies, too, were characterized by certain common features, such as the relative predominance of slavery. Yet such groupings do not satisfactorily explain the major issues that arose in the Congress. The large colonies were pitted against the small ones; colonies with many slaves were in opposition to those with fewer; colonies that had no western lands contended with those that did. On all these issues sectional lines were so broken as to become meaningless. Above all it must be remembered that the constantly shifting bal-

[6] Edmund C. Burnett, ed., *Letters of Members of the Continental Congress* (8 vols., Washington, D. C., 1921–36), 1:35.

ance of politics within each state was reflected in the membership of Congress and in the votes cast by state delegations. It is only as this fact is kept in mind that one can understand the conflicting positions taken by many of the colonies.

The personal biases and interests of the individual members must also be considered. The delegation from each colony was composed of both conservatives and radicals, some being dominated by the one and some by the other group. Moreover, the radicals did not always agree with one another, nor did the conservatives.[7] There were votes that cannot be accounted for by self-interest, political philosophy, or state and sectional interests. Thomas Burke discovered in 1777 that the reason Georgia always voted with Connecticut was that the lone Georgia delegate had once been an inhabitant of the New England state.[8] It is in the light of such exceptions, contradictions, and inconsistencies, and yet in the light of a really fundamental division of interest and political philosophy between conservatives and radicals, that the history of the Continental Congress must be considered.

The Congress met for the first time on September 5, 1774. Its first decision was a straw in the wind indicating the course that events were to take. When Joseph Galloway, as speaker of the Pennsylvania Assembly, offered the statehouse as a meeting place and the radical party in the city offered Carpenters Hall, Congress accepted the latter invitation, a decision which was "highly agreeable to the mechanics and citizens in general but mortifying to the last degree to Mr. Galloway and his party."[9]

The first dispute to engage the Congress was a side issue, but it

[7] Virginia radicals, because Virginia was a large state, insisted that the votes be in proportion to population; the radicals from the small colonies wanted the voting to be by colonies. Two of the most prominent conservatives, John Adams and John Dickinson, differed bitterly on the question of the attitude to be adopted toward England. It may be well to repeat here that the terms "conservatism" and "radicalism" are not used to designate the attitude of the parties toward England, but the more basic attitude toward society and government, which was a continuous factor and of which the attitude toward England was partly a reflection. Most of the radicals ultimately favored the break; most of the conservatives favored staying in the empire, but some, like John Adams, supported the radicals from the beginning so far as the policy toward England was concerned.

[8] Thomas Burke to Governor Caswell, Philadelphia, May 23, 1777, in Burnett, *Letters*, 2:371.

[9] Silas Deane to Mrs. Deane, Philadelphia, September, 1774, in "Correspondence of Silas Deane," edited by J. Hammond Trumbull, in the *Connecticut Historical Collections*, 2:169–170, 172 (Hartford, 1870).

had a vital bearing on the basic problem of the balance of power between the states and the common government which they created. Ironically enough, it was a leading radical who advocated most fluently what was to be the desire of the conservatives a few years later. When Congress met, James Duane moved the appointment of a committee to establish rules of procedure, and in reply to a query of John Adams' suggested that the question of voting, whether it was to be by colonies, by population, or by interest, should be submitted to it. At once Patrick Henry arose to say that since it was the first general congress and since there would be occasion for more, a precedent ought to be established. He felt that it would be a great injustice to the large colonies if the small ones were to have the same weight in the council. This was a simple plea for consideration of Virginia's vast size and greater population, and not, as has been suggested, the result of "national vision." When Major Sullivan of New Hampshire insisted that the small states had their all at stake as well as the larger,[10] Henry burst into a flight of oratory quite inconsistent with his earlier plea for consideration of Virginia's size. Government was dissolved, he said. The colonies were in a state of nature. Where were the boundaries and landmarks between colony and colony? "The distinctions between Virginians, Pennsylvanians, New Yorkers, and New Englanders, are no more. I am not a Virginian, but an American." Later he said again that he proceeded on the supposition that all government was at an end, that all distinctions were eradicated, and that all America was thrown into one mass.[11] This statement alarmed the conservatives. John Jay refused to believe that the Congress had come together to frame an American constitution instead of correcting the faults of the old one, or that all government was at an end.[12]

The fact that no delegate had the data upon which to evaluate the relative weight of the colonies according to either numbers or property was "an objection that coud not be answered."[13] And, as John Rutledge pointed out, the Congress had "no coercive or legislative authority." Theodorick Bland remarked pointedly that

[10] John Adams, Diary, September 5, 1774, in *Works*, 2:365.
[11] John Adams, Notes on Debates, *ibid.*, 366–367, 368.
[12] *Ibid.*, 368.
[13] James Duane, Notes of Proceedings, September 6, 1774, in Burnett, *Letters*, 1:13.

"the question is, whether the rights and liberties of America shall be contended for, or given up to arbitrary powers." [14] The motion to appoint a committee on rules failed, as did a motion to appoint a committee to evaluate the weight of each colony. In the end each colony was given one vote.[15]

On the same day it was agreed to appoint a committee to "state the rights of the Colonies in general, the several instances in which these rights are violated or infringed, and the means most proper to be pursued for obtaining a restoration of them." [16] A second committee was appointed to examine and report on the various laws affecting the trade and manufacture of the colonies.[17] Immediately a wide difference of opinion was manifest between those whom we may call conservatives and those whom we may call radicals. As Joseph Galloway wrote later, the one party "intended candidly and clearly to define American rights, and explicitly and dutifully to petition for the remedy which would redress the grievances justly complained of — to form a more solid and constitutional union between the two countries"; the other party consisted of "persons, whose design, from the beginning of their opposition to the Stamp Act, was to throw off all subordination and connexion with Great Britain; who meant by every fiction, falsehood and fraud, to delude the people from their due allegiance, to throw the subsisting Governments into anarchy, to incite the ignorant and vulgar to arms, and with those arms to establish American Independence. The one were men of loyal principles, and possessed the greatest fortunes in America; the others were congregational and presbyterian republicans, or men of bankrupt fortunes, overwhelmed in debt to the British merchants." [18] Biased though Galloway was, there is in his analysis of the party division some truth that is worthy of consideration.

[14] John Adams, Notes on Debates, in *Works*, 2:367.

[15] *Journals*, 1:25. "Resolved, That in determining questions in this Congress, each Colony or Province shall have one Vote. — The Congress not being posses'd of, or at present able to procure proper materials for ascertaining the importance of each Colony." The last part of the resolution was added "to prevent its being drawn into precedent in future" after an objection to the inequality was made. Connecticut Delegates to the Governor of Connecticut, Philadelphia, October 10, 1774, in Burnett, *Letters*, 1:69.

[16] *Journals*, 1:26.   [17] *Ibid.*

[18] Joseph Galloway, *Historical and Political Reflections on the Rise and Progress of the American Rebellion* (London, 1780), 66.

As he said, the parties formed immediately. As one measure after another came up for consideration, party lines were more and more clearly drawn. The practical problem before the Congress was the selection of means by which to secure a redress of colonial grievances. That problem the conservatives wanted to meet by passing resolutions and presenting petitions,[19] the radicals by adopting the policy of nonintercourse which was so distasteful to the conservatives, especially those from the towns.[20] On the theoretical side the problem was to select grounds upon which to base colonial rights and the measure of authority to be conceded to Parliament. The conservatives wanted to exclude the law of nature as a basis of rights and to grant to Parliament the right to regulate trade.[21] The radicals insisted upon the law of nature and the denial of any parliamentary authority over the colonies whatsoever.[22]

The attitude taken and the measures proposed in Congress were largely the reflection of attitudes and measures that had been taken in the individual colonies. But there was a vital difference. Now measures were being considered by the colonies as a whole, and the decision of the Congress would be binding on all of them, not as a matter of law but as a matter of practical politics. It would be sufficient justification for one party or the other in each of the colonies to carry out its program. This had been the tacit understanding when the two parties agreed to meet for a common purpose.

Radicals and conservatives were approximately balanced in the Congress, and nothing was done during the first few weeks. The committee appointed to formulate a statement of the rights and grievances of the colonies debated heatedly, but came to no decision until the deadlock was broken by the political strategy of

[19] See the letter of the New York Committee in answer to that of the Boston Committee proposing nonintercourse, May 23, 1774, in Jay, *Correspondence and Public Papers*, 1:13–15.

[20] See above, ch. 2.

[21] John Dickinson was "full and clear for allowing to Parliament the regulation of trade, upon principles of necessity, and the mutual interest of both countries." James Duane insisted that the colonies could not regulate trade and that therefore Parliament must do so. John Adams, *Works*, 2:379, 389, 397.

[22] Radicals like Christopher Gadsden were "violent against allowing to Parliament any power of regulating trade, or allowing that they have anything to do with us." John Adams, Diary, September 14, 1774, *ibid.*, 2:379.

Sam Adams.[23] As Galloway said, Adams was "a man, who though by no means remarkable for brilliant abilities, yet is equal to most men in popular intrigue, and the management of a faction. He eats little, drinks little, sleeps little, thinks much, and is most decisive and indefatigable in the pursuit of his objects. It was this man, who by his superior application managed at once the faction in Congress at Philadelphia, and the factions in New England," [24] an achievement made possible by the employment of expresses between the two places.[25]

On September 16 Paul Revere arrived in Philadelphia with a series of resolutions that had been passed in Suffolk County, Massachusetts. These resolutions, penned by Joseph Warren, whom Sam Adams had left in charge during his own absence in Philadelphia,[26] recommended the policy of nonintercourse and denied the legality of recent parliamentary legislation. When they were presented to Congress on the day after their arrival, the conserva-

[23] The New Englanders were an object of suspicion to all the colonies. They had been warned that if they showed any desire for independence they would lose their influence in Congress. Stillé, *Dickinson*, 135. Accordingly they set about to win the confidence of the other delegates as a necessary preliminary to securing aid for Boston. Their task was explained by John Adams in a letter to Judge William Tudor: "We have had numberless prejudices to remove here. We have been obliged to act with great delicacy and caution. We have been obliged to keep ourselves out of sight, and to feel pulses, and to sound the depths; to insinuate our sentiments, designs, and desires, by means of other persons, sometimes of one province, and sometimes of another." September 29, 1774, in *Works*, 9:348. Sam Adams wrote to Joseph Warren that they had been accounted intemperate and rash but that they were now applauded as "cool and judicious." September 25, 1774, in *Writings*, 3:158. The New Englanders were helped by the relatively more fiery attitude of the Southerners. See Silas Deane to Mrs. Deane, September 8, 1774, in *Connecticut Historical Collections*, 2:175; Caesar Rodney to Thomas Rodney, September 9, 1774, in *Letters to and from Caesar Rodney, 1756–1784*, edited by George H. Ryden (Philadelphia, 1933), 45–56.

[24] Galloway, *Historical and Political Reflections*, 67–68. "Whatever these patriots ni [*sic*] in Congress wished to have done by their colleagues without . . . Mr. Adams advised and directed to be done; and when done, it was dispatched by express to congress."

[25] *Ibid.*, 67–68; Governor Gage to Lord Dartmouth, Boston, October 30, 1774, in Force, *American Archives*, 4th series, 1:950. Writing of the relations between the provincial congress in Boston and the Continental Congress in Philadelphia, he says: "expresses are frequently going from the one to the other, and they are very secret in both; and from what has transpired, there is opposition in both."

[26] Richard Frothingham, *Life and Times of Joseph Warren* (Boston, 1865), 360–361, 365–366.

tives were placed in a difficult position. To agree to them would be to give up everything for which they had been arguing in the committee on the statement of colonial rights. To refuse to do so would be to approve tacitly the measures of the British government, to which they were as much opposed as the radicals. The result was that the resolutions were approved.[27] It was a great victory for the radicals, for it committed the Congress to the radical plan of nonintercourse, and indirectly to a denial of the authority of Parliament.[28] John Adams wrote in his diary that it was the happiest day of his life. He was now convinced that America would support Massachusetts or perish with her.[29]

The coercive methods that had so often been used in Boston by the radicals seem to have been applied in Philadelphia to induce members to vote as they wished. John Adams wrote to his wife that when the resolves were presented to Congress, he saw tears gush from "the eyes of the old grave pacific Quakers of Pennsylvania." [30] They may well have wept if Galloway's account of the proceedings is true. After the resolves were presented, he wrote, a warm debate ensued, but "the republican faction in Congress had provided a mob, ready to execute their secret orders. The cruel practice of tarring and feathering had been long since introduced. This lessened the firmness of some of the loyalists: the vote was put and carried." [31]

[27] *Journals*, 1:31–39.

[28] The Suffolk Resolves are printed in the *Journals*, 1:32–37. The essential parts are these: that George III is recognized as sovereign of the colonies "agreeable to compact"; that the late acts of Parliament closing the port of Boston, etc., are infractions of the rights of the colonies according to the law of nature, the British constitution, and the provincial charter; that no obedience is due said acts; that the Quebec Act is a danger to the Protestant religion and the civil rights and liberties of America; that the citizens will act only on the defensive; that commercial intercourse with Great Britain, Ireland, and the West Indies should be stopped; that arts and manufacturing should be encouraged; and that a provincial Congress should be called.

[29] *Journals*, 1:39; John Adams, Diary, September 17, 1774, in *Works*, 2:380. Sam Adams wrote to Joseph Warren on September 25 (*Writings*, 3:158–159) that he had had assurances in private conversations that if the Massachusetts people should be driven to a defense of their lives and liberty, the constituents of the people he had talked with would openly support Massachusetts.

[30] John Adams to Mrs. Adams, September 18, in *Familiar Letters of John Adams and His Wife Abigail Adams during the Revolution*, edited by Charles F. Adams (New York, 1875), 40.

[31] Galloway, *Historical and Political Reflections*, 69. In his examination before a committee of the House of Commons, Galloway said that in the

Congress was now definitely committed to the radical plan of action. A few days later it adopted a resolution asking merchants to suspend further importations "until the sense of the Congress, on the means to be taken for the preservation of the liberties of America, is made public." [32] On September 24 Congress deliberated upon these "means," and three days later it resolved that there would be no importation from the British Isles or any exportation thereto after the first of December, 1774. [33] The form of this "Association" was agreed to on October 18 with a change in the date of its application. [34]

The idea of nonintercourse was of course not new. What was new in the Association was the plan for the uniform application of its provisions throughout the colonies. There was to be no importation after December 1, 1774, and no exportation after September 10, 1775. [35] The Associators agreed to have no commercial dealings with those who broke the agreement. Merchants who imported after December, 1774, and before February, 1775, might either reship or store their goods with local committees, who would sell the goods and pay the owners. Profits, if any, were to go to those suffering from the Port Bill. Goods imported after February, 1775, were to be shipped back. Counties, towns, and cities were to select committees to observe the conduct of all persons with regard to the Association. Names of violators were to be published in the public gazettes. [36] Thus those who refused to conform were to be punished by "social ostracism, commercial boycott, and confiscation of property." [37] Recommendations such

course of the Congress he had received a halter with an anonymous letter threatening to put him to death if he did not make use of it. Thomas Balch, ed., *The Examination of Joseph Galloway* (Philadelphia, 1855), 54.

[32] *Journals*, 1:41, September 22, 1774.   [33] *Ibid.*, 42, 43.

[34] *Ibid.*, 75. The Association is printed *ibid.*, 75–80. The original resolution set December 1, 1774, for beginning the policy. The final agreement set September 10, 1775, for the beginning of nonexportation. The clash of interests which the formulation of a policy produced among the radicals and among the conservatives, as well as between the two groups, may be followed in John Adams' Notes on Debates and in his Diary, in *Works*, 2:381–385.

[35] *Journals*, 1:77.   [36] *Ibid.*, 77–79.

[37] Becker, *Political Parties in New York*, 154. Chapter 6 of Becker's study, "The First Continental Congress," is a brilliant analysis of the work of the first congress from a somewhat different point of view than that of this study. See also Arthur M. Schlesinger, "The American Revolution Reconsidered," in the *Political Science Quarterly*, 34:73 (March, 1919).

as these gave a sanction of sorts to revolutionary organizations. It gave them a common purpose, and hence made for a unity of action that would otherwise have been impossible. As Professor Becker suggests, the Association emphasized the question of allegiance.[38] One had to choose between obedience to the measures proposed by Congress and allegiance to the British government. Refusal to accept the Association as a practical measure of opposition was evidence of lack of "patriotism" and implied support of British measures, whether one approved of them or not. To the conservatives, who cared as little for the one as for the other, it was a question of choosing the lesser of two evils. The middle-of-the-road policy, home rule within the empire,[39] became increasingly difficult as the Continental Congress was steered in the direction of independence, and the British government made plain its intention of continuing a policy of coercion.

In the meantime the form of the Declaration of Rights was being argued. The radicals insisted that the statement of colonial rights be based on the law of nature. The conservatives displayed an understandable predilection for basing their rights on the English constitution,[40] or at least upon something more specific than the law of nature. Richard Henry Lee argued that colonial rights were built upon the fourfold foundation of nature, the British constitution, the charters, and immemorial usage. John Jay, supporting the radical point of view for the moment, maintained that emigrants had the right to set up whatever form of government they pleased. Lee said that their ancestors had found no government here. Sherman denied the contention of the ministry that the colonies were like corporations in England and hence subject to the will of Parliament; on the contrary, he insisted, the colonies were bound to the king or crown only by their consent, and only their respective assemblies had power to legislate for them. They "adopt the common law, not as common

---

[38] Becker, *Political Parties in New York*, 155.

[39] The defeat of the Galloway plan and the adoption of the Association marks the practical end of the influence — so far as policy toward England was concerned — of that wing of the conservative party represented by Galloway. Both wings were agreed upon the nature of government in general, but the Galloway party wanted closer union with Britain. The wing of which Dickinson was the leader wanted home rule.

[40] John Adams, Autobiography, in *Works*, 2:373–374.

law," he said, but as "the highest reason." [41] It was John Adams, political realist that he was, who saw how necessary it was for the radicals to find a theoretical foundation for their position. He was, he wrote, "very strenuous for retaining and insisting on it [*the law of nature*], as a resource to which we might be driven by Parliament much sooner than we were aware." [42]

Given the law of nature as a foundation, any political innovation or experiment was possible — a possibility most alarming to the conservatives. John Rutledge denied that emigrants could set up any constitution they pleased and that any subject could alienate his allegiance; American claims were better founded on the British constitution than on the law of nature.[43] James Duane, who gave a clear exposition of the conservative position in a long address to the committee, argued that according to the English constitution the king was the executive and hence had the right to establish governments in the colonies. True, the rights of Englishmen were inherent and could not be denied them without their consent nor withheld except by lawless oppression. But that did not mean that the colonies were independent and exempt from the authority of the British Parliament, "and free from all Obligations to render to the Parent State those advantages which ought to be the Recompence of Protection, to result from the very nature of Colonization, and to be Justified from the Usage of every commercial Nation." Rights might be derived from two sources, he argued: the common law and the statutes coeval with the founding of the colonies and their charters. The first principle, he said, was the more general if not the more solid. It was essential to place colonial rights on "some solid and Constitutional Principle which will preserve us from Violations." The English courts and the king in council had admitted that the common law and the statutes existing prior to emigration "are fundamentals to our Colony Constitution. Upon this grand Basis the prerogatives of the Crown and the Rights of the Subjects are as fully ascertained in the Plantations as in the parent State." He concluded by saying that he would not forget that they were colonies, "that we are indebted to her for the Blessings of Protection, and that

[41] John Adams, Notes on Debates, *ibid.*, 370–371.
[42] John Adams, Autobiography, *ibid.*, 374.
[43] John Adams, Notes on Debates, September 8, *ibid.*, 370–371.

she ought to derive from us every commercial Advantage which is the Result of our Connection and Dependence." [44]

The most serious weakness in the conservative argument was the contention that the colonies were not bound by any laws of Parliament passed since their founding. Essentially this was the radical argument that the colonies were in no way bound by Parliament. Galloway realized that it was a tacit admission of colonial independence which impaired the conservative argument that "there must be some absolute power to draw together all the wills and strength of the empire." [45] He had looked for colonial rights, he said, in the law of nature and had not found them there, but in a state of political society, and particularly in the constitution of the English government. It was Galloway also who stated another conservative contention, later elaborated by Madison. "Power results from the real property of society," he said. "The states of Greece, Macedon, Rome were founded on this plan," and the English is founded on the same principle, the principle of the representation of landed property in the government of the state. [46]

The final statement of the foundation upon which American rights rested was a victory for the radicals. The rights of the colonies, was the argument, were based on "the immutable laws of nature, the principles of the English constitution, and the several charters or compacts." [47] Thus while the Bill of Rights included the conservative contention that the English constitution was a basis of those rights, both the basic radical doctrines were likewise included: the law of nature implying unlimited rights and little restraint, and the idea of a compact involving the concept of voluntary association and the right of revolution. These ideas are of vast importance in American constitutional history. They were a force from the moment the colonies began to cooperate and remained so throughout the revolutionary period.

The second question of major importance disputed by the committee was "whether we should deny the authority of Parliament in all cases; whether we should allow any authority to it in our

[44] James Duane, "Address before the Committee to State the Rights of the Colonies," September 8, 1774, in Burnett, *Letters*, 1:23-25. See also John Adams, Notes on Debates, September 8, in *Works*, 2:371-372.

[45] John Adams, Notes on Debates, September 8, *ibid.*, 373.

[46] *Ibid.*, 372.   [47] *Journals*, 1:66-67, October 14.

internal affairs; or whether we should allow it to regulate the trade of the empire with or without any restrictions." [48] This, said John Adams, was "the essence of the whole controversy; some were for a flat denial of all authority; others for denying the power of taxation only; some for denying internal, but admitting external, taxation." [49] James Duane, speaking for the merchants of the colonies, insisted on conceding to Parliament the right of regulation, "grounding it on compact, acquiescence, necessity, protection, not merely on our consent." [50] Radicals like Gadsden, on the other hand, were against allowing Parliament any power of regulation, and insisted that such power was the power to ruin the colonies, "as bad as acknowledging them a supreme legislative in all cases whatsoever; a right of regulating trade is a right of legislation, and a right of legislation in one case is a right in all; this I deny." [51]

The disputes dragged on interminably. Finally John Adams was assigned the task of drafting a statement. Not one of the committee was fully satisfied with it, but "they all soon acknowledged that there was no hope of hitting on any thing in which we could all agree with more satisfaction." [52] According to Adams' version the foundation of English liberty and of all free government was the right of the people to participate in their legislative council, and since the English colonists, because of local and other circumstances, could not be represented in Parliament, they were "entitled to a free and exclusive power of legislation in their several provincial legislatures, where their right of representation can alone be preserved, in all cases of taxation and internal polity," subject only to the royal veto in the customary way. "But, from the necessity of the case, and a regard to the mutual interest of both countries, we cheerfully consent to the operation of such acts of the British parliament, as are bona fide, restrained to the regulation of our external commerce, for the purpose of securing the commercial advantages of the whole empire to the mother country, and the commercial benefits of its respective members; excluding every idea of taxation, internal or external, for raising a revenue on the subjects in America, without their consent." [53]

[48] John Adams, Autobiography, in *Works*, 2:374.   [49] *Ibid.*
[50] John Adams, Diary, October 13, *ibid.*, 397.   [51] September 14, *ibid.*, 379.
[52] John Adams, Autobiography, *ibid.*, 374–375.
[53] *Journals*, 1:68–69, October 14.

It was a hodgepodge of conservative and radical views, designed to give comfort to both sides. The conservatives, however, thought it aimed at independence.[54] As a matter of fact, the concession of the right to regulate trade as a matter of "consent," which was the result of "necessity," was a denial of that right to Parliament. The result was at least a logical victory for the radicals.

The conservatives made one constructive effort to arrive at an understanding with England, but here again they were defeated by the radicals, who refused to agree to anything resembling a compromise with the mother country. The vote on the Suffolk resolves had shown the conservatives that there was little hope of "stemming the torrent." Yet, since it had been ordered that a petition to the king be brought in, they continued to hope that the rights of America might be based on constitutional principles and that some plan for uniting the two countries might be agreed upon. They also wished to probe "the ultimate designs of the republicans, and to know with certainty whether any proposal short of the absolute independence of the colonies, would satisfy them." A plan of union was accordingly drawn up, approved by the rest of the conservative group,[55] and on September 28 presented to Congress by Galloway, its author.[56] In an introductory speech he pointed out that he had come to Congress with instructions to devise some means of restoring harmony between the colonies and Great Britain, but that a month had been spent in activity more calculated to inflame than to reconcile. His speech clarifies further the views expressed in James Duane's speech to the committee on rights.

Galloway argued that the proposal to restore harmony by a return to the status that existed before 1763 was indecisive because it mentioned no ground for complaint, settled no principle, and proposed no plan for settling the dispute. Laws passed after 1763

[54] Joseph Galloway, *A Candid Examination of the Mutual Claims of Great Britain and the Colonies, with a Plan of Accommodation on Constitutional Principles* (New York, 1775), 25-31. After discussing the Declaration of Rights he wrote that "nothing has been the production of their two months labor, but the ill-shapen, diminitive brat, INDEPENDENCY."

[55] Galloway, *Historical and Political Reflections*, 69-70.

[56] *Journals*, 1:49; Samuel Ward's Diary, September 28, in Burnett, *Letters*, 1:51. The plan is in the *Journals*, 1:49-51.

had precedents in laws passed before that date. Nonimportation and nonexportation were undutiful and illegal, and insulting to the sovereign authority of the state. In defense of the supremacy of Parliament he asserted that "there must be one supreme legislative head in every civil society, whose authority must extend to the regulation and final decision of every matter susceptible of human direction; and that every member of the society, whether political, official, or individual, must be subordinate" to its will as signified in its laws.[57] A second argument for parliamentary supremacy was that parliamentary jurisdiction had always been exercised over the colonies, that the colonists had ever sworn allegiance to the British state, and had been considered by it and by themselves to be subject to the British government. To deny that authority and at the same time to declare their incapacity to be represented in it "amounts to a full and explicit declaration of independence."[58]

Behind Galloway's third argument for the recognition of the authority of Parliament was the same attitude that later prompted the conservatives to demand a government stronger than the Articles of Confederation. It was used to oppose independence; it was used in an attempt to strengthen the Articles after they had been ratified; and it was a powerful motive behind the Constitution of 1787. One of the dangers that alarmed the conservatives most was that there would be no central control, and that thirteen independent states, each with claims against the others, might engage in open hostilities. Galloway pointed out that the colonies were "so many inferior societies, disunited and unconnected in polity. That while they deny the authority of Parliament, they are, in respect to each other, in a perfect state of nature, destitute of any supreme direction or decision whatever, even to the settlement of differences among themselves." The seeds of discord had been plentifully sown in the constitution of the colonies, he said, and more than once they had broken out in open hostilities. "They are at this moment only suppressed by the authority of the Parent State; and should that authority be weakened or annulled, many subjects of unsettled disputes, and which in that case, can

[57] Galloway, *Historical and Political Reflections*, 70–76; John Adams, Notes on Debates, in *Works*, 2:387–389. Galloway's introductory speech is reprinted in the *Journals*, 1:44–48.

[58] Galloway, *Historical and Political Reflections*, 76–77.

only be settled by an appeal to the sword, must involve us in all the horrors of civil war." [59] This argument for a coercive power over the states and, later, over the individual citizens of the states has a vital bearing on both the Articles of Confederation and the Constitution of 1787. One of the fundamental differences between the two documents is the absence of provision for that power in the one and its inclusion in the other.

Galloway admitted freely that the exercise of parliamentary authority over the colonies was not constitutional, for the whole landed interest of Great Britain was represented in Parliament, whereas neither the land nor the people of America were. Representation in the councils of the state, he said, was the foundation of freedom. He wished to see the right to participate in the councils of the British government applied to all the British dominions; lacking this, he prophesied, the "profound and excellent fabrick of civil polity" would crumble.[60]

He therefore proposed a plan of union with Great Britain. As he himself said, it consisted of only the great outlines or principles, but it did furnish, if the colonials really wished to stay within the empire, a foundation upon which something lasting could be built. It provided for a colonial parliament, or Grand Council, composed of members elected by the colonial assemblies. The executive was to be a president-general apppointed by the king and holding office at his pleasure. His assent was to be necessary to the acts of the council. The colonies were to retain control of all their local affairs, but the president-general and Grand Council were to act as administrators and legislators in all affairs of mutual concern to the colonies and Great Britain, and in affairs involving more than one colony. The Grand Council was to be "an inferior and distinct branch of the British legislature," but acts of a general nature affecting both might originate in either body, the assent of the other being required to make them valid.[61]

Galloway says that in the ensuing debates "all the men of prop-

---

[59] Galloway, *Historical and Political Reflections*, 77.   [60] *Ibid.*

[61] *Journals*, 1:49-51, September 28. James Duane seconded the motion. In doing so he argued that the colonies could not regulate trade because of their local circumstances and that the responsibility should be given to Parliament. John Adams, Notes on Debates, in *Works*, 2:389. For a detailed analysis of Duane's reasons for supporting the Galloway plan, see his letter to Samuel Chase, New York, December 29, 1774, in Burnett, *Letters*, 1:87-89.

erty" and most of the ablest speakers supported the motion, "while the republican party strenuously opposed it." [62] The radicals were in a tight position, for, as was pointed out to them, to refuse any attempt at accommodation was to declare their independence. This it was inexpedient to do. Richard Henry Lee's arguments are indicative of the dilemma in the radical mind. He presented no real objection to the plan, but argued that it would involve changes in the legislatures of the colonies to which he could not agree without consulting his constituents.[63] To this evasion Jay replied that there was no intention of changing the constitutions of the colonies and invited Lee to point out wherein the plan denied a single liberty or interfered with a single right.[64] Patrick Henry spoke vaguely to the effect that the "original constitution of the Colonies was founded on the broadest and most generous base," and finished by remarking irrelevantly but revealingly, "I am inclined to think the present measures lead to war." [65]

In replying to Henry, Galloway went over the same ground he had covered in his introductory speech, pointing out that there was no American constitution and that all the colonies were independent of one another. Some power must have the right to regulate trade, for individual colonies could not do it. "There is a necessity that an American Legislature should be set up, or else that we should give the power to Parliament or King." [66]

The plan was finally referred to a committee for further consideration by a majority of the colonies.[67] Galloway was induced

[62] Galloway, *Historical and Political Reflections*, 81.

[63] John Adams, Notes on Debates, in *Works*, 2:389.

[64] *Ibid.*, 389–390.

[65] *Ibid.*, 390. Patrick Henry's remarks as reported by John Adams offer opportunity for further insight into the radical mind. He said that "we shall liberate our constituents from a corrupt House of Commons, but to throw them into the arms of an American Legislature, that may be bribed by that nation which avows in the face of the world, that bribery is a part of her system of government." Even more helpful toward an understanding of the attitude of the radicals toward a central government was Henry's statement that "we are not to consent by the representatives of representatives." Edward Rutledge, on the other hand, thought the plan might be freed from almost every objection. "I think it almost a perfect plan."

[66] John Adams, Notes on Debates, in *Works*, 2:390–391.

[67] Samuel Ward said (Diary, September 28, in Burnett, *Letters*, 1:51), "a plan of union between Great Britain and the Colonies [was] presented by Mr. Galloway, considered, not committed, but ordered to lie on the table." Galloway (*A Candid Examination*, 51–52) said that the plan, "after a long debate,

to sign the Association, which he had always opposed, in the hope that his plan would be taken up again.[68] But it was never again considered, and was finally dismissed[69] and record of it erased from the Journals.[70]

The failure of the Galloway plan meant the defeat of any serious attempt on the part of the colonies to settle their differences with the mother country. The only alternative left to Great Britain, short of granting independence to the colonies, was to fight. She chose to fight. That the radicals wished for such an outcome is uncertain, but that they expected it is obvious. Sam Adams had early felt that a war would be inevitable if matters should come to a crisis, and this at a time when a crisis was by no means imminent.[71] Equally revealing is the remark of Patrick Henry made in connection with the Galloway plan, "I am inclined to think the present measures lead to war."

The Massachusetts delegates complained that Congress moved too slowly in support of their colony. "We hear perpetually the most figurative panegyrics upon our wisdom, fortitude, and temperance," wrote John Adams; "the most fervent exhortations to perseverance, but nothing more is done." [72] The defeat of the Galloway plan marked a turning point in this respect. The Boston committee of correspondence had sent a letter to Congress stating that while Congress was deliberating, fortifications were being built and that there was reason to suspect that Boston would be

was so far approved as to be thought worthy of further consideration, and referred under a rule for that purpose by a majority of the colonies." In his *Historical and Political Reflections*, 81, Galloway wrote that warm and long debates immediately ensued on the question "whether it should be entered in the proceedings of Congress, or be referred to further consideration . . . The question was at length carried by a majority of one colony."

[68] Galloway, *A Candid Examination*, 52.

[69] Samuel Ward, Diary, October 22, in Burnett, *Letters*, 1:80.

[70] Galloway, *A Candid Examination*, 52. "The resolve, plan, and rule referring them to further consideration, so inconsistent with the measures now resolved on, were expunged from the minutes; with what view let America determine; and while the enemies to the gentleman who proposed them, are abusing him for offering and publishing to the world the most infamous falsehood, in representing it was ministerial, and sent over to him by Lord N–h; they have copies of it in their pockets, industriously concealing it from the world."

[71] Sam Adams to Arthur Lee, April 12, 1773, and to Richard Henry Lee, April 10, 1773, in Burnett, *Letters*, 3:22–24, 25–28.

[72] John Adams to Judge William Tudor, in *Works*, 9:347.

made and kept a garrison town. What did Congress advise? Should Boston be evacuated or should the inhabitants remain and become hostages? [73] The letter was read on October 6, and the next day a committee was appointed to write a letter to General Gage. Congress resolved that unless the actions of the soldiers were stopped, it must "involve all America in the horrors of a civil war." The next day Congress passed a resolution approving of the opposition of Massachusetts to the execution of the late acts of Parliament and asserting that if "the same shall be attempted to be carryed into execution by force, in such case, all America ought to support them in their opposition." [74]

The victory of the radicals was more nearly, complete than could have been hoped for from a Congress called in part to thwart their designs. Sam Adams was said to have reported to the radicals at home that the Congress went as much to his liking as if he had been its sole director. [75] The conservative view of what happened was well expressed by a Maryland merchant who wrote that "Adams, with his crew, and the haughty Sultans of the South juggled the whole conclave of the Delegates." [76]

In the Association the radicals secured the adoption of their method of coercion, which served as well to whip the local merchants into line as to force concessions from Parliament. They succeeded in having the law of nature incorporated as one of the foundations of their rights and were thus armed with a theory that would justify opposition to any practical measures the British government might take. They had denied the authority of Parliament in all matters except the regulation of trade, and even this, they argued, was based on the consent of the colonies and the necessity of the case and not on the legislative superiority of Parliament as such. Finally, they secured the tacit approval of Congress for a policy of meeting force with force. Having done these things, Congress resolved that delegates should be elected to a second congress to meet on May 10, 1775, unless the grievances of the colonies should have been redressed before that time. [77]

[73] *Journals*, 1:55–57, October 6, 1774.   [74] *Ibid.*, 57–58, October 7, 8, 1774.
[75] James Lovell to Josiah Quincy, Boston, October 28, 1774, in Force, *American Archives*, 4th series, 1:949.
[76] "Annapolis Merchant to a Philadelphia Friend," January 28, 1775, *ibid.*, 1194.
[77] January 28, 1775, *ibid.*

THE CONSERVATIVE OPPOSITION

No sooner had the first Continental Congress disbanded than the attack upon its proceedings began. The day after adjournment John Dickinson wrote that "the Colonists have now taken such grounds that Great Britain must relax, or inevitably involve herself in a civil War." Though an ardent believer in peace, he did not expect peace to be made. On the contrary, he prophesied that the first act of violence on the part of the British in America would precipitate an armed conflict.[78] The conservative members of Congress were openly charged with having been outwitted and outmaneuvered by the radicals,[79] a charge that was by no means inaccurate. They had too long had things their own way, and too few of them had learned the lessons that would have enabled them to thwart the methods of clever men like Sam Adams.[80] Governor Gage wrote that the proceedings of the Congress astonished and terrified all "considerate men," but that its resolves would, he feared, be generally received for want of "resolution and strength enough among the most sensible and moderate people in any of the Provinces openly to reject them." [81] True, a few of the conservatives, notably those of New York, had wit and ability enough to take hold of the radical organization and to exercise a moderating influence upon its course. But most of them clung to their old governments, which were rapidly being displaced by new organizations in which the old controls no longer counted and the conservatives were largely outvoted.

The attitude of the conservatives toward the Congress was best expressed by one of them who said that the system set up by the Association was worse than the Spanish Inquisition; that it was "subversive of, inconsistent with, the wholesome laws of our happy Constitution; it abrogates or suspends many of them essential to the peace and order of Government; it takes the Gov-

---

[78] John Dickinson to Arthur Lee, Philadelphia, October 27, 1774, in Force, *American Archives,* 4th series, 1:947.

[79] Schlesinger, *Colonial Merchants,* 438.

[80] It would seem to be a maxim of politics that the party in power loses its wisdom and political ability while the party in opposition makes a corresponding gain. At least a part of the success of the conservatives after the Revolution should be attributed to the excellent training they received in the school of political adversity conducted by Sam Adams from 1774 to 1776.

[81] To Lord Dartmouth, Boston, November 15, 1774, in Force, *American Archives,* 4th series, 1:981.

ernment out of the hands of the Governor, Council, and General Assembly; and the execution of laws out of the hands of the Civil Magistrates and Juries." [82] This was no unthinking reaction but a fairly accurate analysis of the revolutionary change in government that was taking place. As usual, however, the conservatives were better at analyzing events than at changing their course.

Three men of old colonial families of substance made brilliant attacks on the Congress. Samuel Seabury, an Episcopal clergyman in Connecticut writing under the name of "Westchester Farmer," tried to show both farmers and merchants that nothing but evil could result from the course that was being pursued. If the controversy continued, he felt sure, the result would be either war or the cessation of British authority over the colonies. The results of war would be equally bad whether the Americans won or lost. If they lost, there would be dreadful scenes of slaughter and violence, confiscations, and executions. If they won, province would turn against province and desolate the land. It would cost the blood of the greater part of the inhabitants of America, he predicted, to determine whether they should have a monarchy or a republic, and a further conflict to establish the government finally decided upon.[83] Joseph Galloway published his *Candid Examination* early in 1775, including his plan of union and the analysis of the causes of its rejection, in which he charged the radicals with aiming at independence rather than at any form of accommodation.[84] Daniel Leonard, writing under the pseudonym "Massachusettensis," upheld the conservative cause in Massachusetts.[85]

One anonymous radical was quite as frank in stating his views, if one may judge from a series of *Political Observations, Without Order; Addressed to the People of America,* published shortly after the adjournment of Congress. These observations began with the statement that all governmental powers are derived from God either through kings or through the people; that the history of kings is the history of the depravity of human nature, and their

---

[82] "To the Americans," Suffolk County, New York, February 4, 1775, *ibid.,* 1211–1213.

[83] Samuel Seabury, "The Congress Canvassed," quoted by Moses C. Tyler in *The Literary History of the American Revolution* (2 vols., New York, 1897), 1:344.

[84] Galloway, *A Candid Examination,* 31, 52.

[85] Tyler, *Literary History of the Revolution,* 1:356–367.

imposition on humanity the result of God's anger. The American Congress, on the other hand, derived its powers from the people, not from scrolls of parchment signed by kings. The least deviation from the "laws" of Congress would be treason against the present generation, against generations yet unborn, and against God. The author looked upon independence as not only desirable but inevitable. Let us neither think, write, nor speak, he wrote, without keeping our eyes on that period "which shall dissolve our connexion with *Great Britain*." The delirium of the present ministry might precipitate the dissolution, but "the ordinary course of human things must accomplish it." [86]

Such expressions of a belief in the depravity of kings, the sovereignty of the people, the supremacy of the "laws" of Congress, and the desire for independence explain why the conservatives felt that the purpose of all the radicals was independence, in spite of public protestations to the contrary by their leaders. One writer replied that he was positive that the "Republicans of North America," particularly those of New England, had long been aiming at independence and that they had "eagerly seized this *golden opportunity*, when discontent prevails throughout the Colonies, to establish a grand *American Commonwealth*." [87]

The Association aroused bitter hostility, especially among the merchants who were to suffer from it. In New York the majority of the great merchants were against it, Lieutenant Governor Colden reported, but he doubted that they could withstand the pressure from the rest of the colonies. [88] So strong was the opposition to the measures of Congress that the Assembly, after some hedging, finally repudiated its proceedings and sent a separate petition to the king. [89]

The situation was much the same in Pennsylvania. It was pre-

[86] "Political Observations, Without Order; Addressed to the People of America," Philadelphia, November 14, in Force, *American Archives*, 4th series, 1:976–977.

[87] "To the Printer of the New York Gazeteer," *ibid.*, 978–979.

[88] Quoted by Becker in *Political Parties in New York*, p. 142, note 1. In a letter of November 2 Colden wrote that the great majority of the province were far from approving of the "extravagant and dangerous measures of the *New England* governments" and that "they abhor the thoughts of a civil war, and desire nothing so much as to have an end put to this unhappy dispute with the mother country." Force, *American Archives*, 4th series, 1:957.

[89] *Journals*, vol. 2, p. 16, notes 1 and 2; Ebenezer Hazard to Silas Deane, New York, February 1, 1775, in *Connecticut Historical Collections*, 2:193;

dicted that the American merchants would be ruined and that half the debts to Britain would never be paid unless obnoxious British laws were repealed.[90] It was felt, however, that if the merchants did not suspend trade at the direction of Congress, "the people of the country will compel them" and there would be "no power capable to protect them."[91] The conservatives insisted that the radicals "aimed at a general revolution, and were promoting every measure to overthrow our excellent Constitution."[92] This "excellent Constitution," which guaranteed the rule of an oligarchy, was the ark of the covenant around which many events were to move in the course of the next year, and to which the conservatives became progressively more attached as independence loomed larger on the horizon.

In Maryland, as elsewhere, the measures of Congress occasioned "warmth and discord." In Anne Arundel County "a turbulent man, of no consideration, unless with the needy and desperate like himself," assembled the people and urged the adoption of the Association and "the other wild, impracticable views of the Congress." This "demagogue fascinated a multitude," but the conservatives were able to defeat his plan of assessing the inhabitants for the purchase of arms in order to "join the treasonable purpose projected by *Adams*, and the Eastern Republicans, to carry on a formal rebellion in the colonies."[93]

In spite of the opposition, the Association was put into operation with remarkable speed and effectiveness. The total decline in imports in 1775 as compared with 1774 has been estimated at ninety-seven per cent.[94] Yet in spite of its effectiveness in the colonies, it failed of the desired result in England. The English merchants dealing with America had been panic-stricken at first and had appealed to Parliament to grant a redress of American

Force, *American Archives*, 4th series, 1:1025, which contains a charge that leading New Yorkers were bought off with British money.

[90] Joseph Reed to Dennis De Berdt, September 26, 1774, in Reed, *Joseph Reed*, 1:81.

[91] Joseph Reed to Lord Dartmouth, September 25, 1774, *ibid.*, 78.

[92] "Extract of a Letter from Philadelphia to Mr. Rivington, New York," February 16, 1775, in Force, *American Archives*, 4th series, 1:1232.

[93] "Annapolis Merchant to a Friend in Philadelphia," January 28, 1775, *ibid.*, 1194.

[94] Schlesinger, in his *Colonial Merchants*, 534–536, gives a detailed account of the ratification and working of the Association until April, 1775.

grievances, though hardly in a spirit of disinterested altruism. The British government insisted that it was no longer a question of mere economics but a question of political supremacy, and refused to recede from its position. The merchants, anticipating ruin,[95] were furious. Presently, however, better economic conditions in Europe opened new markets for British goods, and large shipments of wheat from the colonies brought in larger payments, especially since there was no corresponding exportation to the colonies. These considerations helped to swing the merchants to the support of Parliament, and by the autumn of 1775 their petitions in favor of America had ceased to be based on their own economic necessity.[96]

The firing of the "shot heard round the world" in April, 1775, which marked the official outbreak of hostilities, shifted the argument at last from the pen to the sword, and it was the latter that was to prove decisive. How Lexington and Concord affected popular feeling in the colonies may be illustrated by a comparison of the journeys of the New England delegates to the Continental Congress in 1774 and 1775. In 1774 they had been received with moderate enthusiasm in New England. Their entry into New York was unheralded, though they were entertained by the "first citizens" and "best people." Outside Philadelphia they were met by "carriages and gentlemen" and entered the city very sedately.[97] By the spring of 1775 the scene had changed remarkably. Outside New York the delegates were met by a crowd of men and women who insisted on unhitching the horses and drawing the carriages into the city, in spite of some objection on the part of the horses. In New York, guards dressed in blue and scarlet uniforms were stationed constantly before their lodgings.[98] The journey from

[95] *Ibid*, 536–538. Franklin, in a letter to Joseph Galloway, London, February 5, 1775, said that he gave a copy of Galloway's plan to Lords Camden and Chatham and would give a copy to the ministry if it had none. He thought it might stay bloodshed and initiate some negotiation, but also thought there was little prospect, "for everything is hurried with inconceivable precipitation & everything rejected immediately, the consideration of which occasion Delay. Thus the Commons would not hear the Merchants support their Petition in the same Committee that was to consider the State of America." A photostat of this letter is in the Mason Library.

[96] Schlesinger, *Colonial Merchants*, 539–540.

[97] John Adams, Diary, in *Works*, 2:340–358.

[98] Silas Deane to Mrs. Deane, New York, May 7, 1775, in *Connecticut Historical Collections*, 2:222–223.

New York to Philadelphia was a succession of military receptions. The news of Lexington and Concord had reached Philadelphia on April 24, and the next day a crowd met in the State House yard and resolved to "associate together to defend with arms our property, liberty and lives against all attempts to deprive us of it." The committees of correspondence took charge and money was pried from the reluctant Assembly. By the time Congress assembled the town presented a martial appearance.[99] The New England delegates were met six miles outside town by "two hundred" men with drawn swords, and four miles further on by two companies of troops.[1]

Thus when the second Continental Congress met, military ardor was at a height that it probably never again reached, but the policy pursued by Congress for the next year prevented that ardor from being turned to much account. The conservative party, although it did not dominate the Congress, was still able to act as a brake upon the radicals and to insist upon a largely negative policy while pursuing the will-o'-the-wisp of reconciliation. Since the British government determined to use troops to enforce its laws, the conservatives were faced with the choice of meeting force with force or of submitting abjectly to what they felt, equally with the radicals, to be an infringement upon American rights and liberties. Thus they sanctioned the creation of an army, convincing themselves that it was for the purpose of "defense" alone. At the same time they pleaded with the British government that their intentions were peaceable and that their only desire was for a connection with the parent state on "constitutional principles." The subtlety of these real truths was too much for the British government, which seemed to feel that "their tongues were forked to split the truth that word and deed might take diverging ways." The colonial radical party too, which wanted preparations for war to proceed as fast as possible, charged the conservatives with hypocrisy and self-seeking. Thus the British government and the radical party in the colonies pursued measures which combined to force the conservatives to choose between loyalism and independence. There was no hope for a policy of constitutional union

[99] Lincoln, *Revolutionary Movement in Pennsylvania*, 196.
[1] Silas Deane to Mrs. Deane, Philadelphia, May 12, 1775, in *Connecticut Historical Collections*, 2:227–228.

so long as the British government was bent on subjection and the revolutionary party on independence.

* * *

War was being fought in Massachusetts when the second Continental Congress met on May 10, 1775. An army of sorts was besieging General Gage in the town of Boston, and the provincial congress was appealing for help. Once more the Massachusetts delegates sought aid for their beloved Bay Colony, bringing with them letters describing the "horrors" of Lexington and Concord. A letter from the Massachusetts provincial congress asserted that there was no hope of stemming "the rapid Progress of a tyrannical Ministry" except by the establishment of an army superior to the forces of Britain. With such a force there was hope of ending "the inhuman Ravages of mercenary Troops" and of seeing the "wicked authors of our Miseries, brought to condign punishment." [2] Without it the colonies might expect to become "the Victims of their relentless fury."

Congress did not at once heed the broad hint that the time had come to take up arms and drive out the British. But the presence of British troops and the expected arrival of others forced even the conservatives to realize that a policy of submission would result in the loss of their rights and liberties. A letter from some of the colonial agents made it plain that Great Britain intended to execute her laws with military force.[3] Therefore when New York requested advice, Congress replied that the people should act only on the defensive, yet they were not to permit the erection of fortifications nor the severance of connections between town and country. Furthermore, if British troops committed hostilities or invaded private property, the people were to defend themselves and their property and to repel any attacks.[4]

A second letter from Massachusetts asserted that the establishment of civil government was necessary to control the military gathering around Boston. What should be done? It was also suggested that since the troops gathering around Boston were there

[2] *Journals*, 2:24–42, May 11.

[3] Circular letter from William Bollan, Benjamin Franklin, and Arthur Lee to the Speakers of Colonial Assemblies, London, February 5, 1775, *ibid.*, 22–23.

[4] *Ibid.*, 49–53. Further resolves were passed on May 25, giving more specific advice than was contained in the resolve of May 15. *Ibid.*, 59–61.

for the defense of American rights, Congress should take over their supervision and regulation.[5] While the army seems never to have been adopted formally, Congress was presently so committed to the supervision of the war that after considerable political jockeying it appointed as commander-in-chief a man who had been making himself conspicuous in that eminently civilian body by appearing in uniform.[6]

The conservatives believed with the radicals that the events at Lexington and Concord partook of "butchery." [7] It had been reported in Philadelphia that old men, women, and children had been slaughtered indiscriminately by the minions of the British government.[8] Sorrowfully the conservatives realized that after such measures on the part of Great Britain they had not a political leg upon which to stand. "But what topicks of reconciliation are now left for men who think as I do, to address our countrymen," wrote John Dickinson after the outbreak of hostilities in Massachusetts.[9]

But although they acquiesced in the use of force, the conservatives maintained that it was for defense alone, and they continued to insist that reconciliation be sought. The quarrel, they said, must be considered a family quarrel, and all thought of revenge, of conquest, and of independence must be "banished from every American breast." [10] Their anomalous policy of presenting petitions and at the same time supporting warfare gave a "whimsical Cast to the Proceedings of this Congress," wrote John Adams, "a strange Oscillation between love and hatred, between War and peace — preparations for War and Negociations for Peace." [11] He

[5] Massachusetts Provincial Congress to the Continental Congress, Watertown, May 16, *ibid.*, 76–78, June 2.

[6] John Adams, Autobiography, in *Works*, 2:415–418; *Journals*, 2:79, 89, 91, 92; John Adams to Mrs. Adams, May 29, in *Familiar Letters*, 59.

[7] John Dickinson to Arthur Lee, April 29, in Force, *American Archives*, 4th series, 2:444.

[8] Richard Henry Lee to [William Lee], Philadelphia, May 10, in *The Letters of Richard Henry Lee*, edited by James O. Ballagh (2 vols., New York, 1912), 1:134–135.

[9] To Arthur Lee, April 29, 1775, in Force, *American Archives*, 4th series, 2:445.

[10] James Duane, "Notes on the State of the Colonies" [May 25, 1775], in Burnett, *Letters*, 1:99.

[11] John Adams to James Warren, Philadelphia, July 6, 1775, in *Warren-Adams Letters* (*Massachusetts Historical Collections*, vols. 62, 73, Boston,

believed that "powder and artillery are the most efficacious, sure and infallible conciliatory measures we can adopt." [12]

The radicals wanted preparation for out-and-out warfare. Their strategy soon secured the passage of a resolution advising New York to prepare more vigorously for its defense, since it was "very uncertain whether the earnest endeavours of the Congress to accommodate the unhappy differences between G. Britain and the colonies by conciliatory Measures will be successful." [13] This move was countered the next day by the adoption of a series of resolutions designed to carry out the conservative program. It was stated that inasmuch as the colonies were in a dangerous condition because of the British government's determination to execute by force of arms the oppressive and unconstitutional acts of the British Parliament, it was necessary to put them in a state of defense. Yet they still desired reconciliation; hence a petition was to be sent to the king, and measures were to be taken for entering into negotiations for a settlement of difficulties. [14]

The success of this move was only in part due to conservative control of Congress: it was also a tribute to the personal prestige and influence of the leader of the conservatives, John Dickinson. [15] It was he who drew up the petition, which was accepted by Congress in much the same form as he gave it to them. [16] It pointed to the benefits which both the colonies and Great Britain derived from their connection, attributed the existing difficulties to the

1917, 1925), 1:74–75. John Adams realized the necessity of agreeing to the conservative policy. "We must have a Petition to the King and a delicate Proposal of Negociation, etc. This Negociation I dread like Death: But it must be proposed. We cant avoid it. Discord and total Disunion would be the certain Effect of a resolute Refusal to petition and negociate."

[12] John Adams to Moses Gill, Philadelphia, June 10, in *Works*, 9:356–357.

[13] *Journals*, 2:61–64.

[14] *Ibid.*, 64–66. The addition of the provision that measures should be taken to open negotiations and that such proposals should be included as a part of the petition to the king seems to have been the work of James Duane. See *ibid.*, vol. 2, p. 65, note 1. The committee to draft the petition was elected on June 3 and consisted of John Dickinson, Thomas Johnson, John Rutledge, John Jay, and Benjamin Franklin. *Ibid.*, 79–80. It was reported to Congress on June 19, debated on July 4 and 5, and ordered engrossed. It was signed on July 8. *Ibid.*, 100, 126, 127, 158. It is printed *ibid.*, 158–162.

[15] Thomas Jefferson, Autobiography, in *Writings*, 1:17. "Congress gave a signal proof of their indulgence to Mr. Dickinson, and of their great desire not to go too fast for any respectable part of our body."

[16] *Ibid.*

wiles of George III's ministers, and expressed a desire to prevent any further effusion of blood. There was no inconsistency, it was urged, between the expression of loyalty in a petition and the use of force against his Majesty's troops; this seeming hypocrisy was attributable not to "reprehensible intention, but to the impossibility of reconciling the usual appearances of respect, with a just attention to our own preservation against those artful and cruel enemies, who abuse your royal confidence and authority, for the purpose of effecting our destruction." [17]

The radicals were furious. John Adams wrote that "a certain great Fortune and piddling Genius, whose Fame has been trumpeted so loudly, has given a silly Cast to our whole Doings. We are between Hawk and Buzzard." [18] The thing to do was to prepare for war, not to send petitions which deluded people and kept them from making the preparations they would have to make. Reconciliation was hopeless; "the cancer is too deeply rooted and too far spread to be cured by anything short of cutting it out entire." [19]

At the same time that this second petition to the king was being written, a declaration of the causes that had led the colonists to take up arms was also being prepared. Congress was united in desiring such a declaration, but divided as to its form. Jefferson wrote the first draft, a hard-hitting, clear-cut statement of the radical point of view. Dickinson objected to the violence of the

[17] *Journals*, 2:158–162. The change in Dickinson's attitude may be seen by comparing the first petition to the king (which he is supposed to have written) with the second petition. The first petition is printed in the *Journals*, 1:115–121.

[18] John Adams to James Warren, July 24, in *Warren-Adams Letters*, 1:88–89. John Adams, in his Autobiography (*Works*, 2:412), and Stillé, in his *Life and Times of Dickinson* (pp. 160–161), interpret the reaction to the capture of this letter by the British and its publication by them. Dickinson's own view of the petition to the king is contained in a letter to Arthur Lee, July 7, 1775, in Force, *American Archives*, 4th series, 2:1604. He felt that it offered the administration an opportunity to stop shedding "British blood" if they so desired. See also Thomas Johnson to Horatio Gates, August 18, 1775, in Burnett, *Letters*, 1:190–191.

[19] John Adams to Moses Gill, June 10, in *Works*, 9:356. In spite of his impatience he realized that "this Continent is a vast, unwieldy machine. We cannot force events. We must suffer people to take their own way in many cases, when we think it leads wrong, hoping, however, and believing that our liberty and felicity will be preserved in the end, though not in the speediest and surest manner."

language and took it in hand to revise it.[20] He used much of Jefferson's work and phraseology but paid much more respect to the Deity and modified the discussion of the constitutional foundation of the colonies to agree with conservative ideas. Jefferson had written that the colonists had come over to America, created their governments, and then formed compacts with the mother country,[21] all of which was the heart of the radical creed and the justification for revolution. Dickinson's version was that societies and governments were formed *under* charters *from* the crown and that harmonious relationships were established with the kingdom *from* which the colonies *derived* their origin.[22] However, the "Declaration" remained a spirited precursor of the Declaration of Independence, in spite of its insistence upon reconciliation.

During the rest of the year Congress pursued the negative policy of meeting situations only as they arose. Great was the wrath of the radicals, who wanted to adopt positive measures. When, in July, Franklin submitted a plan of confederation which admitted of reconciliation, it was buried in piles of unfinished business.[23] Lord North's "motion on reconciliation," however, was rejected by Congress because it left all the disputed issues unsettled.[24]

When the British government passed two acts restraining the trade of all the colonies except New York, Delaware, North Carolina, and Georgia, a division of interest appeared that created much heat, though it resulted in no change of policy.[25] The first reaction was the passage of a resolution for the continuance of

[20] The first committee appointed to draft the declaration was composed of John Rutledge, William Livingston, Benjamin Franklin, John Jay, and Thomas Johnson. This committee reported a draft to Congress which was recommitted, John Dickinson and Thomas Jefferson being added to the committee. Jefferson drew up a draft which was "too strong for Mr. Dickinson." Dickinson then took the Jefferson draft and softened its tone. This was the draft presented to and adopted by Congress. *Journals*, 2:105–108, 127, 128, note 1; Jefferson, Autobiography, in *Writings*, 1:17; *Journals*, 2:128–140. Dickinson's two drafts are included in the *Journals*, 2:140–157, the second draft being the final form.

[21] *Ibid.*, 128–130.   [22] *Ibid.*, 142.

[23] *Ibid.*, 195, July 21. The plan is printed *ibid.*, 195–199.

[24] *Ibid.*, 62–63, 225–234.

[25] *Annual Register*, 1775, pp. 78–93, 102–103; Schlesinger, *Colonial Merchants*, 538. The colonies were restrained from trading with any part of the world except the British Isles and the British West Indies after July 1, 1775, and the New England colonies were not to use the fisheries after July 20.

the Association until the acts should be repealed.[26] This was in July. By September, when the nonexportation clauses of the Association were to go into effect, the material profits of trade had begun to appear more attractive to the exempted colonies than the less material profits of patriotism. They made a strenuous attempt to have the Association relaxed, developing all sorts of ingenious arguments to prove that such relaxation would be beneficial to all the colonies and not to themselves alone. The radicals generally, and the conservatives from the colonies subject to the Restraining Acts, insisted on the continuance of the Association and proved themselves strong enough to make its provisions even more rigid.[27]

The conservatives set themselves hard against such radical measures as were proposed by John Adams: the abolition of customs houses, the creation of independent governments in each of the colonies, the formation of a confederation, and the opening of the ports to all the world.[28] Such proposals were of course open defiance of Great Britain and practical independence, and independence was the great bogy of the conservatives. "We do not want to be independent," wrote Joseph Hewes, a North Carolina merchant and a delegate to Congress, "we want no revolution, unless a change of Ministry and measures would be deemed such. We are loyal subjects to our present most gracious Sovereign." Like other conservatives, Hewes realized that his position was difficult to maintain, and he prophesied that unless something were done soon, the colonies would be lost to the mother country.[29] Even the conservatives could see that such measures as the king's proc-

[26] *Journals*, 2:125, July 4.

[27] John Adams, Notes on Debates, in *Works*, 2:452–457, 460, 469–484; *Journals*, 3:268–269, 314–315.

[28] John Adams to James Warren, July 6, October 7, 20, 1775, in *Warren-Adams Letters*, 1:75, 126–129, 155; John Adams, Autobiography, in *Works*, 2:406–407, 412. Adams said in his autobiography that at this time he made no secret either in or out of Congress of his belief that independence was indispensable. His attitude on opening the ports in the autumn of 1775 is evidence that while he was a conservative, he was never really a Federalist. "God helps those who helps themselves," he wrote. The colonies have no real friend to depend upon "but the Resources of our own Country, and the good sense and great Virtues of our People. We shall finally be obliged to depend upon ourselves." *Warren-Adams Letters*, 1:128.

[29] "Letter from a Gentleman in North-Carolina, and one of the Delegates of the Congress [*Joseph Hewes*], to a Principal House in Edinburgh," Edenton, July 31, 1775, in Force, *American Archives*, 4th series, 2:1757.

lamation of rebellion were "putting the Halter about our Necks, and we may as well die by the Sword as be hang'd like Rebels." [30] A few more violent acts on the part of Great Britain, it was predicted, would so arouse the temper of the people that a complete separation would result.[31]

This fear that the colonies would be forced into independence by British measures on the one hand and the designs of colonial radicals on the other led the conservatives to inaugurate a new policy wherever they were in control of the old colonial assemblies or of the new revolutionary organizations. In November the Pennsylvania Assembly adopted a set of instructions which John Dickinson, as a member of the Assembly, had addressed to himself and his colleagues as members of Congress. In these instructions it was argued, as in the second petition to the king, that a resort to arms had been made necessary by the oppressive measures of Britain. Yet the Pennsylvania delegates were ordered to "dissent from, and utterly reject, any propositions, should such be made, that may cause or lead to a separation from our Mother Country, or a change of the form of this Government." [32]

The fatal weakness of this policy lay in the fact that it was a negative one. The radicals in their greater political wisdom refrained from making statements which would lay them open to the charge that they sought independence, whatever their real intentions may have been. Instead they undertook to steer Congress in that direction by advocating such measures as the adoption of the army, by urging confederation, and by moving that

[30] John Morton to Thomas Powell, Philadelphia, June 8, 1775, in Burnett, *Letters*, 1:114; Joseph Hewes to Samuel Johnston, Philadelphia, December 1, 1775, *ibid.*, 266–267: "no plan of Seperation has been offered, the Colonies will never agree to any till drove to it by dire necessity. I wish the time may not come too soon. I fear it will be the case if the British Ministry pursue their present diabolical Schemes."

[31] "A Member of Congress to a Gentleman in London," August 26, 1775, *ibid.*, 191.

[32] Force, *American Archives*, 4th series, 3:1407; Stillé, *Dickinson*, 165; Lincoln, *Revolutionary Movement in Pennsylvania*, 224–227. Lincoln says that Dickinson and his followers did not join the movement for independence at this time because there was no strong central government and they were distrustful of the radical party in the colony. On December 9 Robert Morris, who had recently become a member of Congress, wrote to a correspondent in Cadiz that he would exert all his influence to bring about an accommodation consistent with American claims. Burnett, *Letters*, 1:271.

the ports of the colonies be opened to the world, all of which could be justified on the logical and patriotic ground of being necessary to the defense of colonial rights. Thus Congress was maneuvered into a position in which it was practically fighting for independence though the word was not mentioned.

Unfortunately for the conservatives, the British government continued to play into the hands of the radicals. The king's proclamation of rebellion in August was an instance. Later, when the news arrived that the king had charged, in his speech to Parliament in October, that "the Rebellious war now levied is become more general, and is manifestly carried on for the purpose of establishing an independent empire," [33] the end of conservative control was near. In order to deny this charge James Wilson moved that the Congress declare to its constituents its intentions with regard to the question of independence.[34] The radicals were alarmed. Sam Adams said that Congress had already been explicit enough and that he was afraid they might get on "dangerous Ground." But all that the radicals were able to do was to effect a postponement of the motion.[35]

In the meantime they had brought forward the program of confederation. Sam Adams had written to James Warren early in January, in answer to a request from the latter, that he would hear of the confederation when some gentlemen felt more bold. "It is not dead but sleepeth." [36] So desirous of confederation was Adams that he even considered the idea of uniting New England in a confederation if the other colonies would not join, an idea which seems to have met with the approval of the Virginians.[37] Franklin's plan was dug from the piles of unfinished business, and on January 16 an attempt was made to have a day set for its consideration.

[33] *Annual Register*, 1775, pp. 268–271.

[34] Richard Smith, Diary, January 9, 1776, in the *American Historical Review*, 1:307.

[35] Samuel Adams to John Adams, Philadelphia, January 15, 1776, in *Writings*, 3:259.

[36] Samuel Adams to James Warren, Philadelphia, January 7, 1776, in *Warren-Adams Letters*, 1:197.

[37] Sam Adams to John Adams, Philadelphia, January 15, 1776, in *Writings*, 3:260. Edward Tilghman wrote to his father on February 4, 1776, that "some time since, Judas Iscariot [*Sam Adams*] made a motion, of whose contents I am note quite certain, but it tended towards a *closer confederacy*, and was of such a nature that whole Colonies threatened to leave the Congress." Stillé, *Dickinson*, 174.

The conservatives, led by Dickinson, defeated the motion [38] and continued to gather their forces in anticipation of the discussion of James Wilson's motion for an address to the colonies.[39]

On January 24 a committee of outstanding conservatives was appointed to prepare the address,[40] which was laid before Congress three weeks later.[41] But by this time the political current was running strongly in the direction of radicalism. One delegate wrote in his diary that "Wilson brought in the Draught of the Address to our Constituents which was very long, badly written, and full against Independency (Wilson perceiving the Majority did not relish his Address and Doctrine never thought fit to stir it again)." The failure to adopt the address marked the end of the conservative control of Congress.[42] From that day on, step by step, the radicals adopted measures calculated to establish the independence of the colonies. Nevertheless the conservatives remained a powerful restraining influence, not in preventing independence but in delaying its final declaration.

THE TRIUMPH OF RADICALISM

THE DAY AFTER Congress rejected James Wilson's address John Adams reported a change of opinion, or at least a change in the expression of opinion, in the colonies. "Scarcely a paper comes out without a speculation or two in open vindication of opinions, which, five months ago, were said to be unpopular." [43] On the same day John Penn wrote that independence might be the in-

[38] *Journals*, 3:456; Richard Smith, Diary, January 16, 1776, in the *American Historical Review*, 1:309.

[39] George Read to Caesar Rodney, January 19, 1776, in *Letters to and from Caesar Rodney*, 69.

[40] *Journals*, 4:87; Richard Smith, Diary, January 24, in the *American Historical Review*, 1:495. "Much was said about Independency and the Mode and Propriety of stating our Dependance on the King." The Committee was composed of John Dickinson, James Wilson, William Hooper, James Duane, and Robert Alexander, the first four of whom were outstanding conservative leaders.

[41] *Journals*, 4:134–146. The address was written by James Wilson.

[42] Richard Smith, Diary, February 13, 1776, in the *American Historical Review*, 1:501–502; *Journals*, 4:146, "Ordered, To lie on the table." Wilson later told James Madison that the address was meant "to lead the public mind into the idea of Independence." *Journals*, vol. 4, p. 146, note 1.

[43] John Adams to James Warren, February 14, 1776, in Force, *American Archives*, 4th series, 4:1140.

evitable result of the contraction of alliances, a plan that was being agitated in Congress.[44] Two days later George Wythe offered resolutions to the effect that the colonies had the right to make alliances with foreign powers, and moved the appointment of a committee to prepare a plan of confederation for the consideration of the assemblies and conventions of the several colonies.[45] By February 29 a declaration of independence was being openly discussed, but consideration was deferred because five or six of the colonies had instructed their delegates not to agree to such a step without consulting their constituents.[46] Thus for a time Dickinson's precautionary tactics blocked serious discussion of the question in Congress.

The movement for independence really began with the publication of Thomas Paine's *Common Sense* in January, 1776. No longer could there be any middle ground where one might urge reconciliation and at the same time sanction force. *Common Sense* was a remarkable statement of the radical philosophy of government and of the radical attitude toward Great Britain. It aroused popular opinion, for it crystallized, in language easily understood and appreciated, the emotions and beliefs of the ordinarily inarticulate masses. It began with an attack on government in general, stripping it of all glamour with the statement that "Government, like dress, is the badge of lost innocence." Reverence for monarchial authority was jolted by the assertion that "the palaces of kings are built on the ruins of the bowers of paradise." The common man was exalted above aristocracy in the declaration

[44] John Penn to Thomas Person, February 14, 1776, in Burnett, *Letters*, 1:349.

[45] John Adams, Notes on Debates, February 16, 1776, in *Works*, 2:486–487; Richard Smith, Diary, in the *American Historical Review*, 1:502.

[46] *Ibid.*, 507. A seriocomic division between radicals and conservatives occurred after the funeral oration delivered in memory of General Montgomery. Dr. Smith, an ardent conservative of Philadelphia, preached a sermon in which he asserted that the Congress wished to continue in dependence on Britain. The conservatives attempted to procure the thanks of Congress for the oration, and the radicals opposed it because "the Dr. declared the sentiments of the Congress to continue in a Dependency on G. Britain which Doctrine this Congress cannot now approve." James Wilson, James Duane, and Thomas Willing supported the motion to thank Dr. Smith; Samuel Chase, John Adams, George Wythe, and others opposed it. The motion was finally withdrawn. *Ibid.*, 494, 503–504; Oliver Wolcott to Mrs. Wolcott, March 19, 1776, in Burnett, *Letters*, 1:399.

that "of more worth is one honest man to society, in the sight of God, than all the crowned ruffians that ever lived." Paine scouted the idea that the connection with England was the basis of American prosperity, pointing out that the articles of American commerce were the necessaries of life and that Americans would always have a market "while eating is the custom in Europe." He argued that it was in the true interest of America to keep clear of entangling alliances, but that she could never do so while connected with Great Britain.[47]

The cause of independence was also promoted by the American Prohibitory Bill of December 23, 1775, which provided that the trade and commerce of all the colonies should be totally cut off, and that the goods and ships of Americans on the high seas and in the harbors were to be forfeit to the officers and crews of the British navy. It repealed the Port Bill and Restraining Acts as inadequate for the existing state of warfare.[48] The British opposition and the colonial radicals were agreed that this was a practical declaration of independence by the British government, as formal an act of abdication as could be penned, and that it destroyed all hopes of accommodation. One speaker observed that the bill answered all the purposes of the most violent Americans, and that it might well have been entitled "A bill for carrying more effectually into execution the resolves of Congress." [49]

Richard Henry Lee wrote that it was curious to observe "that whilst people here are disputing and hesitating about independancy, the Court by one bold Act of Parliament, and by a conduct the most extensively hostile, have already put the two Countries asunder. . . . The measure of British crimes is running over, and

[47] Thomas Paine, *Common Sense*, in *The Writings of Thomas Paine*, edited by Moncure D. Conway (New York, 1894), 1:69–120. John Adams' reaction to the pamphlet is clear evidence that he was a conservative politically in spite of the fact that he was one of the most able leaders in the movement for independence. The account of his reaction which he gives in his autobiography (*Works*, 1:507–508) may have been colored by events subsequent to 1776. He says that Paine's ideas on government flowed "from simple ignorance, and a mere desire to please the democratic party in Philadelphia." He regretted that so foolish a plan had been submitted to the people, and to counteract the effects of Paine's work he wrote a pamphlet, *Thoughts on Government, in a Letter from a Gentleman to His Friend*, in which he described the idea of "checks and balances" as well as it has ever been done. Humorously enough, Paine's work was attributed to John Adams himself, much to the latter's regret.
[48] *Annual Register*, 1776, pp. 109, 111.   [49] *Ibid.*, 109, 112.

the barbarous spoliation of the East is crying to Heaven for vengeance against the Destroyers of the Human Race." [50] John Adams, who thought the best title for the act was "Act of Independency," said that it might be fortunate that it had come from the British Parliament, and he thought it very odd that Americans should hesitate to accept the gift.[51]

The act removed the last real objection to the opening of colonial ports to the world, a measure which the conservatives had opposed, as they had confederation, because it was a step in the direction of independence. Now the radicals moved ahead, and on April 6, 1776, the ports of the colonies were declared open to all the world except the dominions of Great Britain, and subject only to such regulations as might be made by the United Colonies or the several legislatures thereof.[52]

The position of the conservatives remained what it had been in the first Continental Congress. They had argued then the necessity of a supreme legislature over the colonies to regulate trade and maintain the peace between colony and colony. The fears which had moved them at that time had since been increased rather than lulled. Connecticut had moved troops into the Wyoming Valley of Pennsylvania. New York was engaged in a dispute with the people who had settled in Vermont under grants from New Hampshire, on lands claimed by New York. Pennsylvania and Virginia were engaged in a bitter dispute over their boundary, the prize being Fort Pitt. Such disputes were extremely alarming to the conservatives, who feared civil war among the colonies if independence should be declared.[53]

A second consideration determining the conservative attitude was what may be called, broadly, the fear of democracy: the fear

[50] To Landon Carter, April 1, 1776, in Lee, *Letters*, 1:173.

[51] John Adams to Horatio Gates, Philadelphia, March 23, 1776, in Burnett, *Letters*, 1:406.

[52] On the question of opening the ports see John Adams to James Warren, July 6, 1775, in *Warren-Adams Letters*, 1:75; John Adams, Autobiography, in *Works*, 3:29, and Notes on Debates, February 16, 1776, *ibid.*, 2:485–486; and the *Journals*, 4:59, 62–63, 113, 148, 153, 154, 159, 256, 257–259. On March 23 Congress had authorized privateering. The movement had been inaugurated by a petition from citizens of Philadelphia, and was pushed through in spite of uncertain objections on the part of the conservatives. See Richard Smith, Diary, in the *American Historical Review*, 1:508, 511, 512–513; *Journals*, 4:229–232.

[53] Carter Braxton to Landon Carter, April 14, 1776, in Burnett, *Letters*, 1:421.

of political revolution within the colonies. It is commonly assumed that all revolutionists were radicals; that as time passed and bitter experience taught them, the fathers of the Revolution repented of their radical beliefs and became conservative.[54] But the fact that a man became a revolutionist is no proof of his political radicalism. Such men as George Washington, James Wilson, Robert R. Livingston, John Dickinson, Edward Rutledge, and Charles Carroll were always conservative in political philosophy and practice. None of them adopted the democratic ideas trumpeted by the radicals, though some of them accepted independence as the only solution of the difficulties with Great Britain.[55]

The conservatives were as strongly opposed to British measures threatening colonial home rule as were the radicals. But most of them desired no rupture in the connection with the empire, which seemed to offer a far less dubious future than independence. Increasingly they opposed a complete break as they became aware that independence might result in a revolution at home, that conservative rule had more to fear from the people of the colonies than from British legislation.[56] But as a group they were slow to awaken to this fact, caught as they were between the twin fires of British legislation and radical activity.

One of the first to see the dilemma of the conservatives and to

[54] Henry Cabot Lodge, in his *Alexander Hamilton* (Boston, 1882), 43–45, states this thesis briefly.

[55] Of the above-named group, George Washington and Charles Carroll were probably the only ones to accept independence willingly. John Dickinson refused to sign the Declaration. Robert Morris did so but regretted it and still hoped for reconciliation. Henry Laurens declared that he wept at the news of independence. Robert R. Livingston opposed the Declaration until the last moment. James Wilson switched his vote at the last moment, a switch interpreted by a fellow conservative as simply an effort to retain his political life.

[56] Herbert Friedenwald, in *The Declaration of Independence* (New York, 1905), 78–80, makes a very clear statement of the difficult position of the conservatives and the effect it had on the question of independence. Louis M. Hacker, in his monograph "The First American Revolution," in the *Columbia University Quarterly*, 27:259–295 (September, 1935), interprets the Revolution as the inevitable outcome of the growth of colonial capitalism, which at last determined to throw off the imperial shackles. The answer to this contention, which in the broad view has much truth in it, is that such colonial capitalists as had political influence in 1776 were dominated by fear of internal revolution. It is true that British measures were bad, but a social revolution was infinitely worse, and "capitalistic" spokesmen voted accordingly in the first and second Continental Congresses.

state his preference was Gouverneur Morris. He admitted that the ruling aristocracy had fooled the masses overlong and that the masses were beginning to realize it. If the attempt to deceive were continued, he wrote, "farewell aristocracy . . . if the disputes with Great Britain continue, we shall be under the worst of all possible dominions; we shall be under the domination of a riotous mob." What could the aristocracy do to save itself? Morris had a ready answer: "It is the interest of all men, therefore, to seek for reunion with the parent State." [57] Morris thus saw what others were not to see for a year, or even two years: that the connection with Great Britain was the guarantee of the aristocratic order within the colonies. The growing realization of that fact did much to determine the attitude of the conservatives toward the idea of independence and toward the idea of a common government once independence could no longer be avoided.

Thomas Wharton, merchant of Philadelphia, was another who hoped for a closer union with Great Britain in order that aristocracy might be maintained. In January, 1775, he saw nothing but gloomy prospects: "our happy days have departed from us; the thoughtful among us cannot help Asking, what is to be the Next step if England sh.ᵈ be Overcome? This Question sinks deep in our minds, for altho' We think our Parent State wrong with respect to some Acts of Parliament, Yet We have reason to believe She will ever redress our Grievances when Properly stated; but what redress is to be Expected what Civil or Religious Liberty Enjoyd, shᵈ others gain the Ascendency." [58] There is no mistaking that by "others" Wharton meant those who in his eyes constituted the "lower classes."

The views expressed by James Allen of the wealthy Allen family illustrate how opinion changed during the two years preceding the Declaration of Independence. In July, 1775, he wrote in his diary that the eyes of Europe were on America, and that if

[57] Gouverneur Morris to Mr. —— Penn, New York, May 20, 1774, in Force, *American Archives*, 4th series, 1:343.

[58] Thomas Wharton to Samuel Wharton, Philadelphia, January 31, 1775, in the Thomas Wharton Letter Book, 1775–1784, pp. 140–141, in Pennsylvania Historical Society Manuscripts. On January 18, 1775, Thomas Wharton had written to Thomas Walpole that he feared "there are some on this Continent whose political Creed is in Opposition to Monarchical Government." His great concern at this time was for a closer constitutional union with Great Britain.

"we fall, Liberty no longer continues an inhabitant of this Globe: for England is running fast to slavery. The King is as despotic as any prince in Europe; the only difference is the mode; & a venal parliament are as bad as a standing army." [59] By 1776 the issue had become one of independence and internal revolution rather than one of resistance. In March of that year Allen recorded, "Thinking people uneasy, irresolute & inactive. The Mobility triumphant." Congress was in a state of equilibrium on the subject of independence. Allen's personal dilemma was great: "I love the Cause of Liberty; but cannot heartily join the prosecution of measures totally foreign to the original plan of Resistance. The madness of the multitude is but one degree better than submission to the Tea-Act." [60]

When Alexander Graydon returned to Philadelphia in 1776, he found that many who had formerly supported Whiggism and liberty were now less ardent. The reason, he said, was that "Power, to use a language which had already ceased to be orthodox, and could therefore, only be whispered, had fallen into low hands . . . It was, in fact, just beginning to be perceived, that the ardour of the inflamed multitude is not to be tempered; and that the instigators of revolutions are rarely those who are destined to conclude them, or profit by them." [61]

Independence was seen as an evil of which internal discord and revolution seemed to be the inevitable twin. "We do not want to be independent," wrote Joseph Hewes, merchant of North Caro-

[59] Diary of James Allen, July 26, 1775, in the *Pennsylvania Magazine of History and Biography*, 9:185 (1885). Even then he reported that many "thinking people" were feeling that America had seen its best days, and even if the outcome were a victorious peace, it would be difficult to restore order. In October, 1775, Allen joined a battalion of Associators; "my Inducement principally to join them is: that a man is suspected who does not." He also believed that "discreet people mixing with them, may keep them [in] Order." *Ibid.*, 184–185, 186.

[60] *Ibid.*, 186, March 6, 1776.

[61] Alexander Graydon, *Memoirs of His Own Times, with Reminiscences of the Men and Events of the Revolution* (Philadelphia, 1846), 283–284. John Adams viewed the matter in somewhat the same fashion. In his autobiography he wrote that "the gentlemen in Pennsylvania, who had been attached to the proprietary interest, and owed their wealth and honors to it, and the great body of the Quakers, had hitherto acquiesced in the measures of the Colonies, or at least had made no professed opposition to them; many of both descriptions had declared themselves with us, and had been as explicit and as ardent as we were. But now these people began to see that independence was ap-

lina and delegate to Congress, "we want no revolution, unless a change of Ministry and measures would be deemed such." [62]

It is in the light of these beliefs that the attitude of the conservatives toward separation from Great Britain must be considered, as well as their attitude toward the creation of another central government, once that separation had become a fact. Their power was centered in the colonies of Pennsylvania, New York, and Maryland, and to a lesser extent in New Jersey and Delaware, which usually followed in the wake of their more important neighbors. In New York and Maryland the conservatives controlled the revolutionary governments which had been set up.[63] In Pennsylvania the old Assembly was still the legal representative of the colony, but its actual authority was gradually ebbing away. It was recognized that a break with England would mean revolution in government, since a major objective of the radical parties in the Middle colonies was the attainment of political power. The conservatives, especially those of Pennsylvania, clung to their old constitution, which guaranteed their position. The few concessions they did make came so slowly, and so obviously as the result of outside pressure, that they had no influence whatever over the revolutionary organization once it had taken over the control of the state.[64]

The radical leaders in Congress knew that they must have united action and so must have the support of the Middle colonies.[65] To attain this end they continued the policy which had resulted in the establishment of revolutionary governments in

proaching, they started back." *Works,* 2:407. What John Adams said of Pennsylvania was equally true of colonies like New York, Maryland, and South Carolina, where the conservatives still retained control in 1775 and 1776.

[62] "Letter from a Gentleman in North-Carolina, and one of the Delegates of the Congress [*Joseph Hewes*], to a Principal House in Edinburgh," Edenton, July 31, 1775, in Force, *American Archives,* 4th series, 2:1757.

[63] Becker says in his *Political Parties,* 272, that the affairs of the province were directed by conservative politicians "who, in the face of an armed foe and surrounded by domestic enemies, were still determined to preserve the essential features of their ancient political system from what they conceived to be monarchial encroachments on the one hand, as well as from rash democratic experiments on the other."

[64] Lincoln, *Revolutionary Movement in Pennsylvania, passim.*

[65] John Adams to Horatio Gates, March 23, 1776, in Burnett, *Letters,* 1:406; Richard Henry Lee to Patrick Henry, April 20, 1776, and to Charles Lee, April 22, May 21, 1776, in Lee, *Letters,* 1:176–180, 181–183, 192–193.

most of the colonies. This movement had begun in May, 1775, when the Massachusetts convention, with suspicious modesty, refused to assume the powers of civil government without the advice and consent of the other colonies.[66] Congress then advised the Massachusetts Provincial Convention to "write letters to the inhabitants of the several places, which are intituled to representation in Assembly, requesting them to chuse such representatives, and that the Assembly, when chosen, do elect counsellors; which assembly and council should exercise the powers of Government, until a Governor, of his Majesty's appointment, will consent to govern the colony according to its charter." This specific advice to follow old procedures was due to the personnel of the committee rather than to any state of opinion characteristic of June, 1775.[67]

When New Hampshire appealed to Congress for advice in October, a committee dominated by radicals was appointed to prepare an answer, and the reply they made was in accord with radical views. No mention was made of charter restrictions. The colony was advised "to call a full and free representation of the people, and that the representatives, if they think it necessary, establish such a form of government, as, in their judgment, will best produce the happiness of the people."[68] In these two letters of advice lies the whole difference between the philosophy of conservatism and the philosophy of radicalism. South Carolina[69]

[66] Massachusetts Provincial Congress to the Continental Congress, Watertown, May 16, 1775, in the *Journals*, 2:76–78. It must be remembered that these requests for "advice" were not dictated by any particular consideration for the Continental Congress nor by any recognition of its authority, but by motives of political expediency. Such a "request" was often the work of members of Congress who wished to obtain action by that body, or, if it originated in the colonial government, to secure support for a policy that one party or another desired to maintain within the colony concerned.

[67] *Journals*, 2:79, 83–84. The committee was composed of Thomas Johnson, John Rutledge, John Jay, James Wilson, and Richard Henry Lee.

[68] *Ibid.*, 3:298, 307, 319. The committee was composed of John Rutledge, John Adams, Samuel Ward, Richard Henry Lee, and Roger Sherman.

[69] *Ibid.*, 326–327; Sam Adams to James Warren, November 4, 1775, in *Warren-Adams Letters*, 1:170. The South Carolina government that was formed in March, 1776, was regarded as temporary. Henry Laurens wrote that "necessity impelled this measure & every faithful heart wishes that its duration may be shortened by a happy accomodation of the present destructive contest between the Mother Country & these United Colonies." To John Laurens, Charleston, March 28, 1776, in Mason Library Manuscripts, Portfolio no. 19.

and Virginia [70] also were advised not long afterward to organize governments in letters identical with that which had been sent to New Hampshire.

This policy of setting up governments was a part of the radical program of steering the colonies in the direction of independence, for, as Sam Adams wrote, the radicals believed that if new governments were set up, "the Colonies will feel their independence, the way will be prepared for a confederation, and one government may be prepared with the consent of the whole." [71] But, as John Adams said, one must never call it independence. "Independency is a Hobgoblin of so frightful Mien, that it would throw a delicate Person into Fits to look it in the Face." [72]

By the spring of 1776, matters had settled down to a "war" between "the New England Delegates" and "the advocates of Proprietary interests in Congress and this Colony." [73] The conservatives, who had begun to look upon independence as inevitable, were now exerting their efforts to delay its declaration, their argument being that they wished to consult "the people." This was a specious argument, coming as it did from those activated chiefly by a desire to delay the rise of "the people" to power. "Those who wish delay, and want nothing done," wrote Richard Henry Lee, "say, let the people in the Colonies begin, we must not go before them, Tho' they well know the language in the Country to be, Let the Congress advise." [74]

The ostensible reason for the delay of the conservative delegates was that some of them, notably those from Pennsylvania, Maryland, and New York, had specific instructions to oppose any measures that might lead to independence. It was these instructions which had made the Pennsylvania Assembly "so ex-

[70] *Journals*, 3:403–404.

[71] Samuel Adams to Samuel Cooper, April 30, 1776, in William V. Wells, *Life and Public Services of Samuel Adams* (Boston, 1865), 2:395. Indicative of the force behind this movement is the statement of John Adams, in a letter to Elbridge Gerry, that New Hampshire and South Carolina have been given leave to assume government, "but this must not be freely talked of as yet, at least from me." *Works*, 9:364.

[72] John Adams to Horatio Gates, March 23, 1776, in Burnett, *Letters*, 1:405–406.

[73] Elbridge Gerry to James Warren, June 25, 1776, in Force, *American Archives*, 4th series, 6:1067.

[74] To Charles Lee, May 11, 1776, in Burnett, *Letters*, 1:442.

ceedingly obnoxious to America in General, and their own Constituents in particular." [75]

The problem of the radical party was to bring about a political revolution in those colonies, since they refused to revoke the instructions they had given a few months before or to instruct their delegates positively to vote for independence. It was obvious that the conservatives in Pennsylvania would not consider setting up a new government when they were quite content with the government they had and were determined to retain it. Therefore the radicals in Congress gave the still submerged radicals in Pennsylvania an opportunity to seize power. On May 10 John Adams offered a resolution that those colonies which had not yet adopted governments "sufficient to the exigencies of their affairs" should be encouraged to adopt such government "as shall, in the opinion of the representatives of the people, best conduce to the happiness and safety of their constituents in particular, and America in general." [76] This was the same advice that had been sent before, but whereas it had formerly been sent at the request of individual colonies, it now took the form of a general recommendation that the revolution be brought about in colonies still under the old system of government.

The preamble, which the radicals added to the resolution, was even more specific than the resolution itself. It stated that the colonies had been excluded from the protection of the crown by acts of Parliament, that no answer had been made to petitions for redress of grievances, and that the forces of Great Britain and of foreign mercenaries were to be used in the destruction of the people of the colonies. Therefore it was irreconcilable with reason and good conscience to take the oaths required for the support of government under the British crown, and it was necessary that "the exercise of every kind of authority under the said crown should be totally suppressed, and all the powers of government exerted, under the authority of the people of the colonies, for the preservation of internal peace, virtue, and good order, as well as for the defence of their lives, liberties, and properties, against the hostile invasions and cruel depredations of their enemies." [77]

[75] John Adams to James Warren, May 20, 1776, in *Warren-Adams Letters*, 1:250.
[76] *Journals*, 4:342; John Adams, in *Works*, 2:489.
[77] *Journals*, 4:357–358, May 15. The colonists claimed allegiance to the

Both preamble and resolve gave a sanction to the desires of the revolutionary party in Pennsylvania by frankly stating that no government which still held authority from the crown was satisfactory. The preamble was opposed by the Pennsylvania delegates and by the conservatives generally. James Duane urged delay on the ground that no one could say that a redress of grievances would not be made by Great Britain. He argued that it was no more the concern of Congress than of Parliament how the governments of the colonies were administered, an argument that was later to be used by the radicals.[78]

James Wilson spoke for the Pennsylvanians. He argued that the members of Congress were merely servants of the people acting under delegated authority. Some of the delegates were under restraint, he said. What if they should be called to account? Could not the resolve be published and the preamble delayed? Finally, getting to the heart of the matter, he admitted that if the preamble were published there would be an immediate dissolution of all authority in Pennsylvania and the people would be in a state of nature. "Before we are prepared to build the new house, why should we pull down the old one, and expose ourselves to all the inclemencies of the season?"[79] Unfortunately for Wilson and the rest of the Pennsylvania conservatives, they were not to have a part in building the new house, although once it had been built, they united in tearing it down.

The resolve with the preamble passed, and John Adams wrote that it was "the most important Resolution that ever was taken in America."[80] James Duane wrote to John Jay that he should compare the resolve with the preamble. "Compare them with each other and it will probably lead you into Reflections which I dare not point out."[81] Robert R. Livingston reported to Jay that it had occasioned great alarm in Philadelphia and that "cautious

crown alone, and it was now declared that all authority holding from it should be suppressed. The Resolve and Preamble were in effect a declaration of independence, and were so regarded.

[78] John Adams, Notes on Debates, in *Works*, 2:489–490.   [79] *Ibid.*, 490–491.

[80] John Adams to James Warren, May 15, in *Warren-Adams Letters*, 1:245–246. John Adams felt that the resolve was a declaration of independence; "confederation among ourselves, or alliances with foreign nations, are not necessary to a perfect separation from Britain." To Mrs. Adams, May 17, in *Familiar Letters*, 173–174.

[81] Jay, *Correspondence and Public Papers*, vol. 1, p. 61, note 1.

folks" were fearful that it would be attended with ill consequences when the assembly met.[82]

The publication of the resolve brought about immediate and, to the radicals, eminently satisfying action in Pennsylvania. When the Assembly met, it refused to revoke the instructions against independence given its delegates in November, 1775, and appointed futile committees to consider the demands of both radicals and conservatives in the colony. Dickinson, Wilson, and Robert Morris argued for the retention of the old charter and the formation of a new national government before severing connections with England.[83]

The radical party then took action. At a general meeting of the inhabitants of Philadelphia held on May 18 it was asserted that the Assembly had no power to form a new government and that any government formed under it would be a means "of subjecting us and our posterity to greater grievances than any we have hitherto experienced." The Philadelphia committee, acting under authority from the provincial convention of January, 1775, issued a call for another convention to meet in June for the purpose of forming a new government for the state.[84] It also prepared a memorial to Congress in which the radical view of what was being done by the radical members of Congress was set forth with great clarity.

The memorial expressed concern over the withdrawal of Pennsylvania from the union of the colonies through the refusal of her Assembly to act on the measures of Congress. The committee therefore "apprehended" that the resolve of May 15 was an appeal to the people, and with this in mind it had issued a call for a provincial convention to obtain the "sense of the people" and to form a new government, which would bring about a reunion of the province with the other colonies. The committee said it was determined to carry out the resolve of May 15 and declared

---

[82] Jay, *Correspondence and Public Papers*, 59–60.

[83] Lincoln, *Revolutionary Movement in Pennsylvania*, 251; James Duane, in a letter written to John Jay on May 25 (Jay, *Correspondence and Public Papers*, vol. 1, p. 63, note 1), said that the assembly was averse to any change and that the people of the town were for change. He expressed a fear that the dissension might spread to "adjoining colonies." Duane referred, of course, to New York, where the same issue was a live one, but where the conservatives had control of the revolutionary organization.

[84] Lincoln, *Revolutionary Movement in Pennsylvania*, 254–255, 264.

that the Assembly had not been chosen for that purpose. "Their unwillingness to appeal to the vote of the people, and the pains they have taken to prevail upon the Congress to interfere in our 'Domestic police' betrays a fear, that in refusing to comply with the resolve of Congress they will act contrary to the inclinations of a majority of their constituents." The Assembly did not possess the confidence of the people, composed as it was of men holding office under the crown. From such a government there was as much to fear as from "the unlimited exertions" of Great Britain. The committee could not believe that the Congress had meant to include the Pennsylvania Assembly in its recommendations to assemblies and conventions to form new governments, for "the Origin and present tenure" of the power of Congress can never allow it to forget that it was "by making names yield to things & forms to substantial justice, that it acquired the confidence of America." [85]

While engaged in removing the obstruction to independence resulting from continued conservative control in the Middle colonies, the radicals had been pursuing another necessary policy: that of securing positive instructions to work for independence. In March, Elbridge Gerry asked James Warren to "originate" instructions in the Massachusetts General Court indicating that that body was favorable to separation. Gerry felt that it would strengthen many timid minds and procure a reversal of some of the instructions against independence.[86]

When General Charles Lee wrote to Richard Henry Lee, "For God's sake, why do you dandle in Congress so strangely? Why do you not at once declare yourselves a separate independent State?" [87] the latter answered that they were "heavily clogged with instructions from these shamefully interested Proprietary people," and that this state of affairs would continue until Virginia set an example by creating a government and sending peremptory orders to its delegates to "pursue the most effectual measures for the Security of America." Only when this was done would the people of the proprietary colonies force through simi-

[85] Memorial of the "Committee of Inspection and Observation" of the city and liberties of Philadelphia, May 24, 1776, in Papers of the Continental Congress, No. 41, vol. 2, ff. 9–12. It is endorsed as read in Congress on May 25.
[86] March 26, 1776, in Burnett, *Letters*, 1:410.
[87] April 5, 1776, in Force, *American Archives*, 4th series, 5:794.

lar measures.[88] John Adams wrote to James Warren: "You say the Sighs for Independence are Universal . . . As to the Sighs, what are they after? Independence? Have We not been independent these twelve Months, wanting Three days?" Citing the resolves opening the ports and authorizing privateering, he asked if such measures were not independence enough for his beloved constituents. Why did not the general court send instructions to its delegates to promote independency if they were so unanimous in the matter? [89]

This maneuvering between the radicals in Congress and those in the colonies resulted in new instructions from various governments to their delegates in Congress. On April 12 the North Carolina Provincial Congress empowered its delegates in Congress to unite with the other colonies "in declaring Independency and forming foreign alliances, reserving to this Colony the sole and exclusive right of forming a Constitution and laws for this Colony." [90] On May 4 Rhode Island formally declared its independence of Great Britain. Its legislature repealed the act for securing allegiance to the king, justifying its action on the grounds that "in all states existing by compact, protection and allegiance are reciprocal, the latter being only the consequence of the former," and that George III was now actually trying to destroy rather than to protect this condition. Henceforth the name and authority of the governor and Company of Rhode Island were to be substituted for that of the king.[91] The Rhode Island delegates were instructed to cooperate with those of other colonies in promoting confederation and in taking all steps necessary to secure the rights and liberties of the colonies, taking care, however, to secure to Rhode Island "in the strongest and most perfect Manner, its present established Form, and all the Powers of Government, so far as relates to its internal Police and Conduct of our own Affairs, civil and religious." [92]

Virginia took the step that led to the final separation by declaring her independence of Great Britain [93] and specifically in-

[88] April 22, 1776, in Lee, *Letters*, 1:182–183.
[89] April 16, 1776, in *Warren-Adams Letters*, 1:227.
[90] *North Carolina Colonial Records*, 10:512.
[91] *Rhode Island Colonial Records*, 7:522–523.
[92] *Journals*, 4:353–354, May 14.
[93] Eckenrode, *Revolution in Virginia*, 161–162.

structing her delegates in the Congress to move that the United Colonies were "free and independent States, absolved from all allegiance to, or dependence upon, the Crown or Parliament of Great Britain." Assent was given also to the formation of alliances and of a confederation of all the colonies, "*Provided*, That the power of forming Government for, and the regulations of the internal concerns of each Colony, be left to the respective Colonial legislatures." [94]

On May 27 the Virginia and North Carolina delegates laid their instructions before Congress [95] and on June 7 Richard Henry Lee rose in Congress and moved that "These United Colonies are, and of right ought to be, free and independent States, that they are absolved from all allegiance to the British Crown, and that all political connection between them and the State of Great Britain is, and ought to be, totally dissolved. That it is expedient forthwith to take the most effectual measures for forming foreign Alliances. That a plan of confederation be prepared and transmitted to the respective Colonies for their consideration and approbation." [96]

[94] Proceedings of the Virginia Convention, May 15, 1776, in Force, *American Archives*, 4th series, 6:1524.

[95] *Journals*, 4:397.

[96] *Ibid.*, 5:425.

THE WRITING AND RATIFICATION
OF THE ARTICLES OF CONFEDERATION

IV

The Problem of Union

THE IDEA of union had long been part of colonial political thought and activity. The New England Confederation and the Dominion of New England had been unions of part of the colonies, though impermanent ones. From the beginning of the eighteenth century plans for a union of all the colonies had been proposed fairly frequently, and they make a rather imposing list, but to suppose that they were the subject of much concern either because of their number or their good sense would be a mistake.[1]

All these earlier plans reveal a preoccupation with military affairs, as was only natural, since their chief purpose was to increase the efficiency of military operations against the French and Indians. The first proposal for a colonial union was that of William Penn in 1698. It called for regular meetings of deputies from the colonies, to be presided over by an appointee of the king, who in time of war was to be commander-in-chief. This congress was to settle differences between colony and colony in certain specified matters: the return of fleeing debtors and of fugitives from justice; injuries arising from disputes over commerce; ways and means of protecting the common union against enemies; the apportionment of quotas of men and money among the colonies.[2] All these matters, placed at the disposition of the central body, found their place in the Articles of Confederation.

A Virginian writing three years after the publication of Penn's plan raised certain objections which were to be voiced frequently

[1] Richard Frothingham's *Rise of the Republic*, 107–121, has an excellent discussion of the idea of union in the colonies, as does Charles M. Andrews' *The Colonial Period* (London, 1912), ch. 9, "Attempts at Colonial Union." Copies of the various plans for colonial union are to be found in Hampton L. Carson, ed., *History of the Celebration of the One Hundredth Anniversary of the Promulgation of the Constitution of the United States* (Philadelphia, 1889), 2:439–486.

[2] Frothingham, *Rise of the Republic*, p. 111, note 1.

by Virginians in discussions over the Articles of Confederation. He urged that as the colonies grew, a common council would be necessary to regulate currency and weights and measures, to collect debts, to settle boundary disputes, and to provide for some uniformity in colonial laws. He objected specifically to the equality of representation in Penn's plan and proposed an apportionment that would have given Virginia the largest number of delegates.[3]

No substantially different plan was offered until the meeting of the Albany Congress. This convention, called at the behest of the British government for the purpose of uniting the colonies against the French and Indians, proposed a plan which comprehended certain political and economic as well as military features. Control over Indian affairs, Western lands, and new settlements, and the right to levy taxes for the execution of these powers were given to the central body.[4] This plan was unanimously rejected by the colonial legislatures because they thought it subversive of their independence.

The Galloway plan of 1774 had much in common with earlier ones, but its purpose was quite different. The council for which it provided represented a constitutional union between the colonies and Great Britain; it was in reality an American parliament, which was to have a veto on the acts of the British Parliament affecting both countries, as the British Parliament was to have on similar legislation by the American parliament.[5] This was far different from a simple union for military purposes such as the Albany plan, which, in spite of the extensive powers given to the

[3] Frothingham, *Rise of the Republic*, pp. 109, note 3, 112–113.

[4] In *The Writings of Benjamin Franklin*, edited by Albert H. Smyth (New York, 1905–07), 3:207–226, is printed the plan agreed upon by the Congress at Albany, with the reasons stated by the Congress for each of the provisions agreed upon. Franklin's "Short Hints towards a Scheme for Uniting the Northern Colonies" is printed on pages 197–198.

[5] *Journals*, 1:49–51. On the relationship between the Albany plan, the Galloway plan, and Franklin's plan of confederation of 1775, and on Franklin's relations with Galloway, see Franklin to Galloway, London, February 5, 1775, photostat in the Mason Library Manuscripts; "Aspinwall Papers," in the *Massachusetts Historical Collections*, 4th series, 10:729; Eliphalet Dyer to Joseph Trumbull, May 18, 1775, in Burnett, *Letters*, 1:93–94; Samuel Wharton to Benjamin Franklin, Portsmouth, England, April 17, 1775, in the *Pennsylvania Magazine of History and Biography*, 27:151; Lois K. Matthews, "Benjamin Franklin's Plans for a Colonial Union, 1750–1775," in the *American Political Science Review*, 8:393–412 (August, 1914).

central body, was still primarily concerned with frontier problems.

The Declaration of Independence wrought a fundamental change in the problem of writing a constitution for the thirteen states. All the earlier plans of union contemplated, from necessity if not desire, the superior authority of the British government. Independence, nominal if not actual, placed before the electorate of the thirteen states the task of disposing of the political authority which had been wielded by Great Britain. This was a practical matter which could not be decided by legal theories or precedents, nor achieved by some process of historical osmosis whereby the sovereign powers of the British government would be transferred to the Continental Congress. The ultimate decision was the result of social conditions, of certain political beliefs, and of the workings of practical politics.

In 1776 a radical party came into power as the result of a successful fight against (among other things) the power of a central government which they felt had denied them their political and economic heritage. The new system of government created was designed in part to remedy those defects which radical leaders saw in the British connection. The central government became the agent of the states which created it and which remained superior to it.[6]

The fundamental difference between the Articles of Confederation and the Constitution of 1787 lies in the apportionment of power between the states and the central government. In the first the balance of power was given to the states, and in the second to the central government. The first constitution was one of a federal organization; the second was in essence that of a national government, although political realities demanded the retention of federal features. The difference between the two was the result of the shifting balances of political power within the thirteen states, which enabled first one party and then the other to write its desires, its beliefs, and its interests into the colorless language of a constitution. Hence it was the nature of union, and not its desirability, that was the major issue between the parties in 1776. The conservatives wished for the re-creation, as nearly as might

[6] See Schuyler, *Constitution of the United States*, 26–27, for an excellent statement of the radical case against a centralized government in 1776.

be, of the system that had existed before the Revolution. The radicals tended to desire a union chiefly for the purpose of carrying on the war, but a union that would not infringe upon the sovereign authority of the individual states. They believed profoundly that only under such a system was democracy possible.[7]

The necessity of fighting the war and the desire for a central government by many of those conservatives who became revolutionists were the chief forces behind the movement for a political union of the thirteen states. On the whole the radicals were indifferent to union after 1776. From 1765 to 1776 the idea of union had been most popular with them for the reason that effective opposition to Great Britain required a measure of intercolonial unity, whether the policy was that of nonimportation, nonconsumption, or nonintercourse. Moreover, they probably realized that the local governing classes could never be overcome permanently so long as they were supported by the British government, and that to remove the British government from colonial affairs and topple the local aristocracies from their seats of power all the colonial radical forces must combine.

The Galloway plan of union had been an ultraconservative scheme for uniting the colonies more closely with the British Empire. It involved no fundamental internal changes. The centralized organization for which it provided was to control the military and naval forces, and it would have been able to suppress local disturbances much more effectively than the British government was able to do at the time. Such a system, whatever

[7] An example of this is the first reaction of Sam Adams to the Constitution of 1787. He wrote to Richard Henry Lee on December 3, 1787, "I confess as I enter the Building, I stumble at the Threshold. I meet with a National Government instead of a Federal Union of Sovereign States." He asks if a national legislature can make laws "for the *free* internal Government of one People living in Climates so remote," whose "Habits & Particular Interests" will always be so different. He questioned whether laws could be passed which would suit both New England and the South. He prophesied discontent and frequent insurrections which would require standing armies. His own belief was that "should we continue distinct sovereign States, confederated for the Purposes of mutual Safety and Happiness, each contributing to the federal Head such a Part of its Sovereignty as would render the Government fully adequate to those purposes and *no more*, the People would govern themselves more easily, the Laws of each State being well adapted to its own Genius & Circumstances, and the Liberties of the United States would be more secure than they can be . . . under the new Constitution." *Writings*, 4:324–325.

its effect on the constitutional relationship between the colonies and Great Britain, would have solidified the position of the conservatives in the colonies. But the radicals defeated the plan, for it threatened death to their hopes. It is not certain that they realized its significance for the internal history of the colonies, but they were keen politicians and it is doubtful whether conservative arguments could have misled them. Indeed, some of those arguments were positive proof of this point of view.

As the loyalist wing of the conservative party disappeared and the radical party grew in strength, the latter pushed the idea of confederation as a political expedient which would make the colonies actually independent without a formal declaration. Because they recognized this to be the real aim of the radicals, the conservatives opposed confederation. In 1775 they defeated Franklin's plan, which offered them far more than they were later to obtain in the Articles of Confederation. Only when independence could no longer be avoided were they converted to the idea of union. They had wished to stay with Britain because they recognized the benefits of a centralized government and feared revolt should the break be made. That hope gone, they became the most ardent protagonists of a national union. They insisted that a confederation must precede any formal declaration of independence. The radicals, on the other hand, their goal of independence almost within their grasp, became less and less interested in the idea of union.

In a general way the conservatives knew what kind of government they wanted: a centralized government that would take the place of the British government — a government that would regulate trade, control the disposition of Western lands, and settle disputes between one state and another; a government having power to act coercively against any citizen who displayed tendencies subversive of the established conservative order. They did not need the experiences of the Revolution to demonstrate what were for them the benefits of such a government. They had been stating their ideas on the subject ever since the meeting of the first Continental Congress.[8]

[8] The arguments used by the conservatives in the first Continental Congress have been discussed. The idea of a central government as a check on the democracy of the colonial legislatures had been urged all through the eighteenth

Thomas Wharton, whose Letter-Book contains many a plea for a central government over the colonies, had written Thomas Walpole in May, 1774, that when he considered how extensive were the colonies, how various their jurisdictions, and how unhappy a situation would result from a disunion between them and the parent state, he wished that a magistrate superior to the governors could be appointed by the king to act in conjunction with a central body elected by the colonial assemblies. To this body he would have given the power "to make Laws relative to the General Police of America, this I conceive would have a tendency of checking a Turbulent Spirit in any one of the Colonies & giving England as well as the colonies a greater Security then they can otherwise have." [9] Edward Biddle told Alexander Graydon that "the subjugation of my country, . . . I deprecate as a most grievous calamity, and yet sicken at the idea of thirteen, unconnected, petty democracies: if we are to be independent, let us, in the name of GOD, at once have an empire, and place WASHINGTON at the head of it." [10]

By the spring of 1776 the course of events had heightened rather than allayed the fears expressed by the conservatives in the first Congress in 1774. As the old controls were weakened, new men rose to power [11] and the masses vented their spite upon those who had once been considered their betters. In April Carter Braxton, summing up the arguments of his class for delaying inde-

---

century, so its expression was not new in 1774. Frothingham, *Rise of the Republic*, 114–115.

[9] Thomas Wharton to Thomas Walpole, Philadelphia, May, 1774, and May 31, 1774, in Thomas Wharton Letter-Book, 1773–1784, pp. 34–35, in the Pennsylvania Historical Society Manuscripts; Thomas Wharton to Samuel Wharton, July 5, 1774, *ibid.*, 50–51, in which he expresses a desire for a constitutional union with an upper house to control the affairs of the continent and to be "a Proper Check to the forward or Ambitious Views of any one Colony." Other letters written in 1775 to Thomas Walpole and to Samuel Wharton reiterate the desire for a union and express a deep gloominess as to the probable outcome of affairs. Wharton felt that the greater part of the inhabitants wanted reconciliation, but that "there are some on this Continent whose political Creed is in opposition to Monarchical Government."

[10] Graydon, *Memoirs*, 285.

[11] John Adams felt that the new governments being created would "require a purification from our vices, and an augmentation of our virtues, or they will be no blessings. The people will have unbounded power, and the people are extremely addicted to corruption and venality, as well as the great." To Mrs. Adams, July 3, 1776, in *Works*, 9:418.

pendence, wrote that independence and total separation were subjects of interest for all ranks of men, but that it was "in truth a
delusive Bait which men inconsiderately catch at, without knowing the hook to which it is affixed." Though he admitted that it
was an objective to be wished for if it could be obtained with
safety and honor, he felt that that time was yet in the future. In
the first place, the conservatives still awaited the arrival of commissioners from Great Britain.[12] Moreover, the Americans were
in too defenseless a position to declare their independence, having neither an alliance with a naval power nor any fleet of their
own. A third reason for delay was the fear of New England
democracy. Monarchy had always hung heavily on the New
England colonies, Braxton declared, and he was satisfied that they
meant to avoid any reconciliation; "the best opportunity in the
World being now offered them to throw off all subjection and
embrace their darling Democracy they are determined to accept it."

Above all, there was the danger of civil war over rival land
claims. Braxton reported that Connecticut had eight hundred men
in the Wyoming Valley who were peaceable only because of the
influence of Congress; New York was apprehensive of the temper of her neighbors, "their great swarms and small Territory";
Virginia had claims on Pennsylvania, and Maryland on Virginia.
The Virginia delegates carried their land claims so far to the east
that some of the Middle colonies feared being swallowed up between the claims of Virginia and of the easterners.

And yet, without the adjustment of these claims, some were for
"lugging" the colonies into independence. If independence were
to be declared then, wrote Braxton, "the Continent would be torn
in pieces by Intestine Wars and Convulsions." Before independence could be declared, "all disputes must be healed and Harmony prevail. A Grand Continental league must be formed and

[12] The American Prohibitory Act of December, 1775, had provided that
the crown could appoint commissioners who might pardon individuals and
decide when colonies had returned to a state of obedience. See the *Annual
Register*, 1775, p. 109. The hope that commissioners might come was an argument for delay continually used by the conservatives. See John Adams to
James Warren, April 2, Robert Morris to Horatio Gates, April 6, and Oliver
Wolcott to Mrs. Wolcott, April 17, in Burnett, *Letters*, 1:413, 416, 427; *Journals*, 4:328–329; and John Adams, Autobiography, in *Works*, 3:43.

a superintending Power also. When these necessary Steps are taken and I see a Coalition formed sufficient to withstand the Power of Britain, or any other, then I am for an independent State and all its Consequences." [13]

The demand that a union be formed before independence was declared was strongest in the Middle colonies, particularly in Pennsylvania, where the conservatives were on the verge of losing control. John Dickinson, who had led the successful attempt to defeat consideration of Franklin's plan of confederation, was now in the fore of those demanding a union before a declaration of independence. John Adams was delighted over the conversion of his leading opponent. "What do you think must be my Reflection," he wrote to James Warren, "when I see the Farmer himself now confessing the Falsehood of all his Prophecies, and the Truth of mine, and confessing himself, now for instituting governments, forming a Continental constitution, making alliances with foreigners, opening Ports and all that." [14]

On June 8 Richard Henry Lee's motion for independence and confederation was debated by Congress. "The sensible part of the House opposed the Motion," wrote Edward Rutledge to John Jay. "The sensible part" did not object to the formulation of a plan for a treaty with France nor to the creation of a confederation, but they felt that independence would only place them in the power of the enemy and render them ridiculous in the eyes of foreign powers, who would not unite with the colonies before they had united with one another. "For daily experience evinces that the Inhabitants of every Colony consider themselves at liberty to do as they please upon almost every occasion." Rutledge added that the only reason that had been offered for declaring independence was "the reason of every Mad-man, a shew of our spirit." [15]

[13] Carter Braxton to Landon Carter, Philadelphia, April 14, in Burnett, *Letters*, 1:420–421. See also Joseph Hewes to Samuel Johnston, March 20 and July 28, *ibid.*, 1:404; 2:28; Thomas Stone to Daniel of St. Thomas Jenifer, April 24, *ibid.*, 1:431–432; and William Whipple to John Langdon, May 18, *ibid.*, 1:456.

[14] Letter of May 20, in *Warren-Adams Letters*, 1:251. See also Graydon, *Memoirs*, 283–285, and Charles Thomson to W. H. Drayton, in Reed, *Joseph Reed*, 1:153.

[15] Letter of [June 8] in Burnett, *Letters*, 1:476–477. Rutledge wrote that a man must have "the Impudence of a New Englander" to propose a treaty honorable to the colonies in their present disjointed state.

In the debate Robert R. Livingston, James Wilson, John Dickinson, Edward Rutledge, and James Duane, supporting the conservative point of view,[16] argued for delay. Congress must wait for the "voice of the people," which, they asserted, had not spoken in the Middle colonies. True enough, but the people were trying to speak and were only prevented from doing so by such organizations as the Pennsylvania Assembly, from which Dickinson and Wilson were delegates.[17] A better argument was that some of the colonies had not given their consent to independence and that Congress could not declare it for them. This concern for "state rights" on the part of the conservatives was of course a matter of expedience, not conviction, and it was so recognized at the time. Finally, the conservative leaders threatened to retire from Congress and warned that their colonies might secede from the union.[18] Consideration of the motion was thus delayed for three weeks because some of the delegates lacked instructions.[19] When it did come up for a final vote on July 1, John Dickinson once more set forth the views of the conservatives. Again he pleaded the necessity of creating a confederation before declaring independence and pointed out that the committee on confederation was having a difficult time in coming to an agreement. He particularly urged the need for a central control over the Western lands of the various states.[20] But his arguments availed him nothing, and nominal independence, at least, was established.

[16] James Duane to John Jay, June 8, in Jay, *Correspondence and Public Papers*, vol. 1, p. 66, note 1; Jefferson, Notes on Debates, in *Writings*, 1:19.

[17] Clear evidence of this is the action of the Pennsylvania Provincial Convention on June 23. The members declared unanimously that the delegates (of the Assembly) should vote for independence on July 1, the members declaring *seriatim* that such was the opinion of the towns and counties they represented. John Adams to Samuel Chase, June 24, in *Works*, 9:413. On June 25 Elbridge Gerry reported that all were for independence except New York and Maryland, and that the people would be for it even if the conventions and delegates of those colonies voted against it. To James Warren, in Force, *American Archives*, 4th series, 4:1067.

[18] Jefferson, Notes on Debates, in *Writings*, 1:19–21.

[19] *Ibid.*, 21–24; Charles Thomson, History of the Confederation, p. 6, in Papers of the Continental Congress, No. 9; Elbridge Gerry to the President of the Massachusetts Provincial Congress, June 11, in Burnett, *Letters*, 1:484; Maryland Delegates to the Maryland Council of Safety, June 11, *ibid.*, 485–486; John Adams to Zabdiel Adams, June 21, in *Works*, 9:399–400.

[20] John Dickinson, "Arguments ag^t. the Independance of these Colonies — in Congress," in the Pennsylvania Historical Society Manuscripts.

Even then Robert Morris still expressed a hope for reconciliation,[21] but as the war continued the hopes of the conservatives
were increasingly centered on a national government. Those
hopes none stated more plainly than Joseph Reed, secretary to
George Washington, when he declared to Morris that "private
opinions and those of mere local authority should be subservient
to the supreme decision of Congress." He admitted frankly that
his own hopes of political safety depended on a supreme Congress: "From the purity and extent of its intelligence, and the
abilities of its members, I deriv[d] my hope of political safety, and
therefore beheld with concern every attempt to control the
Judgment and bind down the opinions of any of its members by
instructions and other devices formed as they must be on the
partial intelligence of some and the interested or timid views of
others." [22]

The second major force making for a union of the colonies was
the exigency of the situation or, as one of the colonials put it,
the necessity of hanging together or hanging separately. Radicals
and conservatives alike were agreed that united efforts were necessary to fight the war with Great Britain and to secure assistance
from foreign countries, raise funds, and provide for a common
policy.[23] By common consent these matters were placed in the
hands of Congress, which exercised the necessary powers throughout the war without the formality of a constitutional union. The
lack of such a union seems not to have hampered the conduct of
the war in spite of the jeremiads so often pronounced.

The greatest obstacle to a union of almost any kind was the
states' independence of one another. The colonies had been

---

[21] Robert Morris to Joseph Reed, July 20, 1776, in Reed, *Joseph Reed,* 1:201.
[22] Joseph Reed to Robert Morris, New York, July 18, 1776, *ibid.,* 1:199.
[23] "To the Freeborn Sons of America in General, and of Connecticut in
Particular," New York, March 21, 1776, in Force, *American Archives,* 4th
series, 5:450, urges the establishment of confederation. A plan of confederation was printed in the *Pennsylvania Evening Post* of March 5, 1776, with the
statement that it was proposed to the public "rather to draw their attention
to the subject, than as a perfect *model.*" John Adams, in writing to James
Warren on May 15, stated that confederation must now be pursued with all
the "Address, Assiduity, Prudence, Caution, and yet Fortitude and Perseverance, which those who think it necessary are possessed of." *Warren-Adams
Letters,* 1:246. William Whipple wrote to John Langdon on May 18 that "a
Confederation, permanent and lasting, ought, in my opinion, to be the next
thing." Burnett, *Letters,* 1:456.

founded individually and had developed different traditions and attitudes in spite of a common heritage of language, law, and government. Their relations with one another were often unfriendly, especially after the middle of the eighteenth century, as a result of rival land claims. Actual warfare had been prevented only by the external power of Britain, which subdued them but did not eliminate their animosity toward one another. While the pressure of British legislation after 1763 gave them unity, it was a unity only for protection against Great Britain, not for the administration of internal affairs. Now their animosities and enmities, far from having been subdued, were intensified by the possibility that they might have to fight it out after they had been released from the power of Great Britain.

This separatism of the colonies was not only legal but, what was more important, psychological as well. Much of the argument against England had been devoted to proving that colonial legislatures were independent of any outside legislative power. Inasmuch as the revolt was in part an effort to maintain that position, it was hardly to be expected that another such power would be set up by the radical party which had brought about the revolt. Some momentary radicals like Patrick Henry declared themselves Americans rather than Virginians, but there is more than a suspicion that they were inebriated by their own rhetoric, especially since their actions so often gave the lie to their professions. Above all, the radicals believed that the independence of the states was the guarantee of the kind of government they desired. Speaking broadly, it was democracy they wanted, and they knew full well that the kind of democracy they wanted was incompatible with centralization. Their experience with the British Empire had taught them that much, and they were not soon to forget the lesson.

The psychological difficulty was manifest also in the attitudes of various sections of the country, or of classes within those sections. Conservative Southerners had a very real distrust of the New Englanders, whose supposed democracy and seeming desire to extend "mob rule" to other parts of the country they greatly feared.[24] The New Englanders, on the other hand, condemned the "slow-

[24] John Adams, Diary, August 22, 1774, in *Works*, 2:351; John Adams to James Warren, July 6, 1775, in *Warren-Adams Letters*, 1:76–77; Samuel Ward

ness" of the Southerners, which they attributed to their reluctance
to accept democratic government.[25] New Englanders had a profound conviction of their own ineffable superiority, both personal
and geographical. Silas Deane was certain that the grass was
greener, the fruit better, the girls prettier, and the cows fatter in
New England than in Pennsylvania, and did not hesitate to insist
upon it to the Pennsylvanians, who, complacent in the knowledge
of their own superiority and advantages, were unable to appreciate
his point of view.[26] John Adams stated the New England opinion
of itself in both its sublime and its ridiculous aspects. He wrote
in his diary in 1774 that "Philadelphia, with all its trade and
wealth and regularity, is not Boston. The morals of our people
are much better; their manners are more polite and agreeable;
they are purer English; our language is better, our taste is better,
our persons are handsomer; our spirit is greater, our laws are
wiser, our religion is superior, our education is better." [27]

The belief in and insistence upon the independence of the individual states was not confined to the radicals alone. Many conservatives as well insisted upon it.[28] This was true of Marylanders
as well as of some of the New Yorkers. When the Maryland con-

to Henry Ward, November 21, 1775, in Burnett, *Letters*, 1:256; Carter Braxton
to Landon Carter, April 14, 1776, *ibid.*, 420–421.

[25] John Adams to Horatio Gates, March 23, 1776, *ibid.*, 1:406; "all our
Misfortunes arise from a single source – the Reluctance of the Southern
Colonies to Republican Government. The success of this war depends on a
skillful steerage of the political vessel."

[26] Silas Deane to Mrs. Deane, September 8, 1774, and July 15, 1775, in *Connecticut Historical Collections*, 2:167, 287.

[27] *Works*, 2:395. In a letter to Joseph Hawley, November 25, 1775, he wrote
that "Gentlemen, men of sense or any kind of education, in the other colonies,
are much fewer in proportion than in New England." Burnett, *Letters*, 1:259–
260. On the other hand, it seemed to have been a case of love at first sight
between the Massachusetts radicals and the Virginia radicals. See Silas Deane
to Mrs. Deane, September 19, 1774, in *Connecticut Historical Collections*,
2:181; John Adams, Diary, September 2, 1774, in *Works*, 2:362; Richard
Henry Lee to Samuel Adams, Chantilly, June 23, 1774, in Lee, *Letters*, 1:113.
Lee exclaimed that the political salvation of America depended on Massachusetts.

[28] The conservatives who demanded a national legislature in 1776 were
from the states where the conservatives were in greatest danger of losing control completely. Where the conservatives were in control, they were hesitant
about surrendering any of the independence of the states. As they faced the
danger of losing control, they switched their politics. The most notable example was that of South Carolina. In 1776 South Carolina delegates were
ardent supporters of state sovereignty. Not until 1783, when the radical move-

vention authorized its delegates to vote for independence, it specifically retained the right of the state to control its internal affairs.[29] New York, having refused to give its delegates permission to vote for independence, declared its independence of Great Britain after it had been declared by Congress.[30] Hence John Alsop, who became a loyalist, did not resign as a New York delegate to Congress when that body declared independence, but only after he heard that New York had declared its independence.[31] We have seen how most of the states, in the instructions permitting their delegates in Congress to vote for independence and for a confederation, reserved to themselves the complete control of their internal affairs and particularly of their "internal police." [32] The instructions of Virginia had been the most explicit. There the conservatives, who felt able to maintain their accustomed position, were actually more concerned than the radicals over the maintenance of their local independence. Thus Virginia reserved not only her own independence but the independence of the rest of the states in all matters of government.[33]

ment in South Carolina became dangerous, did the South Carolina conservatives change their views, and then they became ardent "Federalists."

[29] June 28, 1776, in Force, *American Archives*, 4th series, 6:1491. The delegates were authorized to concur with the other colonies in declaring them "free and independent States" and in forming a confederation, provided that "the sole and exclusive right of regulating the internal Government and Police of this Colony be reserved to the people thereof." On July 6 the Maryland convention passed its own declaration of independence, maintaining that it was not because of a desire for independence that Maryland was uniting with the other colonies but to maintain its liberties. This was the first wish of the convention; the second was "to continue connected with, and dependant on, Great Britain." *Ibid.*, 1506–1507.

[30] Alexander C. Flick, ed., *History of the State of New York* (New York, 1933), vol. 3, ch. 8, "The Provincial Congress and the Declaration of Independence"; Becker, *Political Parties in New York*, 272–273. The reason, as Becker points out, was that the conservatives in New York were not taking any steps which might result in a loss of control.

[31] John Alsop to the New York Convention, July 16, 1776, in Burnett, *Letters*, 2:12–13.

[32] Instructions to the Delaware delegates, in *Letters to and from Caesar Rodney*, 82; credentials of the Rhode Island delegates, in *Journals*, 4:353–354; *North Carolina Colonial Records*, 10:512.

[33] Force, *American Archives*, 4th series, 6:1524. Patrick Henry had proposed separation and had also proposed that the task of forming a new government for the colonies be left to the Continental Congress. The conservatives insisted on a simple declaration of independence by Virginia, without any reference to Congress. Eckenrode, *Revolution in Virginia*, 161–162.

The immediate issue which held up the ratification of the Articles of Confederation from November, 1777, until March, 1781, was the disposition of the region west of the Appalachians, to which most of the states laid claim in one way or another.[34] The chief factor in the whole dispute was that certain of the states had definite western limits, whereas others had claims that extended westward for unknown distances, usually to the "South Sea." The most favored among these latter was Virginia, which had more or less explicit charter claims to the region west and north of the Appalachians. Furthermore, the great get-rich-quick activity of the eighteenth century was land speculation. From north to south there were land companies, great and small, in operation, each for the ultimate purpose of enriching its members at no particular personal sacrifice to any of them. Obviously the citizens of colonies with western claims would have more influence with their local assemblies and their governors than would their equally ambitious but less fortunately placed fellows in colonies having definite western limits and hence relatively few opportunities for speculation.

Various members of the Virginia aristocracy had been granted huge slices of the unsettled West. They were quite certain that it all lay within the bounds of Virginia.[35] The only recourse for speculators from other colonies was to evade Virginia's charter claim in some way. They evolved two ideas: the limitation of the colonies with indefinite boundaries, an idea which found its first expression in the Albany plan;[36] and the creation of independent land companies for the establishment of new colonies in the West. For this purpose they turned to the British govern-

[34] On this controversy over the West see Merrill Jensen, "The Cession of the Old Northwest" and "The Creation of the National Domain, 1781–1784," in the *Mississippi Valley Historical Review*, 23:27–48 (June, 1936); 27:323–342 (December, 1939).

[35] Clarence W. Alvord, in *The Mississippi Valley in British Politics* (2 vols., Cleveland, 1917), 1:88–89, discusses the beginning of this land-granting by the Virginia government.

[36] The Grand Council under the Albany plan was to have the power to make all purchases for the crown from Indians of land "not now within the bounds of particular colonies, or that shall not be within their bounds when some of them are reduced to more convenient dimensions." The Grand Council was to have power to make new settlements on such lands and to provide laws for them until established as separate governments. Franklin, *Writings*, 3:218–220.

ment, since it was clearly the only power which could shear from Virginia some of the territory she claimed.

There were many abortive schemes for independent colonies and many an abortive land company.[37] Two of the companies, however, pursued a policy of obstruction and attack, the most obvious result of which was to delay the ratification of the Articles of Confederation for more than three years. These two companies were the Indiana Company and the Illinois-Wabash Company, both of which were made up largely of speculators and politicians from the states of Pennsylvania, Maryland, and New Jersey. By 1776 they had staked out extensive areas within Virginia's charter limits. The Indiana Company's claim south of the Ohio River covered much the same area as had been granted to the Ohio Company of Virginia. The Illinois and Wabash claims lay north of the Ohio in regions as yet untouched, though not unknown to Virginia speculators.

As the speculators of the landless colonies had turned to the British government for help before the Revolution, so they now turned to the agency which they regarded as the logical successor to the power of the British government — the Continental Congress. The Congress may have been a weak reed, but it was a far more stable support than the Virginia government, which soon made it plain that it intended to dispute all deeds and purchases from Indians. Just how intimate the connections between the land companies and the members of Congress became at the outbreak of the Revolution is difficult to determine. Sufficient evidence exists, however, to indicate that land speculation played an important role. Shares were provided in a proposed land purchase north of the Ohio, and some of them were given to Thomas Wharton to distribute among the members of Congress in the hope of inducing that body to make a declaration in favor of the

[37] The oldest of these was the Ohio Company, which was founded by Virginians. The expansion program indicated by the activity of the Ohio Company aroused opposition centering largely in Philadelphia, whose Indian traders had hitherto monopolized the trade of the Ohio Valley. Franklin was fertile with schemes for new colonies. For accounts of these companies see Alvord, *Mississippi Valley in British Politics*, 1:87–89, 93–95, 99–101, 314–315, 316–323; 2:92–94; Albert T. Volwiler, *George Croghan and the Westward Movement, 1741–1782* (Cleveland, 1926), 39–40, 77, 82, 235, 263–264; Abernethy, *Western Lands*, chs. 1–3, 8–10.

validity of Indian purchases.[38] Patrick Henry, who had early fallen in with the schemes of the Pennsylvania speculators, later testified that he had been offered and had rejected shares in all the various purchases from Indians.[39] Franklin entered Congress upon his return from England in 1775 and participated both in its work and in the reorganization of the Indiana Company, which assumed its original status upon the collapse of the Vandalia project.[40] In July, 1775, he presented a plan of confederation in which the Congress was given the power of "planting new Colonies when proper," thus implying congressional control over the West.[41] In March, 1776, John Adams wrote that union was being delayed by "that avarice of Land, which has made upon this Continent so many votaries to Mammon, that I sometimes dread the Consequences." [42] The first draft of the Articles of Confederation, in the handwriting of John Dickinson of Pennsylvania and Delaware, elaborated Franklin's plan in that it gave to Congress the power of limiting and defining state boundaries, of setting up new governments in the regions set aside, and of settling disputes between states over rival land claims.[43] The issue was thus placed squarely before Congress for the first time. And for years it was to remain there as an impediment and even as a threat to union and common action.

It was during this time that the Virginia convention was beginning to define its attitude toward the control of the West. On June 24, in response to petitions from settlers in the West, the

[38] Volwiler, *Croghan*, 297–298.

[39] Thomas Wharton to Thomas Walpole, September 23, 1774, in the *Pennsylvania Magazine of History and Biography*, 33:444–446 (1909). In 1775 Henry gave it as his opinion that grants from Indian nations were valid. See William Trent, Opinions Regarding the Grant to William Trent, 1775, in the Pennsylvania Historical Society Manuscripts. Henry's deposition is in the *Calendar of Virginia State Papers and Other Manuscripts, 1652–1781*, edited by William P. Palmer (Richmond, 1875), 1:289–290. James Wilson, member of Congress from Pennsylvania, was paid a fee to give an opinion in favor of the Indiana Company. Edmund Pendleton also declared in its favor. Abernethy, *Western Lands*, 143–144.

[40] Minutes of meetings of the Indiana Company, September 21–22, 1775, and March 20, 1776, in the Ohio Company Papers, vol. 2, in the Pennsylvania Historical Society Manuscripts; Volwiler, *Croghan*, 299–300; Max Savelle, *George Morgan, Colony Builder* (New York, 1932), 82–86.

[41] *Journals*, 2:196.

[42] John Adams to Horatio Gates, March 23, in Burnett, *Letters*, 1:406.

[43] *Journals*, 5:549–551.

convention resolved that all people holding lands within Virginia which were also claimed by those who pretended to derive title through purchase or deed from the Indians should continue to hold those lands until the validity of such purchases could be passed upon by the Virginia legislature. The convention also resolved that no purchase of lands from the Indians within the charter limits of Virginia should be made without the approval of the legislature.[44] On July 4 commissioners were appointed to collect and to take in writing in behalf of the government evidence against persons claiming lands under deed and purchases from the Indians.[45]

The Virginia constitution was adopted with an amendment taken in large measure from a draft constitution by Jefferson. This amendment provided that the boundaries of the state were to remain as they had been defined in the Charter of 1609, except that the territories of Maryland, Pennsylvania, and South and North Carolina were "ceded, released, and forever confirmed" to the people of those colonies with all the rights that might have been claimed by Virginia. This was an exasperating magnanimity on the part of Virginia, implying as it did that the other states existed only by the sufferance of their larger neighbor. The northern and western boundaries of the states were to remain as fixed in the Charter of 1609 and the Treaty of Peace in 1763, "unless by act of legislature, one or more territories shall be hereafter laid off and governments established westward of the Allegheny mountains."[46]

Thus Virginia made plain her intention of maintaining jurisdiction within her charter bounds, and of denying the validity of the Transylvania purchase, the Illinois and Wabash purchases, and the Indiana Company deed. The Virginia commissioners began the collection of "evidence" while Congress was debating

[44] *Proceedings of the Convention of Delegates* . . . (Richmond, 1816), 63.
[45] *Ibid.*, 83–84; Abernethy, *Western Lands*, 162–164.
[46] *Ordinances Passed at a General Convention of Delegates and Representatives from the Several Counties and Corporations of Virginia* (Richmond, 1816), ch. 2, p. 6, "The Constitution or Form of Government." Jefferson's draft is evidence of a split in Virginia's attitude toward the West. His draft reads that the boundaries were to remain as of the charter until by act of the legislature one or more territories should be set off for new colonies, where new colonies should be established on the same laws "and shall be free and independent of this colony and all the world." *Writings*, 2:26.

whether or not it should be given control over the West in the proposed confederation.

It is against this complex background that the disputes over this part of the Confederation must be considered. An additional factor was the fear and jealousy of Virginia's smaller neighbors, whose attitude was that of small nations toward a large and powerful, and potentially even more powerful, neighbor. Thus the activity of Maryland was dictated both by jealousy and by prominent land speculators. Certainly the events of the next few years were to prove that the motivating force behind the conduct of the landless states was not "national vision."

It may thus be seen that the problem of union was an exceedingly difficult one. Economic disputes, political theories, and the inherited prejudices of one state against another all worked in the direction of separatism and the complete independence of each state. And, above all, the Revolution itself was a revolt against centralization of political authority. On the other hand, a common heritage, opposing political theories, different economic interests, class influences, and the external pressure of the war all worked in the direction of a political union of the states and, even more, the creation of a constitutional entity superior to the clashing interests of states and of class groups. But centralization was so contrary to the theoretical foundations of the Revolution that it was not and could not be too openly sought.

The Articles of Confederation, like any constitution, may be analyzed in various ways. One may be concerned with the historic origins of its phrases and clauses and of the political theories upon which it is thought to be based. Or one may be concerned with the purpose of its writers and with those features which permit of "interpretation," either by the popular mind or by legal and judicial processes. The committee appointed to draft articles of confederation doubtless had various plans at its disposal. Franklin's plan of confederation was a part of the records of Congress. Another had been printed in the *Pennsylvania Evening Post* in March, 1776. These plans had a superficial framework that was more or less similar, for the problems contemplated by them were very much alike, but they are of little importance for an understanding of the basic problems involved in the creation of a common constitution.

It was generally agreed that a central organization was necessary to handle such matters of common or general concern as war and peace, the army and navy, and Indian affairs. There was likewise rather general agreement that matters of local concern should be decided by the states. But controversy soon arose over the demarcation of the boundary between the two areas of responsibility and authority. What affairs were of "general" or "national" concern? What affairs were purely "local" in nature? That question arose in the first Continental Congress. With respect to that question, the writing and ratification of the Articles of Confederation is merely the first chapter in the constitutional history of the United States. In the years to come, section was to be arrayed against section, class against class, and party against party in an effort to determine the province of the central government and that of the states.

V

The Dickinson Draft of the Confederation

FEW SOURCES remain for study of the work of the committee appointed on June 12, 1776, to draft articles of confederation. Much must be inferred from the political views of the thirteen committeemen and from the document they presented to Congress on July 12. The weight of influence as well as of numbers lay with the conservative party, which up to May, 1776, had spent its efforts in opposing independence and then, when that appeared inevitable, in trying to delay a declaration of independence until a government could be created for the thirteen colonies and foreign alliances could be obtained. Three outstanding opponents of independence, John Dickinson, Edward Rutledge, and Robert R. Livingston, were members of the committee, and of these John Dickinson was the recognized leader. Thomas McKean, though in favor of independence, was on the whole also a conservative, as were Francis Hopkinson and Thomas Stone. Joseph Hewes was a North Carolina merchant and a business associate of Robert Morris. Button Gwinnett was English-born. Thomas Nelson was a product of Trinity College, Cambridge, and closely connected with the royal government of Virginia. Roger Sherman and Josiah Bartlett may be described as middle-of-the-road men. This leaves only two whose radicalism is unquestioned. One was Stephen Hopkins, a very old man. The other, Sam Adams, was unquestionably a radical, but his talents were hardly suited to the work of drafting articles of confederation.

There is little doubt that Dickinson was dominant in the committee. His prestige as a writer and the honesty of his convictions led men to respect him whether they agreed with his political views or not. To him was given the task of writing the Articles which were presented to Congress, and it would seem that, in spite of many compromises, the draft presented was an embodiment of the views of the conservatives, and of his own views in particular.

Dickinson himself admitted that every article was bitterly fought over,[1] and the existing evidence indicates that the disputes were long and sharp. Five days after the committee was appointed Josiah Bartlett wrote that "as it is a very important business, and some difficulties have arisen, I fear it will take some time before it will be finally settled."[2] On June 29 Edward Rutledge wrote to his friend John Jay that he had lately been much engaged upon a plan of confederation which Dickinson had drawn and that it had "the Vice of all his Productions to a considerable Degree; I mean the Vice of Refining too much."[3]

Rutledge's attitude toward Dickinson's draft of the Articles illustrates the division of opinion which had been the undoing of the conservative party during the past two years. Unlike the radicals, whose single-minded devotion to one end overcame most of the obstacles they faced, the conservatives were divided, and, being timid and largely on the defensive, they had been helpless in the face of a determined minority. The conservatism of Rutledge was the conservatism of the South, of an aristocracy that had the situation well in hand at home and was determined not to surrender to democratic influences from New England. If South Carolina supported Massachusetts because she feared that her own legislative independence might be endangered once Massachusetts had been conquered,[4] it was not to be expected that she would surrender it to a government such as the conservatives of the Middle states wished to create.

To Rutledge, who feared the democratic pretensions of the New Englanders, it seemed that "the Idea of destroying all Provincial Distinctions and making every thing of the most minute kind bend to what they call the good of the whole, is in other Terms to say that these Colonies must be subject to the Government of the Eastern Provinces." He had no respect for the military prowess of New England, but he spoke from deep conviction and some experience when he said that he dreaded "their

[1] John Dickinson, "Arguments ag.ᵗ the Independence of these Colonies — in Congress," Dickinson MSS., in the Pennsylvania Historical Society.
[2] Josiah Bartlett to John Langdon, June 17, in Burnett, *Letters*, 1:495.
[3] Edward Rutledge to John Jay, June 29, *ibid.*, 517.
[4] McCrady, *South Carolina in the Revolution*, 1:171–172.

overruling Influence in Council . . . their low Cunning, and those levelling Principles which Men without Character and without Fortune in general possess, which are so captivating to the lower class of Mankind, and which will occasion such a fluctation of Property as to introduce the greatest disorder." Rutledge was determined that the reins of power should remain in the hands of the states, for if their power were to be surrendered, he was convinced, a "most pernicious use" would be made of it.[5]

Rutledge saw in the Dickinson plan the ruin of some of the states, should it be adopted. He prophesied that unless greatly modified it would never be accepted, since it had to be submitted to men in the several states who could not be led nor driven into measures which might lay the foundation of their ruin. Thus Rutledge's belief in the independence of the individual states, along with his fear of New England democracy, led him to deny to a central government the powers which the conservatives of the Middle states wished to give to it. To Rutledge the danger seemed to be external, but to the conservatives of the Middle states the danger was from within. Therefore they talked much of "the good of the whole" and presented a constitutional program to provide for what was in effect a "national" government. It cannot be said that they believed unreservedly in doing away with the states. They were as ready to preserve state individuality as were the radicals, but not at the cost of an internal revolution which might throw the colonial governing classes from power. Hence where the conservatives remained in power as the revolutionary tide rose, as in Virginia and South Carolina, they were chary of surrendering any powers to a central government.

Thus while the conservatives dominated the committee on confederation, they were divided among themselves, and even in their own minds. It is difficult to say how much of a leaven the few radicals on the committee were. Certainly the compromises are evident in the Dickinson draft. Congress was not, for example, specifically given the right to regulate trade, although it was implied in the provision prohibiting the states from levying imposts conflicting with treaties made by Congress. The states were on a footing of equality in voting measures in Congress, yet by

[5] Rutledge to Jay, June 29, in Burnett, *Letters*, 1:517–518.

and large the Dickinson draft met the wishes of the conservatives, particularly those of the Middle states. James Wilson so testified in the Convention of 1787, where he argued that the Continental Congress had constituted a single state and that the interests of individual states had been unknown, but had crept in only after the formation of the confederation. "The original draft of confederation," he said, "was drawn on the first idea [of Congress as a single state] and the draft concluded on how different!" [6]

Two things should be kept in mind in considering the form and phraseology of Dickinson's draft. In the first place, it has been said of his "Farmer's Letters" that they were able by "argument, subtle but clear," to derive "the nature of an act from the intention of its makers, and the intention of its makers from the nature of the act." [7] In the second place, the draft was presented to a body dominated by lawyers for whom subleties of phraseology undiscernible by the lay mind were pregnant with meaning for the future.

The first article of the draft in Dickinson's handwriting [8] provided that "THE Name of this Confederacy shall be 'THE UNITED STATES OF AMERICA'." [9] The second defined the terms of union. The colonies were to unite so as never to be divided by any act, and "hereby severally enter into a firm League of Friendship with

[6] Robert Yates, "Notes in the Convention of 1787," in Charles Tansill, ed., *Documents Illustrative of the Formation of the Union of the American States* (Washington, 1927), 759; James Madison's notes, *ibid.*, 177.

[7] Carl Becker, *The Eve of the Revolution* (New Haven, 1918), 133.

[8] Charles Thomson, "History of the Confederation," p. 7, in the Papers of the Continental Congress, No. 9. The Dickinson draft uses the word "colonies," but uses the term "United States" whenever speaking of the colonies in a collective sense. The draft seems to have been finished at least as early as July 4, for Dickinson probably did not attend Congress after that date. See Burnett, *Letters*, 1:lix. He resigned from Congress after he failed to stem the tide of independence, feeling that he had sacrificed his popularity to his principles, and that he had been unjustly treated by "those unkind Countrymen, whom I cannot forbear to esteem as fellow Citizens amidst their Fury against Me." To Charles Thomson, August 7, 10, 1776, in the Charles Thomson Papers, vol. 1, Library of Congress Manuscripts. Thomson replied that he regretted "that by a perseverance which you were fully convinced was fruitless, you have thrown the affairs of this state into the hands of men totally unequal to them" and as for Dickinson's "unkind Countrymen . . . They did not desert you. You left them." To Dickinson, August 16, 1776, in the Logan Papers, vol. 8, f. 78, in the Pennsylvania Historical Society Manuscripts.

[9] *Journals*, 5:546–547.

each other, for their common Defence, the Security of their Liberties, and their mutual and general Welfare, binding the said Colonies to assist one another against all Force offered to or attacks made upon them or any of them, on Account of Religion, Sovereignty, Trade, or any other Pretence whatever." [10] In other words, sovereign states were entering "severally" into a league of friendship for protection against attack from the outside. On the face of it this appears to be a concession to the radicals, but the rest of the document is a practical negation of the idea.

The greater part of the Dickinson draft dealt with the apportionment of powers and duties between the states and the Congress. In this matter of the distribution of power lies the fundamental difference between this and the final draft of the Articles of Confederation, as also between the latter and the Constitution of 1787. The Dickinson draft, while by no means as explicit as the Constitution of 1787, made the constitution of the central government the standard by which the rights, powers, and duties of the states were to be measured. Congress was theoretically, if not practically, the supreme authority. In contrast, the final draft of the Articles of Confederation was a pact between thirteen sovereign states which agreed to delegate certain powers for specific purposes, while they retained all powers not expressly delegated by them to the central government.

A comparison of the powers of the states and the guarantees made to them with the limitations on the powers of Congress in the Dickinson draft will make this point clear. The draft contained one general clause providing that each state should retain and enjoy "as much of its present Laws, Rights and Customs, as it may think fit, and reserves to itself the sole and exclusive Regulation and Government of its internal police, in all matters that shall not interfere with the Articles of this Confederation." [11] Each state might lay imposts or duties on importations and exportations, provided they did not conflict with any stipulations in treaties thereafter entered into by the United States with the King of Great Britain or any foreign prince or states.[12] The states were to maintain a well-regulated and well-supplied militia. When troops were to be raised in any of the colonies for the common

[10] *Journals*, 5:546–547.   [11] *Ibid.*, 547, Art. III.   [12] *Ibid.*, 547–548, Art. VIII.

defense, the state legislatures were to appoint "Commission Officers," but Congress was to appoint the general officers.[13]

These and no other powers were allotted to the states by the Dickinson draft, and even these few contain provisos which in effect nullified them. In Article III, which is a general guarantee to the states, there are two such provisos negating its legal effectiveness. The states were to enjoy their *present laws*, nothing being said about future state legislation. The control of internal police is qualified, if not negated, by a stipulation that it must "not interfere with" the Articles of Confederation.[14] The same interpretation may be applied to Article VIII, which provided that each state might lay imposts and duties, but treaties made by Congress were to be superior to such state regulation. The privilege of maintaining militia was a duty as well as a privilege, and the right to appoint the subordinate officers of troops raised for the Continental Army was little more than a guarantee of patronage. The third article was really the heart of the matter, as Thomas Burke was to convince Congress nearly a year later. He saw that since it granted only the power of regulating internal police, it clearly assigned every other power to Congress.[15]

If, by implication and interpretation, the states could thus be made to resign all powers but one, and that one was to be subject to interpretation by Congress, what were the restrictions on the power of Congress? There was only one unqualified restriction, that Congress might never impose taxes or duties except in managing the post office. A qualified restriction was that which forbade Congress from interfering in the internal police of a state "any further than such Police may be affected by the Articles of this Confederation."[16] One other restriction, which was really protection for the larger states rather than a limitation of the powers of Congress, was the requirement that the votes of nine

[13] *Ibid.*, 548, Arts. IX, X.

[14] The states are to control their internal police "in all matters that shall not interfere with the Articles of this Confederation." Dickinson's "Quaere" attached indicates his state of mind: "Quaere. The Propriety of the Union's garranteeing to every colony their respective Constitution and form of Government? J. D." *Journals*, vol. 5, p. 547, note 1.

[15] Thomas Burke to Richard Caswell, April 29, 1777, in Burnett, *Letters*, 2:345–346.

[16] *Journals*, 5:552, Art. XVIII.

states were necessary to make war, grant letters of marque and reprisal in peacetime, enter into treaties and alliances, coin money and regulate its value, fix the sums necessary for the "common defence and general welfare," emit bills and borrow money on the credit of the united colonies, raise naval forces, and agree upon the number of land forces to be raised.[17] Thus the sole restraint upon the power of Congress was that it might not lay taxes and duties, which was logical enough if the American Revolution was in any sense a revolt against taxation by an external and superior political agency.

The reverse of the picture is to be found in a consideration of the restrictions placed on the power of the states and of the powers specifically granted to the Congress. The states might not send or receive embassies nor enter into negotiations with any foreign powers.[18] No two or more states were to enter into any treaty, confederation, or alliance without the previous consent of Congress, which was to specify the purpose and duration.[19] The inhabitants of each state were to have all the "Rights, Liberties, Privileges, Immunities and Advantages" in the other states which they then had [20] and the same "Rights, Liberties, Privileges, Immunities, and Advantages, in Trade, Navigation, and Commerce" in any other state, and in going to and from them to any part of the world.[21] The states were to keep no standing armies nor bodies of forces except such as were necessary to garrison forts for the defense of the colony; and each state was to keep up a militia with arms and public stores.[22] Every state was to abide by the decisions of the Congress "concerning the Services performed and Losses or Expences incurred by every Colony for the common Defence or general Welfare," and in no case was any state to attempt to secure by force a redress of any injury supposed to have been done by Congress in denying such satisfactions, indemnifications, etc.[23] No state or states were to engage in war without the consent of Congress unless danger from invasion was so imminent as to admit of no delay. Neither were the states to

[17] *Journals*, 5:552, Art. XVIII; Samuel Adams to James Warren, June 30, 1777, in *Writings*, 3:380–381.

[18] *Journals*, 5:547, Art. IV.

[19] *Ibid.*, 547, Art. V.

[20] *Ibid.*, 547, Art. VI.

[21] *Ibid.*, 547, Art. VII.

[22] *Ibid.*, 548, Art. IX.

[23] *Ibid.*, 548–549, Art. XII.

grant commissions to ships of war, or letters of marque and reprisal, except after a declaration of war by the United States and only under regulations established by the latter.[24] None of these restrictions was considered excessive by the states, since war and foreign affairs were admittedly the province of a confederation and, at the time, one of the chief forces promoting a union of the states.

But the Dickinson draft gave to Congress, by indirection in two articles and directly in another,[25] the control of Indian affairs and of the boundaries of the states with charter claims to the "South Sea." The question of the control of the West was a powder magazine so far as interstate relationships were concerned. Its inclusion speaks for Dickinson's courage and his faithfulness to the interests of the landless states, but hardly for his political acumen. These clauses must have been the subject of some dispute in committee, and of some remaining doubt, for in a note attached to those provisions giving Congress jurisdiction over the West, Dickinson attached the cryptic note, "these clauses are submitted to Congress," and signed it with his initials.[26]

The powers granted to Congress by the eighteenth article are a remarkable list, when one considers that this was the first earnest attempt to bring all the states together into some form of union and that the war was, in one sense, a revolt against centralization. It provided that the United States "shall have the sole and exclusive Right and Power" of determining peace and war; of establishing the legality of, and rules for, captures on land and water; of dividing prizes taken by land or naval forces in the service of the United States; of granting letters of marque and reprisal in times of peace; of appointing courts for the trial of all crimes, frauds, and piracies committed on the high seas or on navigable rivers not within any county or parish; of establishing courts for the final determination of appeals in all cases of captures; of sending and receiving ambassadors "under any Character"; of entering into treaties and alliances; of settling all disputes

[24] *Ibid.*, 549, Art. XIII.

[25] *Ibid.*, 549, 550–551, Arts. XIV, XV, XVIII. In July, 1775, Congress had organized Indian departments and had appointed commissioners for their administration. *Ibid.*, 2:174–177.

[26] *Ibid.*, vol. 5, p. 551, note 1, Art. XVIII.

that exist or may arise between two or more states concerning boundaries, jurisdictions, or any other cause whatever; of coining money and regulating its value; of regulating trade and managing affairs with the Indians; of limiting the bounds of colonies claiming by charter or proclamation to the South Sea, and of ascertaining bounds of colonies whose bounds appeared indeterminate; of assigning territories for new colonies from the lands thus separated or purchased by the Crown of Great Britain from the Indians, or to be hereafter purchased from them; of disposing of all such lands for the benefit of the United Colonies; of fixing the boundaries of new colonies within which forms of government are to be established "on the Principles of Liberty"; of establishing and regulating post offices; of appointing general officers of the land forces in the service of the United States; of commissioning such other officers as should be appointed by the tenth article; of appointing all the officers in the service of the naval forces of the United States; of making rules for the government and regulation of the land and naval forces of the United States, and directing operations; of appointing a Council of State and such committees and civil officers as might be necessary for managing the general affairs of the United States while assembled in Congress, and during its recess, of the Council of State; of appointing a presiding officer and a secretary; and of adjourning at any time during the year.[27]

Besides these "sole and exclusive" powers Congress was to "have Authority for the Defence and Welfare of the United Colonies and every one of them" to fix the amounts of money to be spent, to emit bills and borrow money on the credit of the United States, to raise naval forces, to determine the number of land forces, to request each legislature to raise and equip its quota, which was to be based on the number of white inhabitants,[28] and to establish uniform weights and measures.[29]

Some of these powers had long been conceded without ques-

[27] *Journals*, 5:550–551.
[28] *Ibid.*, 551–552. Congress was allowed to vary the quotas of the individual colonies. Legislatures might take exception to the demand for more than their normal share of troops if in their opinion the extra number might not be safely spared.
[29] *Ibid.*, 552.

tion to the empire: war and peace, the post office, foreign affairs, and Indian affairs; and it was therefore natural enough, in view of past practice and immediate necessities, to give them to Congress. Certain others were the result more particularly of immediate needs and of conservative attitudes, such as the control over the troops, the power to issue bills and borrow money on the credit of the colonies, and to coin money and regulate its value. If war was to be waged with any hope of success, some central power had to take charge of such matters.

The express grant of certain judicial powers to Congress was less unusual than it might seem in the light of the objections to British judicial relations with the colonies. The British government had acted often as an arbiter between classes in a given colony, and in intercolonial disputes.[30] The Dickinson draft provided that Congress should settle all disputes between the states, although it did not provide the machinery for doing so. As we have seen, such delegation of power was eminently desirable in the eyes of the conservatives, who viewed with alarm disputes over boundaries and land claims. The right to abrogate charter claims had never been expressly conceded to the British government in theory, although practice had compelled its concession in fact. If Virginia was moved to revolt, in part, by attempts to mutilate her charter claims to the West, it is obvious that she and other states with charter claims would never consent to placing control over the West in the hands of a central body. Such centralized control was most desired by speculators, who had nothing to hope for from the state governments, and its inclusion was a clear expression of the desires of the landless states in general and of their speculators in particular.

In keeping with conservative ideas, the Dickinson draft provided the foundation of an executive organization. Among the "sole and exclusive" powers of Congress was that of appointing a "Council of State, and such Committees and civil Officers as may be necessary for managing the general Affairs of the United States, under their Direction while assembled, and in their Recess,

[30] Evarts B. Greene, "American Opinion on the Imperial Review of Provincial Legislation," in the *American Historical Review*, 13:104 (October, 1917).

of the Council of State." [31] This Council, whose functions were detailed in a separate article, could make no commitments binding upon the United States, but it was to have certain definite powers which were to be permanent, since they were embodied in a "perpetual" document. It was to have charge of all military and naval operations when Congress was not in session. Although it could not alter the objectives of expeditions agreed upon by Congress, yet an "Alteration of Circumstances" would permit it to do so. It was to "expedite" such measures as might be agreed upon by Congress in pursuance of the powers given to the Council. It could make contracts and draw upon the treasury for payment of them. It was to "superintend and controul or suspend" both civil and military officers acting under the authority of the United States. It was to prepare "matters for the Consideration of the United States" and to summon Congress earlier than the appointed time when it was believed to be necessary. The business of the Council might be carried on by seven members.[32]

The Dickinson draft thus really provided for the establishment of a bureaucratic staff and a continuity of policy in the central government. The implication in the term "Council of State" was that it was the executive arm of a single state, whereas in the draft of the Confederation finally adopted the term "Committee of the States" was applied to a body which was designed to sit only during the recess of Congress and which was given only the most limited functions. It would seem that it was the intention of the Dickinson draft to create a permanent executive body which could do most of the executive work of a centralized government. Its tenure was to be permanent. Its power to spend money and to control the army and navy during the recess of Congress, and its control over civil and military officers, combined to give this body a vast influence for centralization. Although it was not superior to the legislative branch, its powers could not be touched by that branch. The complete change effected in the final draft is evidence — in the absence of contemporary opinion — that such were the possibilities inherent in the "Council of State." [33]

[31] *Journals*, 5:551.
[32] *Ibid.*, 553–554, Art. XIX.
[33] See below, ch. 8. See also Jennings B. Sanders, *Evolution of the Executive Departments of the Continental Congress, 1774–1789* (Chapel Hill, North Carolina, 1935), *passim*.

The failure to grant Congress the power to regulate trade has been thought strange,[34] but when viewed in the light of the disputes among the states over the restraining acts in 1775, and the opening of the ports in 1776, it seems quite natural. There seems also to have been a belief that trade would regulate itself, and that in any case the treaty-making power was sufficient for the purpose.[35]

We have then, so far as the constitution itself is concerned — and it must be considered as a tool rather than as a source of power — a Congress with practically unlimited powers. The states are guaranteed only a conditional control over their internal police. Basically the Dickinson draft was a limitation of the power of the states, a natural expression of the conservative philosophy; yet it was a flat contradiction of the Revolution as a movement against irresponsible centralized political authority. As will be seen, the final form of the Articles of Confederation reversed this situation and made the constitution the measure of the powers of the central organization, and gave to the states the field of undefined authority.

The balance of power between the states on the one hand and the Congress on the other is the most significant aspect of the Dickinson draft. The second important feature is the balance of power among the states themselves. Equality was provided for in the provision that each state was to have one vote in Congress.[36] Expenses were to be paid from a common treasury, to which each state was to contribute in proportion to its population of every age, sex, and quality, except Indians not paying taxes. The taxes were to be levied by the authority and direction of the several legislatures.[37]

The remainder of the Dickinson draft deals with the organiza-

[34] McLaughlin, "Background of American Federalism," in the *American Political Science Review*, 12:239.

[35] This seems to have been the belief of so ardent a "nationalist" as James Wilson. See his "Considerations on the Nature and Extent of the Legislative Authority of the British Parliament," in Adams, *Selected Political Essays of James Wilson*, pp. 81–82, note 44. This view held by Wilson contradicts that held by such men as James Duane, another conservative whose views were expressed in the first Continental Congress.

[36] *Journals*, 5:550, Art. XVII.

[37] *Ibid.*, 548, Art. XI. On July 29, 1775, Congress had agreed to include negroes and mulattoes in each colony. Since population could not be ascertained

tion of Congress and methods of procedure. No matter was to be decided unless seven colonies voted in the affirmative.[38] On certain important questions, such as entering into treaties and alliances, coining money and regulating its value, fixing sums for expenses, and borrowing money, the affirmative votes of nine states were necessary.[39] Congress was to meet on the first Monday of each November.[40] Its journals were to be published except such parts relating to treaties or military operations as must necessarily be kept secret, and they were to be furnished to the delegates of any colony to lay before the legislatures. The colony's yeas and nays were to be entered in the journal at the request of any delegate or delegates.[41]

The delegates to Congress were to be appointed annually as the legislatures of the several colonies might direct. Each colony was to support its own delegates, who were to be subject to recall and replacement at any time during the year.[42] No person could be a delegate for more than three in any six years. No person holding any office under the United States for which he received pay of any kind could be a delegate.[43]

Canada was to be allowed to enter the Confederation on equal terms, but no other colony was to be admitted except with the consent of the delegates of nine states.[44]

The Articles were to be submitted to the several legislatures, which were to approve them and authorize their delegates to ratify them; this being done, the Articles were to be perpetual. No alteration was to be made unless agreed to by the Congress and afterwards confirmed by the legislatures of all the colonies.[45]

The immediate attacks on the Dickinson draft were not the result of its general nature but of certain specific features. Three provisions especially excited dissension. The equal representation of all the states in Congress aroused the antagonism of the larger states. The apportionment of common expenses according to

at the time, an arbitrary proportion was agreed upon. The occasion was the emission of three million dollars in bills of credit by Congress. See the *Journals*, 2:221–222.

[38] *Ibid.*, 5:552, Art. XVIII.   [39] *Ibid.*

[40] *Ibid.*, 549–550, Art. XVI.   [41] *Ibid.*, 552–553, Art. XVIII.

[42] *Ibid.*, 549–550, Art. XVI. This was in a measure a guarantee to the states, for they could control their delegates and thus insure a reflection of the prevailing political atmosphere at any given time.

[43] *Ibid.*, 552, Art. XVIII.   [44] *Ibid.*, 554, Art. XX.   [45] *Ibid.*

total population aroused the bitter opposition of the states with large slave populations. The grant to Congress of broad powers over Western lands and boundaries was resisted stubbornly by the states whose charters gave them large claims to the West.

These three features of the confederation were debated bitterly in July and August of 1776, before the second draft was printed. The second draft, agreed to by Congress on August 20,[46] contained only sixteen articles, whereas the Dickinson draft had contained twenty. The most significant change was the omission of the article which gave Congress control of boundaries, charter claims, and unlocated lands. The two articles which erased state lines with respect to legal and commercial privileges and rights were likewise omitted. The right to fix the standards of weights and measures was placed in the category of the "sole and exclusive" powers of Congress. The provisions for a council of state were removed from this category and placed in that giving Congress "the authority." [47] In addition there were many verbal changes simplifying the Dickinson draft, which had contained much involved and ambiguous phraseology and which would have lent itself to multiple interpretation. But completion of the final draft came only after long and bitter disputes over the major issues of representation, the basis of taxation, and the control of the West. Over the most vital problem of all — the distribution of power between the states on the one hand and Congress on the other, the problem of "sovereignty" — there was only a short discussion, though a sharp and illuminating one.

[46] Charles Thomson, "History of the Confederation," p. 19, in the Papers of the Continental Congress, No. 9; *Journals*, 5:689.

[47] In the *Journals*, 5:674–689, the Dickinson draft of the Articles and the draft agreed to by Congress on August 20 are printed in parallel columns.

VI

The Solution of the Major Issues

REPRESENTATION IN CONGRESS

THE DISPUTE over the basis of "representation," as it was
called at the time, was a controversy between the large and
the small states. Should the vote of the states in Congress
be in proportion to their population, or should all, whatever their
size, have an equal voice in deciding matters of common concern? [1] Tied up with this problem was the far more subtle and
more important question of the fundamental nature of the union
to be created. Was it to be a national state or was it to be a federation of independent states?

The members of Congress from the larger states developed
many ingenious theories to support their demand for a prepon-
derating influence in the union. They discoursed much on "the
good of the whole," explaining that the Declaration of Independence had thrown all the people of the thirteen colonies into one
great mass. Therefore, they argued, representation should be
based on population: that is, in proportion to the population of
each state as a political organization. This solution they felt to
be synonymous with justice and good government.

Obviously their arguments were dictated by a desire to give
their states a dominant voice in the affairs of the union. Their
opponents from the small states knew this and dwelt upon it persistently, for they feared that they would be "swallowed" by
their great neighbors. They fell back upon the solid fact that the
states were legally independent of one another. To retain that

[1] Estimates of population vary. Evarts B. Greene and Virginia D. Harrington, *American Population before the Federal Census of 1790* (New York,
1932), 7, gives the following estimates for 1775: New Hampshire, 100,000;
Massachusetts, 350,000; Rhode Island, 58,000; Connecticut, 200,000; New York,
200,000; New Jersey, 130,000; Pennsylvania, 300,000; Delaware, 30,000; Maryland, 250,000; Virginia, 400,000; North Carolina, 200,000; South Carolina,
200,000; Georgia, 25,000 (1783). Virginia, Massachusetts, and Pennsylvania
were thus the "large" states.

independence they must have an equal vote in Congress, otherwise three or four large states would rule the rest.[2]

The delegates from the large states, whether conservative or radical in political philosophy, used "national" arguments and sought to prove by theoretical abstraction the justice of their material interests. They argued that the members of Congress were the delegates of the people of the United States and not of the individual states.[3] This argument was an obvious contradiction of the facts, for the delegates in Congress were elected, paid, instructed, and, where necessary, recalled by the state governments whose wishes they were expected to reflect in Congress. But their arguments have more than an academic interest, for they were to be used in the Convention of 1787 by James Wilson, Alexander Hamilton, and other conservatives in their efforts to evade the fact of state sovereignty. It was as obvious in 1776 as in 1787 that in a national government representation must be according to population. But in 1776 the issue was confused by the politicians representing large states like Virginia, who were anxious to exert an influence in Congress somewhat in proportion to the population of their respective states. Hence they used arguments that tended in the direction of "nationalism," although they had no intention of surrendering any of their local independence.

The controversy between the large and small states over this question of representation had developed at once in the first Continental Congress. There it had been decided that each colony should have a single vote, since the data for determining the relative weight of each colony were not available.[4] This method of voting was continued in the second Continental Congress, although the plan of Confederation proposed by Franklin in July, 1775, provided for the apportionment of representation in Congress according to population, and for the passage of measures by a majority of the delegates present voting as individuals.[5]

The Dickinson draft had embodied the accepted practice in giving each state one vote on all questions before Congress for

[2] John Adams, Notes on Debates, in *Works*, 2:496, 499, 501; Jefferson, Notes on Debates, in *Writings*, 1:46; William Williams to the Governor of Connecticut, July 5, 1777, in Burnett, *Letters*, 2:399–400.

[3] Jefferson, *Writings*, 1:45.   [4] *Journals*, 1:25.   [5] *Ibid.*, 2:196–197.

decision.[6] When this article came up for discussion on July 31, the delegates from the large state of Pennsylvania led in the attack upon it. They had the able assistance of John Adams and of a scattering of delegates from other states. Franklin placed the matter on a material basis. The small states, he asserted, should have an equal vote with the larger only if they contributed an equal amount toward the support of the union. He prophesied that a confederation based on so "iniquitous" a principle as equality among the states would not last long. In accordance with his arguments he submitted a motion to the effect that voting should be on the basis of population.[7] Middleton of South Carolina suggested that voting should be according to the amounts of money paid in support of the central government.[8]

Dr. Benjamin Rush appealed to "history" to prove the contentions of the larger states. He assured Congress that the failure of the Dutch Republic had been due to the fact that voting by states had been required, and that members had to consult their constituents whenever any question arose. He prophesied that the article as it stood would bring evils in its train, and that the growth of freedom would be prevented, although he failed to explain why such a result was to be expected. He argued plausibly but speciously that if the whole people could come together, they would decide by a majority vote. Therefore Congress, as representative of all the people, should decide by majority vote. Rush informed Congress that he was not really pleading the cause of Pennsylvania. When he entered the door of the room, he said, he no longer considered himself a citizen of Pennsylvania, but a citizen of America. In answer to the small states that feared oppression by the larger ones, he declared that the latter were so scattered that they could never combine for this purpose,[9] an argument that was a tacit admission of the contention of the small states.

On their part, the small states again fell back upon the inescapable fact that the members of Congress were the representatives of the states and not of the people of the United States. Chase of Maryland saw clearly that it was by no means merely a question

[6] *Journals*, 5:550, Art. XVII.　　[7] John Adams, *Works*, 2:496, 499.
[8] *Ibid.*, 499.　　[9] Jefferson, *Writings*, 1:46; John Adams, *Works*, 2:499–500.

of money, as men like Franklin were inclined to argue. Chase agreed that in questions involving property the larger states should be protected, but he urged that it was more than a question of property; that it was a question of life and liberty as well, and that in these the smaller states needed protection. To secure protection for both groups he proposed that in votes relating to money the voice of each colony should be proportionate to the number of its inhabitants.[10] This solution seems to have remained unconsidered, as did that of Sherman of Connecticut, who proposed that on any question the vote of both a majority of the states and a majority of "individuals" should be obtained.[11]

Franklin also made one of those appeals to "history" to which the delegates resorted so often when they desired to prove a point in their favor. He argued that there was no danger of oppression in uniting as one state. That had been one of the arguments against the union of Scotland with England, he said; what had happened was that Jonah had swallowed the whale, and the Scotch now controlled England and made its laws.[12] Such flimsy reasoning was riddled by a Scotchman, who voiced the views of both the radicals and the small states. This was the Reverend John Witherspoon, president of Princeton, whose keen intelligence punctured many a shallow "historical" argument. He could appeal to "history" as well as others, and he cited examples to prove that the subjects of free states were always the most enslaved. He then went to the heart of the issue by making it plain that there was a difference between a federal union and what he termed an "incorporating" union. The union of Scotland with England was of the latter kind. The Congress was not discussing that kind of union at all. The Congress was discussing a federal union, hence no matter concerning an individual could come before it. This was as clear a statement as could be made of the radical view of the government they were seeking to create. It was to be a federal union of sovereign states, not a national government. "Every Colony," said Witherspoon, "is a distinct person."[13]

[10] John Adams, *Works*, 2:499; Jefferson, *Writings*, 1:42–43.
[11] John Adams, *Works*, 2:499.
[12] *Ibid.*, 501; Jefferson, *Writings*, 1:43–44.
[13] John Adams, *Works*, 2:496, 501; Jefferson, *Writings*, 1:44–45.

The most realistic argument from the conservative ranks was made by John Adams. He reiterated that the delegates were the representatives of the people; that in some states the people were many, in others they were few. Therefore the votes should be in proportion to population. He then made a profession of his political skepticism by saying that "Reason, justice, & equity never had weight enough on the face of the earth to govern the councils of men." It is "interest" alone — and he meant economic interest — that governs men, and interest alone is to be trusted. Therefore the interest indoors should be a mathematical representation of the interest out of doors.[14] What he really objected to, of course, was that Rhode Island would be on terms of equality with Massachusetts. "Thus," he wrote, "we are sowing the seeds of ignorance, corruption, and injustice in the fairest field of liberty that ever appeared upon earth, even in the first attempts to cultivate it."[15]

But the members from the large states and the conservatives, who wanted a central power superior to that of the states, were not able to defeat the members from the small states and the radicals who believed in the independence of the individual states. The printed draft of August 20, 1776, included the article in the form it had been submitted to Congress.[16]

Neither side gave up, and the issue remained one of major importance. In May, 1777, Jefferson wrote John Adams that he considered representation the greatest issue and that neither the great nor the small states would make concessions in the matter. He suggested that Adams offer an amendment providing that any proposition might be defeated by a majority of the people represented, or by a majority of the states. The first method would protect the large states, and the second the small states.[17] Adams promised to try to have it introduced, but nothing seems to have been done.[18] Finally a compromise was reached in which it was agreed that on certain measures the votes of nine states should be necessary for passage. This was a concession to the interests of the larger states.[19]

[14] Jefferson, *Writings*, 1:45.
[15] John Adams to Joseph Hawley, August 25, in *Works*, 9:435.
[16] *Journals*, 5:681, Art. XIII.
[17] Williamsburgh, May 16, 1777, in *Writings*, 2:130.
[18] John Adams to Jefferson, May 26, in *Works*, 9:467.
[19] Samuel Adams to James Warren, June 30, in *Writings*, 3:380–381. The

No new arguments were advanced. The question was debated occasionally during the summer of 1777, but was not taken up seriously until October 7. At that time the large states proposed several amendments, each of which was voted down. The first of these would have given Rhode Island, Delaware, and Georgia one vote each, and the other states one vote for each fifty thousand population. This amendment received only the votes of Virginia and Pennsylvania.[20] A second amendment proposed to give each state one delegate for each thirty thousand population, each delegate to have one vote. This also failed, Virginia alone supporting it.[21] Finally it was proposed that each state be given representatives in Congress in proportion to the amount of money it contributed to the common treasury. Virginia again was the sole supporter of this motion.[22] The question was then put on the article as reported in the Dickinson draft. It was agreed to, Virginia alone dissenting. The minority negative votes in their respective delegations were those of John Adams, of Arthur Middleton of South Carolina, and of John Penn of North Carolina.[23]

The large states made one last attempt to change the mode of representation and thus to secure an influence in Congress somewhat proportionate to their size. It had been decided earlier that the votes of nine states should be necessary to secure the passage of such important measures as the declaration of war and provisions for the coinage of money and the apportionment of expenses. An amendment was offered to this portion of the Articles stipulating that the nine states so agreeing should contain a majority of the people of the United States, excluding Indians and negroes. Virginia, the largest state, was alone in supporting the proposal.[24] The victory of the small states and of the radicals was complete.

THE BASIS OF TAXATION

A SECOND MAJOR ISSUE was the apportionment of common expenses among the several states. Upon what basis should each state be expected to pay money into the common treasury? The Dick-

Dickinson draft had provided this same measure, as had the second printed draft of August 20, 1776. See the *Journals*, 5:685.

[20] *Journals*, 9:779–780. [23] *Ibid.*, 781–782.
[21] *Ibid.*, 780–781. [24] *Ibid.*, 849, October 30.
[22] *Ibid.*, 781.

inson draft provided that the states were to supply funds in proportion to their total number of inhabitants of every age, sex, and quality except Indians not paying taxes.[25]

This proposal met with the determined opposition of the states with a large negro population; they demanded that taxation be based on land values. The controversy that ensued between the North and the South had little of the humanitarian about it. It was a matter of simple addition and subtraction. If negroes were to be included in the population on which the apportionment of expenses was based, the South's share would be much larger in proportion to its white population than that of the North. If, on the other hand, the value of granted and surveyed lands was to be the basis of assessment, the Northern states, so their delegates believed, would pay more than a fair share of the common expenses. The arguments used by both sides are readily understood if these facts are kept in mind.

Maryland was the first to oppose the method suggested in the Dickinson draft. On July 30, 1776, Samuel Chase moved that each state's quota of taxes be in proportion to the number of white inhabitants only. He said he realized that in theory taxation should be according to wealth, but that the value of property in every state could never be estimated. Negroes, however, were property, indistinguishable from land and personalty. Where the Northern farmer invested his profits in cattle and horses, the Southern farmer invested in slaves; and there was no more reason for taxing the one than the other.[26] John Adams replied to Chase in a long disquisition which amounted to a statement of a labor theory of value. He argued that population should be taken as an index of wealth. Whether labor is free or slave makes no difference: in either case it adds just so much to the wealth of the state, since it is the number of laborers that produces the surplus for taxation. He then went on to say that the application of the word "property" to some members of the state was a fallacy, be-

---

[25] *Journals*, 5:548, Art. XI. On July 29, 1775, Congress had resolved that each colony's proportion of the bills emitted by Congress should be determined according to the total population, including negroes and mulattoes. *Journals*, 2:221–222.

[26] Jefferson, Notes on Debates, in *Writings*, 1:39–40.

cause from the point of view of the state all population is equally its wealth.[27]

James Wilson supported Adams' contentions with the ingenious argument that freemen do not produce the surplus for taxation that slaves do, since they work more and consume more than slaves. Then, too, slaves consume the food of freemen. Therefore, he argued, dismiss the slaves and let freemen take their place. To this piece of stupidity John Witherspoon replied that, according to Wilson's reasoning, horses, which likewise ate the food of freemen, should also be taxed. He pointed out that in including slaves the Congress was not doing what the Southern states did when they counted slaves in determining the amount of taxes an individual must pay, because "in the Southern colonies slaves pervade the whole colony; but they do not pervade the whole continent." Witherspoon urged that the value of lands and houses was the best basis for estimating the wealth of a nation and the easiest to ascertain.[28]

The attack upon the idea of slaves as property aroused Lynch of South Carolina, who said plainly that if it were to be debated whether or not slaves were property, confederation would be at an end. Where other states taxed their lands, Carolina taxed its negroes.[29] Rutledge expressed himself as willing to be rid of slavery, but said that the proposal involved the taxation of Southern property (slaves), whereas the property of other colonies was not to be drawn upon.[30] Hooper of North Carolina pointed to the fact that North Carolina was a striking exception to the theory that riches are proportional to population.[31]

After still further debate Chase's amendment was brought to

[27] *Ibid.*, 40–41.

[28] *Ibid.*, 41–42. Benjamin Harrison of Virginia proposed a compromise: that two slaves be counted as a freeman. He said that he doubted whether two slaves did the work of one freeman.

[29] John Adams, Notes on Debates, in *Works*, 2:498.

[30] *Ibid.* Both Lynch and Rutledge said that slaves were taxed as property in the South. If they were to be included in apportioning taxes, the property of other states, such as the shipping interests of New England, should be taxed. Rutledge prophesied that "the Eastern Colonies will become the carriers for the Southern; they will obtain wealth for which they will not be taxed."

[31] John Adams, Notes on Debates, in *Works*, 2:498; Cornelius Harnett, in a letter written to William Wilkinson on November 30, 1777, said that propor-

a vote and defeated by a solid sectional division. New Hampshire, Massachusetts, Rhode Island, Connecticut, New York, New Jersey, and Pennsylvania voted against the amendment; Maryland, Delaware, Virginia, North and South Carolina for it; the votes of Georgia were divided.[32] Chase and his colleagues swore that they would have nothing more to do with the taxation article and that Maryland would never agree to it.[33] Yet the printed draft of August 20 contained the article substantially as written by Dickinson.[34]

The basis of taxation was debated occasionally in the summer of 1777 and taken up seriously in October, when three plans of taxation were proposed: (1) in proportion to the total population, the original proposal; (2) according to the value of lands in each state; and (3) according to the value of property in general. Henry Laurens wrote on October 10 that they had been discussing the matter for two days, and that "some sensible things have been said, and as much nonsense as ever I heard in so short a space." [35]

By this time the original plan as proposed by Dickinson had come to be bitterly opposed by all except the New England delegates. After five days of debate it was moved that taxes be based on the value of all property except household goods and wearing apparel.[36] On the failure of this motion, the vote on which is not recorded, it was moved that public expenses be apportioned according to the estimated value of all lands granted to or surveyed for individuals, including the improvements thereon.[37] The four New England states voted against this motion without a single dissenting vote. New Jersey, Maryland, Virginia, North and South Carolina were as unanimously in favor of it. The two delegates from Pennsylvania were divided, as were the two from New

tioning taxes according to population "would have ruined Poor North Carolina. she has as many Inhabitants as Connecticut (almost) tho' the Land in that state would sell for five times as much as the Lands in ours." Burnett, *Letters*, 2:578.

[32] Jefferson, *Writings*, 1:42.

[33] William Williams to Oliver Wolcott, August 12, 1776, in Burnett, *Letters*, 2:48.

[34] *Journals*, 5:677–678.

[35] Henry Laurens to John Laurens, in Burnett, *Letters*, 2:515.

[36] *Journals*, 9:785, 788–789, 793, 797–798, 800.

[37] *Ibid.*, 800–801.

York. It was thus carried by a five to four vote that each state's contributions to the common cause were to be based upon the value of its lands and improvements.[38]

The opposition of the New England states to this basis of apportionment was founded on the belief that their lands were much more valuable than those of any of the other states and that they would therefore pay more than a just share of the costs of the war. "The Eastern people," wrote a North Carolina delegate, "were much against this. knowing their Lands to be very valuable, they were for settling the quota by the number of Inhabitants including slaves." [39] The Southern delegates, on the other hand, still maintaining that the most adequate tax base was total property, felt that compliance with New England's desire would have, as Cornelius Harnett explained it, "ruined Poor North Carolina. she has as many Inhabitants as Connecticut (almost) tho' the Land in that state would sell for five times as much as the Lands in ours." [40]

The New Englander's attitude was set forth by Nathaniel Folsom in a letter to the president of New Hampshire. He was unable, he wrote, to see any justice in the rule laid down for the apportionment of expenses, for a third of Southern wealth, consisting of negroes, was thus left out of consideration in determining the South's ability to pay taxes. Furthermore, the Southern states were to have the advantage in supplying troops, since these were to be apportioned on the basis of white population only. Thus their negroes were to be left at home, and "they can till their lands and get bread and riches, while some other States may be greatly distressed." [41] It must be remembered in evaluating the

---

[38] *Ibid.*, 801–802. Duane of New York, who was heavily interested in lands, voted against the measure. William Duer voted for it. Of the Pennsylvania delegation, Robert Morris was for the measure and Daniel Roberdeau, a radical, was against it.

[39] Cornelius Harnett to William Wilkinson, November 30, in Burnett, *Letters*, 2:578.

[40] *Ibid.*

[41] Nathaniel Folsom to Meshech Weare, November 21, 1777, *ibid.*, 564. In a letter to Richard Henry Lee, Roger Sherman reiterated that wealth was generally in proportion to the number of people that could be supported in a state and that "wealth principally arises from the labour of men." He was willing to exclude all negroes under ten or any other age that could be agreed upon. He wished to have the confederation delayed for a time rather than to

position of the New Englanders that their section was more densely populated and that land values were, as they contended, higher than in the South. Hence the assessment of expenses according to the value of lands granted to or surveyed for individuals seemed to bear much more heavily upon them than on the states to the south, where there were vast areas of unappropriated lands which could not be considered in making assessments.

Richard Henry Lee pointed out rightly enough that "in this great business . . . we must yield a little to each other, and not rigidly insist on having everything correspondent to the partial views of every State. On such terms we can never confederate." He went on to say that in the history of the world numbers had never been a just criterion of wealth, but that wealth was really reflected in the land values of a country, and prophesied that Virginia would probably end by paying more taxes than if population had been made the basis.[42] In the end, though the decision of Congress was to meet with opposition, New England yielded without much objection when the Confederation came up for final ratification.

THE CONTROL OF THE WEST

THE CONTROL OF THE West was the issue around which revolved the most bitter controversy during the writing and ratification of the Articles of Confederation. Certain of the states, like Virginia, had charter claims to lands extending to the "South Sea" or at least to the Mississippi River. The boundaries of others — Maryland, Pennsylvania, Delaware, New Jersey, and Rhode Island — had been definitely set by their charters. These "landless" states insisted that Congress be given control of all the lands beyond the boundaries which were to be set by Congress. The "landed" states refused to grant such vast powers to Congress and were successful in writing their point of view into the final draft of the Articles. Maryland, however, persisted in the fight and re-

make a perpetual rule and prophesied that "the States can neither agree to nor practise the mode voted by Congress, and nothing effectual can be done to fix the credit of the currency or to raise necessary supplies until some rule of proportion is adopted." Hartford, November 3, in Burnett, *Letters*, 2:541.

[42] Richard Henry Lee to [Meshech Weare], November 4, 1774, in Burnett, *Letters*, 2:569.

fused to ratify the Articles until Congress was given the desired power and thus delayed the adoption of the Confederation until March of 1781.

Maryland's refusal to ratify the Articles of Confederation was long interpreted as evidence of her national vision and patriotism. This point of view is hardly tenable.[43] The conflict over the West was primarily an economic one. Virginia's western claims seemed unlimited, and her speculators found it easy to stake out vast areas west of the Alleghenies through their influence upon or presence in the Virginia legislature. The speculators from the landless states could not hope for such favors. Hence they appealed to whatever authority they could conceive of as superior to that of Virginia. Before the Revolution it had been the British government to which they appealed for a share in "the West" of the eighteenth century. Once the Revolution had begun, they turned from London to Philadelphia, where, armed with legal opinions, shares of stock, and entertainment of various kinds, they sought to convince the Continental Congress of the justice of their claims. They soon evolved the theory that the Continental Congress had inherited the sovereign powers of the British government and, particularly, the power of disposing of Western lands.

In leaning upon the Congress they leaned upon a weak reed, but it was the only alternative to a certainly futile appeal to the Virginia legislature, although even that appeal was made in the last extremity. The Virginia legislature soon made it plain that it intended to preserve the state's charter claims intact. Eventually, and in express terms, it declared null and void the claims of the speculators of the landless states.[44]

[43] For over a half century Herbert Baxter Adams' *Maryland's Influence upon Land Cessions to the United States* (*Johns Hopkins University Studies in Historical and Political Science*, 3d series, no. 1, Baltimore, 1885) set the pattern for the interpretation of this significant episode in American history. Frederick Jackson Turner gave it somewhat vague approval in his essay on "The Significance of the Frontier in American History," published in 1893, and ever since it has been the standard. A different interpretation based on a wider study of the evidence and following the lead of such writers as Burke A. Hinsdale in *The Old Northwest* and Clarence W. Alvord in *The Illinois Country, 1673–1818*, is to be found in Jensen, "Cession of the Old Northwest," in the *Mississippi Valley Historical Review*, 23:27–48.

[44] See Jensen, *ibid.*, 23:30–32, 34–36.

In their first dealings with Congress the speculators had a measure of success. There is no sure way of determining whether the provisions of the Dickinson draft of the Confederation were a deliberate or an accidental response to their desires. But John Dickinson was a Pennsylvanian, and it is natural to suppose that he would have embodied as best he could the views of the landless states. Such a conclusion is warranted at least by the background and the result. Much earlier, in his Albany plan, Franklin, who was a Pennsylvanian and a land speculator, provided that the Congress should control Indian affairs. He also provided somewhat vaguely for congressional control of the western limits of the colonies.[45] This idea was further elaborated in the draft of a confederation which he made in July, 1775.[46] Finally, in the Dickinson draft, the elements of the Western problem were treated in various places, but on the whole the proposed government was given such extensive powers that it was sure to arouse the ire of the landed states and of those interested in keeping a severe check upon the powers of the central government.

Article XIV of the Dickinson draft provided that Congress should enter into alliances with the Six Nations and neighboring Indian nations, determine their boundaries, and guarantee their lands to them. In the same article state and individual land purchases from Indians were declared invalid until the boundaries of the states should be established. Once this was done, purchases of lands beyond state boundaries were to be made only by the United States in council with the Indians.[47] Thus, by implication, constitutional status was given to the contention of the landless states and of their speculators that there were lands lying outside the bounds of any state. Furthermore, congressional control of such bounds was also implied, for Article XV provided that once the boundaries of any state had been established, the states were to guarantee free and full possession of all remaining lands to any state thus having its boundaries drawn.[48]

Such clauses are rather general and indicate congressional con-

[45] Benjamin Franklin, *Writings*, 3:198, 217–220.
[46] *Journals*, 2:196, 197–198. Abernethy, in his *Western Lands*, 148, says that Dickinson "incorporated" Franklin's proposals. "Elaborated" would be a better word.
[47] *Journals*, 5:549.   [48] *Ibid.*

trol only by implication. But in another part of the Dickinson draft, among the "sole and exclusive powers" given to Congress by the eighteenth article, were the powers of regulating Indian trade and of managing all affairs with the Indians; of limiting the bounds of those states claiming to extend to the South Sea and of fixing such other state boundaries as seemed indefinite; of setting up new states in the lands so separated, and previously purchased by the British crown from the Indians, or to be thereafter obtained from them; of disposing of all such lands for the benefit of all the states; and, finally, of providing that "Forms of Government are to be established on the Principles of Liberty" within the state so established. To this grant of extensive powers, John Dickinson attached the cryptic note: "These clauses are submitted to Congress." [49]

It may be argued that such powers belong to a central government, but it is from the point of view of constitution-making as a practical art that the opposition to them is to be explained. One must keep in mind the "interests" which demanded that they be placed in the hands of Congress. The landed states may be pardoned their refusal to sacrifice their interests to the "good of the whole" when it is recognized that they saw nothing in such phrases but the program of the speculators of the landless states, or, at best, the jealousy of these states. Above all is the fact that the citizens of the landed colonies had been vastly irritated by the British government's exercise of just such powers as the Dickinson draft now proposed to give to Congress. The Indiana-Vandalia scheme and the Quebec Act had contributed greatly to the Virginians' growing irritation over the imperial connection. Thomas Jefferson penned an eloquent protest in his *A Summary View of the Rights of British America* in 1774,[50] and in 1776 he was in Congress to oppose the allocation of sweeping powers to another central government which obviously was intended to perform functions similar to the government of Great Britain. Hence when Article XIV came up for debate on July 25, Jefferson attacked it as equivocal and indefinite, stated that the bounds of the Southern colonies were fixed, and offered an amendment designed to give that assumption constitutional status: "No pur-

[49] *Ibid.*, pp. 550-551, note 1.   [50] *Writings*, 1:441-445.

chases to be made by the individual states or persons of lands on this continent not within the boundaries of any of these United States, shall be valid." All purchases outside the boundaries of the states were to be made by Congress. Jefferson added a significant detail when he proposed that the lands so purchased by Congress "shall be given freely to those who may be permitted to seat them." [51]

Chase of Maryland, later to become a member of the Illinois-Wabash Company, stated the case for the landless states.[52] He declared that the article as drafted by Dickinson was plain and right and the amendment wrong. He frankly admitted that it was the intention of certain members of Congress to limit the boundaries of some of the states, inasmuch as no state then had, ever had, or ever could have a right to extend to the South Sea. Such extensive boundaries would render the position of their neighbors unsafe. Jefferson's reply was that he believed the states would limit themselves, and demanded to know what guarantee even the present settlements would have against congressional encroachment if such extensive powers were given to Congress.

James Wilson of Pennsylvania, who was to become president of the Illinois-Wabash Company, declared that the claims to the South Sea were extravagant and founded on mistakes: that when the original charters had been granted it had been supposed that the South Sea was only a hundred miles from the Atlantic Ocean. He cited an opinion of Lord Camden's, given to the land company speculators who some years earlier had appealed to him for aid, to the effect that such claims could never be practical. Wilson was enough of a legalist, however, to admit that Pennsylvania had no right to interfere with such claims. But he did forecast the method later adopted by Maryland to realize the desire of the landless states: Pennsylvania did have a right to say that she would not confederate until such claims were cut off.[53]

When the debate was resumed, Chase of Maryland once more denied the right of any state to extend to the South Sea. The

[51] Papers of the Continental Congress, No. 47, f. 13.

[52] Chase was a member at least as early as 1781. See the list of members of the Illinois-Wabash Company in the James Wilson Papers, 10:100, in the Pennsylvania Historical Society Manuscripts.

[53] John Adams, Notes on Debates, in *Works*, 2:492–493.

reply of the Virginians was much more pointed than it had been before. Benjamin Harrison maintained that Maryland had a right to its land only by virtue of its charter, and that Virginia, by virtue of her charter, owned the land to the South Sea. Jefferson probed a sore spot in the relations between Virginia and Maryland when he spoke of Virginia's release of her claim to all the land settled by Maryland. To the reiterated argument that the small states would be endangered by the growth of their large neighbors, the reply was made that, granted the danger, it did not follow that Congress could limit the bounds of Virginia. "A man's right does not cease to be a right, because it is large." [54]

Much the same lines were drawn in the debate on the articles giving Congress control over trade with the Indians. James Wilson pointed out, correctly enough, that the Indians refused to recognize any superior political authority, but he went on to argue that no power except the United States should be allowed to deal with Indians either within or outside the bounds of any state. The Georgians, who were in danger from the Indians and who did not feel equal to buying enough presents to keep them peaceful, were willing to shift the burden to Congress. The Virginians were willing to agree to congressional control if the Indians within a state were excepted, and ultimately an amendment to that effect was secured.[55]

As Samuel Chase remarked, "a considerable Diversity of opinion prevails," [56] but those opposed to such wide congressional powers were able to have all the disputed items postponed — except the one relating to Indian affairs — and they were not printed in the draft of August 20. Nevertheless the problem continued to be a source of dispute when the question of bounty lands came up. In this first test of strength the state of Maryland won an empty victory, but the event illustrates what were the relations between the states and Congress when any important issue arose. On September 16 Congress decided to raise eighty-eight new battalions to serve for the duration of the war. Each soldier enlisting was promised a bounty of twenty dollars and a hundred acres of land, the cost of which was to be apportioned in the

[54] *Ibid.*, 500–502.
[55] *Ibid.*, 494–496.
[56] Samuel Chase to Philip Schuyler, August 9, in Burnett, *Letters*, 2:44.

same manner as the other expenses of the war.[57] Maryland decided that her quota of eight battalions was unjust and declared that Congress must have made out the quota on the basis of both white and black population, whereas it should have been done on the basis of white population only. The Maryland Convention therefore decided to re-enlist all its previously enlisted citizens, and for that purpose commissioners were appointed to search all the camps for Maryland soldiers. In addition, it was agreed to offer a ten-dollar bounty in lieu of the land bounty offered by Congress, "because there are no lands belonging solely and exclusively to this State," and because the purchase of lands would eventually involve the state beyond its ability to pay.[58]

The Maryland delegates told Congress that their state had no land for the purpose, and "that an Expectation was formed by the People of our State that what was conquered from an Enemy at the joint Expence of Blood and Treasure of the whole should become their joint property but as Claims had been set up opposite to our Ideas of natural Justice it became a wise people rather to prepare for the worst by giving ten Dollars now than trust to the mercy of a few Venders from whom they would be obliged to purchase (having pledged their Honour) at any price, the Case of all Monopolies." [59] Congress then asked Maryland not to give the additional ten-dollar bounty and reiterated that the lands would be supplied at the expense of the United States.[60] The Maryland Convention replied that if the honorable Congress would specify any lands belonging to the United States, it would be glad to enlist troops on the terms set by Congress. The Convention expressed the belief that the lands claimed by the British Crown ought to be common stock.[61] If they were not, some of

[57] *Journals*, 5:762–763, September 16. Officers received more, depending upon their rank.

[58] Proceedings of the Maryland Convention, October 9, in Force, *American Archives*, 5th series, 3:120–121.

[59] Benjamin Rumsey to James Tilghman, October 24, in Burnett, *Letters*, vol. 2, p. 140, note 3.

[60] *Journals*, 6:912–913, October 30.

[61] On October 30 the Maryland Convention had passed the following illuminating resolution: "That it is the opinion of this Convention, that the very extensive claim of the State of Virginia to the back lands hath no foundation in justice, and that if the same or any like claim is admitted, the freedom of the smaller States and the liberties of *America* may be thereby greatly

the states would set a price on their lands and thus pay off their debts and have their territory settled by the soldiers of other states, "whilst this State and a few others must be so weakened and impoverished, that they can hold their liberties only at the will of their powerful neighbors." The Convention finally declared that it was willing to do all in its power to raise its quota; if Congress would not specify the lands belonging to the United States, nor allow Maryland to give the additional ten-dollar bounty, its commissioners would try to enlist the troops on the twenty-dollar bounty alone, "but if the event should prove a disappointment, it cannot be imputed to this state." [62]

Congress was more than equal to the occasion. When Massachusetts began offering additional sums of money to raise its quota of troops, the state was asked to withdraw its offer of extra pay, and it was provided that instead of enlisting for the duration of the war, a man might enlist for three years and receive the same bounty and pay, with the exception of the land bounty, which would be given only to those enlisting for the duration of the war. [63] An exasperated Maryland delegate reported that "Congress has got rid of the difficulty with respect to the land, and has not closed in with either of the propositions made by Our State, nor receded entirely from their own resolution." [64]

Nevertheless the Maryland delegates continued to urge upon Congress that "the procuring Lands at the expense of the united States, and our claim that the back Lands acquired from the Crown of G. B. in the present war should be a common stock for the benefit of the united States, and should remain open for the determination of some future Congress" and that any state

endangered; this Convention being firmly persuaded, that if the dominion over those lands should be established by the blood and treasure of the *United States*, such lands ought to be considered as a common stock, to be parcelled out at proper times into convenient, free and independent Governments." Force, *American Archives*, 5th series, 3:134. It is to be noted that no attack on the legality of Virginia's charter had as yet been made. That came only after appeals to "justice" and to the expense of "blood and treasure" proved to be ineffective.

[62] Proceedings of the Maryland Convention, November 8, 9, in Force, *American Archives*, 5th series, 3:174, 177–178.

[63] *Journals*, 6:944–945, November 12.

[64] Benjamin Rumsey to Daniel of St. Thomas Jenifer, November 13, in Force, *American Archives*, 5th series, 3:660–661.

which might raise its quota of troops and give a bounty in lieu of land, be not chargeable for the land bought for the soldiers of other states.[65] Congress at last acted by a "fence-straddling" resolution declaring that anything theretofore done was not intended "to prejudice or strengthen the right or claim of the United States, or any of them, to any lands in America, nor to determine in what proportion or manner the expences of the war shall be raised or adjusted" except the first emissions of money by Congress.[66]

The Western question dropped from official sight for the time being, but when Thomas Burke of North Carolina arrived in Congress in February, 1777, he reported that Maryland, Pennsylvania, New Jersey, and others were very jealous of the landed states, and gave it as his opinion that they would attempt to make the power of Congress very extensive and then limit the states to the west.[67] In July, 1777, when an expedition to capture West Florida was under consideration, Chase of Maryland made it plain that the issue was not dead, for he demanded to know to whom the area would belong if the expedition should succeed; unless it were first decided that it should belong to the United States, he said, he would be against the expedition.[68]

Late in August, Richard Henry Lee wrote to Thomas Jefferson that he had found that Virginia's charter bounds would be strongly contested on the ground that the charter of 1609 had been vacated and that no transfer from the Company to the people of Virginia could be shown; that therefore all ungranted lands were the property of the crown and that, having been taken by common exertions, they must become common stock.[69]

With the activity in October, 1777, that completed the Confederation, the question of the West was brought to the fore and the lines were sharply drawn between the landed and landless

[65] Samuel Chase to the Maryland Council of Safety, November 21, in Burnett, *Letters*, 2:161–162.

[66] *Journals*, 6:978, November 23; Benjamin Rumsey to Daniel of St. Thomas Jenifer, November 24, in Burnett, *Letters*, 2:162–163.

[67] Thomas Burke to the Governor of North Carolina, February 10, in Burnett, *Letters*, 2:257. He was of the opinion that the states with western claims should not give their delegates any power to bind them in anything concerning bounds.

[68] Charles Thomson, Notes of Debates, July 25, in Burnett, *Letters*, 2:422.

[69] Lee, *Letters*, 1:319–320.

states. On October 15 a motion was made that every state should lay before Congress a description of its claims with a summary of the grants and treaties on which those claims were based, in order that the limits of each territorial jurisdiction might be ascertained by the Articles of Confederation. The motion received the aye votes of only New York, Maryland, and Pennsylvania. It was then moved that the United States should have the sole power to fix the western boundaries of such states as claimed to the South Sea and to dispose of all lands beyond the boundaries so fixed. On the failure of this motion, a third was made, that Congress should have the power to ascertain and fix the boundaries, and to lay out the lands beyond such lines into separate and independent states. On this motion the state of Maryland was the only one to vote favorably.[70]

Whether or not "so persistent an attack alarmed the landowning states,"[71] Richard Henry Lee seems to have provided the way out for them. At the end of a long and complicated article, more calculated to delay than expedite judicial procedure, there was inserted the clause "that no State shall be deprived of territory for the benefit of the United States."[72]

A similar proviso was attached to the "sole and exclusive" power of Congress of "regulating the trade, and managing all affairs with the Indians, not members of any of the States," which had been reported in the draft of August 20, 1776. After some maneuvering the article was made more acceptable to the landed states by an amendment stating that "the legislative right of any State, within its own limits be not infringed or violated."[73]

The victory for the landed states in this portion of the Articles was complete. Though the claims of many states were tenuous and Virginia was the special target of the landless states, yet those states with any claims at all usually sided with Virginia. In addition there were those who were guided by the radical belief in the limitation of the powers of government. But the success of

[70] *Journals*, 9:806, 807, October 15.

[71] John B. McMaster, *A History of the People of the United States*, 3:92 (New York, 1892).

[72] *Journals*, 9:843; Papers of the Continental Congress, No. 47, f. 99. A slip in the writing of Charles Thomson indicates that the proviso was the motion of Richard Henry Lee.

[73] *Journals*, 9:844, 845, October 28.

the landed states in securing constitutional guarantees against attack from the landless states and the land speculators by no means settled the problem. The history of the ratification of the Articles of Confederation is almost entirely the history of the continuation of the struggle. As the conflict continued during the ratification of the Articles, all other issues involved in the control of the West came to be overshadowed by the activity of the land speculators, who themselves came to Congress to represent the landless states. When this happened, the landless states could no longer garb themselves in the cloak of "patriotism," but they could and did continue to play the part they had played since 1775.

VII

The Problem of Sovereignty

THE FUNDAMENTAL issue in the writing of the Articles of Confederation was the location of ultimate political authority, the problem of sovereignty. Should it reside in Congress or in the states? Many conservatives in 1776–77, as in 1787, believed that Congress should have a "superintending" power over both the states and their individual citizens. They had definite reasons for such a desire. They feared mob action and democratic rule. They saw the advantage of a centralized control over the unsettled Western lands, the chief field of economic opportunity, and over trade and trade regulation, which involved, ultimately, taxation. Not all the conservatives, particularly in the Southern colonies, agreed on all these points, but enough of them did to make their attitude plain at the outbreak of the Revolution.

The radicals, on the other hand, were fighting centralization in their attack upon the British Empire and upon the colonial governing classes, whose interests were so closely interwoven with the imperial relationship. Furthermore, the interests of the radicals were essentially local. To them union was merely a means to their end, the independence of the several states. Hence centralization was to be opposed. Finally, the democratic theory of the time was antagonistic to any government with pretensions toward widespread dominion. Theorists believed that democratic government was impossible except within very limited areas. Virginia democrats, for example, were willing to surrender her Western land claims because they believed that their state was too large for democratic government.

Thus the conflict was between those who were essentially "nationalists" and those who were the forerunners of the "states rights" school. The solution was not a matter of legal theory nor yet of a constitutional metaphysics whereby the coercive authority of the British government was transferred to the Continental Congress. On the contrary, it was a matter of practical politics, arrived at by the political maneuvering of two opposing parties having quite different political aims and ideals. No one realized this more clearly than contemporary politicians who believed that the colonists could choose between "a sovereign state, or a number of confederated sovereign states" when they organized their common government.[1]

The real significance of this controversy was obscured during the nineteenth century by historians and politicians who sought to justify the demands of rising industrialism on the central government and the Northern attitude toward the South's secession in 1860–61. The Southern contention that the Union was a compact between sovereign states was opposed by the contention that the Union was older than the states. Northern historians insisted that the first Continental Congress was a sovereign body, and that it represented the people of the United States as a whole, not the people of the several states as represented in their state governments.

To prove their contentions the Northerners cited such documents as the Declaration of Independence and the preamble to the Constitution of 1787. Their method of proof was to state their contention, or reiterate it, and by the use of italics to place undue emphasis on the portions of the documents which seemed to prove their arguments.[2] This is essentially the technique of

[1] John Adams to Patrick Henry, June 3, 1776, in Burnett, *Letters*, 1:471. This was also the opinion of James Wilson. See his "Of Man as a Member of a Confederation," in *The Works of James Wilson*, edited by James D. Andrews (2 vols., Chicago, 1896), 1:307–308. It is to be noted that this statement of Wilson's was made after the Constitution of 1787 had been adopted. Before this, when he was engaged in efforts to overturn the Articles of Confederation, he used quite different arguments.

[2] Joseph Story, *Commentaries on the Constitution of the United States* (5th ed., 2 vols., Boston, 1891), 1:145, 154; Hermann E. Von Holst, *The Constitutional and Political History of the United States* (8 vols., Chicago, 1881–92), 1:4–22; L. Bradford Prince, *The Articles of Confederation and the Constitution* (New York, 1857), 22–25; John W. Burgess, *Political Science and Comparative Constitutional Law* (2 vols., Boston, 1890), 1:100. Professor Claude H. Van Tyne in his article on "Sovereignty in the American Revolution: An Historical Study," in the *American Historical Review*, 12:529–545 (April, 1907), has effectively disposed of the arguments of such writers. He demonstrates conclusively that both psychologically and legally the states were re-

argument used by small boys and would be unworthy of consideration had it not been so effective in shaping certain ideas which have profoundly influenced the interpretation of American history.

The conservatives who had opposed the Revolution and who went with it only when they saw no alternative, as well as many who were not opposed to independence, wanted supreme political authority placed in a central government which could exercise a coercive power over the states and their citizens. As we have seen, they had valued the British connection for the very definite advantages it gave the conservative ruling classes of the colonies. When faced with the fact of independence, they demanded the creation of a government which would in some way function as a bulwark of conservative interests: in other words, as a substitute for the British government.

The radical party, which wanted both internal revolution and independence, insisted that the preponderance of power should be retained by the individual states. The American revolution was in large measure a revolt against the centralized coercive power of Great Britain and the colonial aristocracy. The radicals had no intention of re-creating in America a form of government similar to that which they were fighting to overthrow.[3] They believed in the independence and equality of the several state legislatures, partly because colonial history had so molded men's ideas that they thought in terms of the "nationality" of the individual colony, and partly because experience had taught them that a centralized government was incompatible with their local aims.

The "nationalism" of the individual state is a factor too often overlooked. It was loyalty to one's country that moved men, whether radical or conservative, and one's country was the state in which one lived, not the thirteen more or less united states along the Atlantic Coast. In 1774 John Adams wrote of Massachusetts Bay as "our country" and of the Massachusetts delega-

garded as sovereign throughout the period. He is in error, however, when he states in *The American Revolution, 1776–1783* (New York, 1905), 177, that the theory of the sovereignty of Congress was not developed until long after the American Revolution. The conservative minority, of which James Wilson was the chief, used it as early as 1776 in a somewhat disguised form.

[3] See Schuyler, *Constitution of the United States*, 26–27.

tion in Congress as "our embassy." [4] In 1775 Sam Adams declared that every legislature of every colony "is and ought to be the sovereign and uncontroulable Power within its own limits of Territory." [5] In 1792 the ardent Federalist, Fisher Ames, bewailed the intensity of this patriotic attachment to a particular state. "Government is too far off to gain the affections of the people," he wrote. "What we want is not a change in forms. We have paper enough blotted with theories of government. The habits of thinking are to be reformed. Instead of feeling as a Nation, a State is our country. We look with indifference, often with hatred, fear, and aversion to the other States." [6]

Such being their attitudes and convictions, the radicals particularly opposed the creation of a government which would deprive the states of any of their sovereign powers. They justified their convictions by the democratic theory that any group of people might associate together and create any form of government they wished, and that they might change that government at will. Thus read the Declaration of Independence, which had meaning in the radical thought of the time.

This doctrine of the right of revolution and of self-government, involving as it did even the right to create and destroy governments at the will of the majority, was a shattering attack upon the theoretical foundation of political authority as it had existed in the American colonies. Under the colonial system all power had in theory been handed down from above. By charter the monarchy had delegated a portion of its sovereign authority to a group of people, organized either as trading companies or as actual colonial governments. The people exercised this authority only because they had been allowed to do so by a superior power. The royal veto was superior to the will of the people as expressed in colonial legislatures.

[4] Burnett, *Letters*, vol. 1, p. 35, note 4. It is significant that when the letter to his wife in which these words occur was reprinted after the Civil War, the words "our embassy" were changed to read "ourselves," and thus a misleading slant was given to the sentence. Dr. Burnett most aptly remarks: "Apparently a sentiment permissible to one's ancestor in 1841 required softening in 1876."

[5] Adams, *Writings*, 3:229.

[6] Fisher Ames to George Minot, February 16, 1792, in *Works of Fisher Ames*, edited by Seth Ames (Boston, 1854), 1:113.

To this theory the radicals of the American colonies opposed the ancient doctrine of the sovereignty of the people, with which they coupled the dissenting doctrine of the right of voluntary association in a compactual relationship from which the individual could withdraw at will. This doctrine of voluntary association and withdrawal had been religious in origin, but it had soon been applied to political life. It was the heart of the religious and political philosophy of Separatism. It had received practical if not theoretical application in the Mayflower Compact and been widely used in the creation of revolutionary governments between 1774 and 1776. It was restated in the Declaration of Independence, which was a complete negation of the conservative theory that all authority must proceed in an unbroken legal chain from some superior political power. It was an affirmation of the right of political revolution on the part of the majority of any group of people, and as such was anathema to the conservatives of the American states.

Centralized political authority had been the bulwark of the economic and political aristocracy of the colonies. Hence those conservatives who took part in initiating the Revolution defended the theoretical foundations of their position: authority derived from the king. They pleaded the necessity of a supreme legislature over the colonies in 1774; the Galloway plan was an expression of this desire. When independence became a fact, they were forced to accept the theoretical foundation of the Revolution, the doctrine of the sovereignty of the people, which at the time was understood to be *the people organized as states*, not the people organized in a nation known as the "United States." But while they paid lip service to this theory, they accepted neither its principles nor its implications. Instead they very cleverly used the theory to justify the creation of a supreme authority, by arguing that the Revolution was the work of all the people of the United States. The argument was ineffective in 1776, but in 1787 the conservatives used the theory most subtly to abolish in fact what they upheld in theory.

Thus the disputes between the proponents of state sovereignty and the sovereignty of the central government began, not with Webster and Calhoun, but with the first Continental Congress.

Roger Sherman there stated the radical philosophy. He denied the British contention that the colonies had the same legal status as corporations in England, and hence were the creatures of Parliament. He denied that the colonies were bound by the action of either the crown or Parliament except by their consent. "There is no other legislative over the Colonies but their respective Assemblies." Richard Henry Lee went so far as to deny the right of the crown to grant charters at all.[7] Such contentions were shocking to conservatives like John Rutledge, James Duane, and Joseph Galloway, who denied that emigrants could erect any form of government they chose and that the colonies could alienate their allegiance at will. Above all, the conservatives insisted, there must be a supreme legislative authority over the whole.[8]

The same division of opinion appeared in 1775, during the writing of the "Declaration on Taking Arms." Jefferson wrote the first draft of that document, which set forth the radical theory of the right of voluntary political association and withdrawal. He wrote that "our forefathers" had left their native land to seek civil and religious freedom. At the sacrifice of their blood and the ruin of their fortunes they had settled in the wilds of America "and there established civil societies with various forms of constitution. [But possessing all, what is inherent in all, the full and perfect powers of legislation.] To continue their connection with the friends whom they had left behind, they arranged themselves by charters of compact under the same common king, who thus completed their powers of full and perfect legislation and became the link of union between the several parts of the empire."[9] However historically inaccurate such an interpretation of constitutional beginnings in the colonies might be, it was consistent with the radical theory of the time, and hence useful. The conservatives considered it entirely wrong, and John Dickinson, their acknowledged leader by the summer of 1775, undertook to rewrite the objectionable portions. When Dickinson had finished

[7] John Adams, Notes on Debates, September 8, 1774, in *Works*, 2:371.

[8] *Ibid.*, 370, 371, 372–373; James Duane, "Address before the Committee to State the Rights of the Colonies," September 8, 1774, in Burnett, *Letters*, 1:23–25.

[9] *Journals*, 2:129–130. The portion in brackets was finally omitted in Jefferson's draft.

with the "Declaration," it stated that "Societies or governments vested with perfect legislatures, were formed under charters from the crown." [10] Thus the conservatives supported their contention that all political authority in the colonies derived from a superior power and not from the people.

In terms of practical politics, the outbreak of the Revolution and the acceptance of the Declaration of Independence meant the establishment of the radical theory of the derivation of political authority. It meant that the people of the individual states rather than the British crown were to be the ultimate theoretical source of power. It meant the establishment of the right of a group of people to associate together in the creation of a government which would have legal status by virtue of the fact that it was created by the people, or by representatives in the name of the people.

This revolution in theory was recognized by no less a conservative than John Adams. It was he who proposed the resolution of May 10, 1776, recommending that all governments deriving their power from the king should be replaced by governments deriving their power from the people.[11] He likewise recognized the practical bearing of this revolution in theory upon the creation of a central government. In June, 1776, he wrote to Patrick Henry that the colonies then had the choice before them of declaring themselves "a sovereign state, or a number of confederated sovereign states." [12]

Other conservatives were willing enough to use the popular theory to serve their own ends. When approaching independence confronted them with the possibility of their own removal from positions of economic and political control, as in Pennsylvania, they rationalized their desire to stay in power in terms of the theory of popular sovereignty. They had used it to delay independence. James Wilson had urged that the members of Congress were servants of the people acting under delegated authority. Hence Congress could not declare independence. The argument was specious, for so far as "the people" had had any voice it

[10] *Ibid.*, 142.
[11] John Adams, *Works*, 2:489; *Journals*, 4:342.
[12] June 3, in Burnett, *Letters*, 1:471.

seems to have been for independence, certainly in Pennsylvania. But the argument had been temporarily effective in delaying independence until "the people" could make it plain that those who delayed in their name did not do so at their behest.[13]

Once independence had been declared, the conservatives continued to use radical theories to support their demands for some centralized authority. They insisted that the Congress represented all the people of the thirteen states in their collective capacity. From this assumption they reasoned that Congress was obviously a body superior to the state governments, any one of which could represent only a part of the sovereign people. James Wilson, one of the few really able conservative leaders in Congress during the writing of the Articles of Confederation, made repeated efforts to give Congress powers which would make it superior to the states. On August 1, 1776, he stated the essentials of the doctrine for which Story and Webster and others are usually given the credit. He defined government as a collection of the wills of all and declared that if any government could speak the will of all, it would be perfect. The conclusion he drew from this was quite illogical, though consistent with the real aim of the conservatives. Congress, he said, did not represent the states, but the people of the United States. "It has been said that Congress is a representation of states; not of Individuals. I say that the objects of its care are all the individuals of the states. . . . As to those matters which are referred to Congress, we are not so many states, we are one large state. We lay aside our individuality, whenever we come here." John Adams used the same argument, asserting that the delegates in Congress were there as representatives of the people, that the individuality of the colonies was a mere sound, and that the confederation was to make the colonies into a single individual: "it is to form us, like separate parcels of metal, into one common mass. We shall no longer retain our separate individuality. . . ." Benjamin Rush was equally clear. He argued that a portion of the peoples' rights was deposited in the hands of the legislatures and a portion in the hands of Congress. The members

[13] John Adams, Notes on Debates, May 10, in *Works*, 2:490–491. See also Jefferson's notes on the debates upon Lee's motion for independence, June 8–10, in *Writings*, 1:19–28, where the same argument was used by the conservatives and effectively disposed of by the proponents of independence.

of Congress represent the people. "We are now a new nation." [14]
It is true that at the moment these arguments were being used by
the members from the larger states to justify their demands for
representation in Congress according to population and thus to
defeat the move for state equality. But they were the same arguments that were being used by leading conservatives to justify
their demand for the creation of a central government with superior authority.

The radicals were not befuddled by such arguments. Sherman
of Connecticut pointed to the obvious fact that the delegates in
Congress were the "representatives of States, not individuals." [15]
The radicals made a clear distinction between a national and a
federal government. John Witherspoon of New Jersey stated the
theoretical proposition that "Every Colony is a distinct person."
Nothing concerning the individual citizen of the separate states
could come before Congress. He replied to Franklin — who argued as did Wilson — that Congress was not at work creating a
national government, but a federal government of independent
states.[16]

In spite of this awareness of the distinctions between a national
and a federal form of government, none of the radicals seems to
have sensed the significance of the Dickinson draft when it was
first presented to Congress. In the early stages of the controversy
no one was alive to the necessity of a definite distribution of powers between the states and the central government. This failure
was no doubt due in part to the subtleties and complexities of the
Dickinson draft, of which one of the members of the committee
wrote that it had "the Vice of all his productions . . . the Vice
of Refining too much." [17] Then, too, the first debates were naturally concerned with the easily discernible issues, such as the
control of the West, the basis of taxation, and representation.
Furthermore, there was little time for the deliberation that would
have been necessary to discover underlying implications, for the
confederation was dropped from consideration in August, 1776,

[14] Jefferson, Notes on Debates, in *Writings*, 1:45–47; John Adams, Notes
on Debates, in *Works*, 2:499.
[15] John Adams, Notes on Debates, in *Works*, 2:499.
[16] *Ibid.*, 496; Jefferson, *Writings*, 1:44–45.
[17] Edward Rutledge to John Jay, June 29, 1776, in Burnett, *Letters*, 1:516.

after less than a month's debate, and was not again discussed until April, 1777. Above all, it seems that the radicals were little concerned about the creation of a confederation once the war for independence had begun. Many of them felt a confederation to be neither necessary nor important.[18]

The conservatives, being a minority, were unable to make their desires felt directly. Nevertheless they made repeated efforts to establish precedents from which the superior authority of Congress could be deduced even though by a process of somewhat fragile reasoning. It was this line of tactics, coupled with the arrival of an arch-democrat in Congress, which finally centered radical attention on the problem of the general nature of the proposed union. Early in 1777 Dr. Thomas Burke came to Congress as a delegate from North Carolina. In the controversy which followed, this Irish doctor, trained at Dublin University, led the forces of radicalism; James Wilson, a Scotch lawyer trained in Scottish universities, led the remnants of the conservative forces.[19]

Burke soon reported that during the first part of the year much time had been taken up with debates "whose object on one side is to increase the Power of Congress, and on the other to restrain it." He soon discovered that the landless states were determined to make Congress powerful enough to take the Western lands away from the landed states. This determination excited his suspicions, and a series of debates over the relative power of Congress and of the states aroused him to positive action.[20]

James Wilson tried from time to time to establish precedents for the supreme authority of Congress. The first recorded attempt was made early in 1777. In December, 1776, the New England states had held a convention to consider the progress of the war and to adopt plans for concerted action. They sent a report of this informal meeting to Congress, where Wilson promptly

[18] Samuel Chase to Richard Henry Lee, July 30, 1776, and to Philip Schuyler, August 9, 1776, and Thomas Burke to the Governor of North Carolina, November 4, 1777, in Burnett, *Letters,* 1:32, 44, 542.

[19] William K. Boyd, "Thomas Burke," in the *Dictionary of American Biography,* 3:282–283; Konkle, *James Wilson and the Constitution.* It may or may not be significant that Burke came to America after a family quarrel, whereas Wilson came to America to make his fortune.

[20] Thomas Burke to the Governor of North Carolina, March 11, 1777, in Burnett, *Letters,* 2:294.

made an effort to establish the idea that such meetings must have the approval of Congress. A motion was made questioning whether the meeting had been a proper one and whether it needed the approbation of Congress. Thomas Burke reported that Maryland and Pennsylvania were anxious to have Congress vote on the subject, to the end "that this approbation might imply a right to disapprove." [21] Wilson argued that the New England states had sent the proceedings to Congress in order to secure the approval of Congress, and that since continental business was involved, the approval of Congress was required. John Adams agreed with this interpretation. Benjamin Rush stated that the meeting had actually usurped the powers of Congress.[22]

The radicals at once took the offensive. Sam Adams answered these arguments with the assertion that the right to assemble upon any occasion and to consult on measures for promoting liberty and happiness was a privilege opposed only by tyrants. Richard Henry Lee pointed out that since there was no confederation, no law of the Union had been infringed upon.[23] "After a long metaphysical debate" it was decided that Congress had the right to inquire into the causes of such meetings and to know what transpired, but that it had the power neither to prohibit nor to sanction such measures.[24]

The next tilt between radicals and conservatives came a few days later; "the main question was concerning the jurisdiction of Congress and the States," and the debate was largely between James Wilson and Thomas Burke, two of the ablest of the exponents of the opposing views. The occasion was an amendment to a report on desertion. The report recommended that the states pass laws authorizing constables and others to take into custody any person suspected of being a deserter. To this a significant amendment was moved: that the power to pick up suspected deserters might be given by Congress to local officials without the intervention of the state governments. The amendment passed and Thomas Burke at once demanded that his dissent be placed on the

[21] Thomas Burke, Abstract of Debates, February 12, 1777, *ibid.*, 249.
[22] Benjamin Rush, Diary, February 4, *ibid.*, 234–235.
[23] *Ibid.*, 234.
[24] William Ellery to Gov. Nicholas Cooke of Rhode Island, Baltimore, February 15, *ibid.*, 255; Thomas Burke, Abstract of Debates, *ibid.*, 249.

Journals. He pointed out that Congress was assuming the power to go into the states and seize citizens "and thereby endanger the personal liberty of every man in America."

A motion was made for reconsideration because of his objections. In the debate which followed, Wilson used much the same argument he had used before: that since desertion was a matter of continental concern, Congress certainly had power to authorize persons within the states to execute congressional measures in relation to it. Burke's answer was a long statement of the radical attitude toward a central government. He claimed that if provisions made by Congress were to be enforced by its authority, Congress would have the power to prostrate state laws and constitutions, since it might create within each state an authority which might act independently of it. With such a power, Congress could render ineffectual the barriers provided by the states for the security of their citizens, "for if they gave a power to act coercively it must be against the subject of some State, and the subject of every state [is] entitled to the protection of that particular state, and subject to the Laws of that alone, because to them alone did he give his consent." With respect to deserters, if Congress had the power to appoint persons to decide who were deserters, then it had "power unlimited over the lives and liberties of all men in America." Wilson retreated in the face of this argument and the fact that a majority were with Burke.[25]

The next day another dispute arose over the question of adjournment from Baltimore to Philadelphia. The Southern states were against the move, and Burke moved on the behalf of his state to put off the question. James Wilson and John Adams now argued that a majority of Congress rather than a majority of the states should decide whether or not the rule of voting by states should apply and whether North Carolina might ask for postponement. Richard Henry Lee termed it a "violent Impropriety" and a South Carolina delegate considered it a "very extraordinary kind of proposition to submit to a Majority whether that Majority should be checked by a Power absolutely reserved for that purpose in the Constitution of the Congress."

Burke flatly refused even to debate the matter. He stated that

[25] Thomas Burke, *Abstract of Debates*, February 25, in Burnett, *Letters*, 2:275–279.

if a majority could vote away rules entered into by common consent, then Congress was a body "bound by no rule at all and only Governed by arbitrary discretion." If such a practice were admitted, a majority could vote that any number of states, however few, could form a Congress, although the present rules required nine; that in this manner a few members could take upon themselves the whole authority of Congress. Such assumption would be "an arbitrary tyrannical discrition," and if it were done, Burke would consider it a violent invasion of the rights of his state. Furthermore, he would look on Congress as a body no longer to be entrusted with the liberties of his fellow citizens, and if the matter were put to a vote he would withdraw from Congress. This threat forced the conservatives to retreat once more. [26]

A final instance of the conflict of ideas was the excitement aroused in Congress by General Washington's proclamation requiring that all who had taken an oath of allegiance to Great Britain must either "take an oath of allegiance to the United States of America" or be treated as common enemies. This raised at once the question of "national" citizenship as opposed to the only recognized citizenship — that of the individual states. Radical members of Congress looked upon Washington's proclamation as an assumption of the "Legislative and Executive powers of Government in all the states" and insisted that it must not be regarded as a precedent. But the conservative John Adams, who wrote a committee report on the matter, could not consider it an infringement on the rights of the states.[27] So sensitive did Congress become about the supremacy of civil authority over the military that it even suspended a captain of a continental ship who was guilty of insulting the Governor of Maryland.[28]

Democratic political theory had taught the radicals to distrust uncontrolled governmental authority far removed from the restraint of the electorate. In May, 1776, Richard Henry Lee had

[26] Thomas Burke, Abstract of Debates, February 25, *ibid.*, 282–284. Burke records that he was supported by New Hampshire, Maryland, Virginia, and South Carolina.

[27] *The Writings of George Washington*, edited by John C. Fitzpatrick (Washington, 1931–), 7:62–63; Abraham Clark to John Hart, February 8, 1777, and to Elias Dayton, March 7, in Burnett, *Letters*, 2:243, 292; *Journals*, 7:95, February 6.

[28] Thomas Burke to Governor Richard Caswell, May 2, in Burnett, *Letters*, 2:353–354.

written that "abridged duration, temperate revenue, and every necessary power withheld, are potent means of preserving the integrity of public men and for securing the Community from the dangerous ambition that too often governs the human mind." [29] The controversies centering around the attempt of the conservatives to establish the superior authority of Congress showed a fairly clear division between those who identified state sovereignty with individual freedom and liberty and those whose main concern was the establishment of a coercive political authority whose main function would be the protection of vested property rights. Thus the distrust of uncontrolled governmental authority expressed by Richard Henry Lee was augmented rather than allayed as time wore on. The effect on Thomas Burke and others was to increase in them the conviction "that *unlimited Power can not be safely Trusted* to any man or set of men on Earth." Burke explained to the governor of North Carolina why, in his opinion, the members of Congress sought to increase their power: "Power of all kinds has an Irresistible propensity to increase a desire for itself. it gives the Passion of ambition a Velocity which Increases in its progress, and this is a passion which grows in proportion as it is gratified." [30]

Hence when the Articles of Confederation were once more taken under consideration, Burke was quick to sense that the third article of the Dickinson and of the printed draft of August 20, 1776, was potentially dangerous to the political independence of the states. This third article, he said, "expressed only a reservation of the power of regulating the internal police, and consequently resigned every other power." He was convinced that to leave it thus was to leave it "in the Power of the future Congress or General Council to explain away every right belonging to the States and to make their own power as unlimited as they please." To prevent such usurpation he proposed an amendment to the Confederation which completely altered its whole character and deprived it of the last vestiges of the legal supremacy which Dickinson had given it. He proposed that "all sovereign power was in the States separately, and that particular acts of it, which should be expressly enumerated, would be exercised in conjunction, and

[29] To Edmund Pendleton, May 12, in Lee, *Letters*, 1:191.
[30] To Governor Richard Caswell, March 11, 1777, in Burnett, *Letters*, 2:294.

not otherwise; but that in all things else each State would exercise all the rights and power of sovereignty, uncontrolled." Burke thus placed before Congress the basic constitutional issue of the Revolution.

Members of Congress were so slow to become aware of the vast significance of the proposed amendment that even a second was wanting for a time. James Wilson and Richard Henry Lee furnished most of the opposition, but eventually Burke secured the votes of eleven states for his amendment. He was pleased to find "the opinion of accumulating powers to Congress so little supported" and to find that the delegates from other states held ideas so like his own.[31] The amendment stands as the second article of the Confederation, the first being a statement of the name of the union. In its final form the amendment reads: "Each State retains its sovereignty, freedom and independence, and every power, jurisdiction, and right which is not by this confederation expressly delegated to the united states in Congress assembled." [32]

Thus the states retained their sovereign position and the central government was made a subordinate body of severely and strictly delegated powers. This was natural enough. As had been pointed out in the debates of the summer of 1776, the Congress was composed of the delegates of the state governments. The delegates of the states created a government which left their constituents in the place of supremacy. The failure of the conservatives to create a sovereign congress was due not to lack of knowledge or arguments, but to a simple lack of votes.

No less a conservative than Alexander Hamilton testified that under the Articles of Confederation the states were sovereign and independent. One of his complaints was that "the concurrence of thirteen distinct sovereign wills is requisite, under the Confederation, to a complete execution of every important measure that

---

[31] Thomas Burke to Governor Richard Caswell, April 29, *ibid.*, 345–346. There seems to be no evidence to explain why Richard Henry Lee took a stand so at variance with his prevailing political philosophy. Nor is any explanation offered for the fact that Virginia was the only state to oppose the amendment.

[32] *Journals*, 9:908. Von Holst thought that even the shift in the order of the articles was significant. In the Dickinson draft the article of union preceded the guarantee to the states. In the final draft the article of union followed the delegation of powers to Congress. *Constitutional and Political History of the United States*, 1:22.

proceeds from the union." [33] Hamilton was characteristically much franker than conservatives like James Wilson, who continued to develop the arguments he had used in the debates of 1776 and 1777, and who had them well worked out by 1785. In that year he used such arguments to defend the Bank of North America, of which he was a stockholder and for which he acted as attorney. The Bank had been chartered by Congress and by the Pennsylvania Assembly. But when the conservatives used it as an engine with which to regain control of the state, the Pennsylvania radicals revoked its state charter. In arguing against this act before the Pennsylvania Assembly, Wilson declared that the Assembly could not revoke the charter it had given earlier, because the congressional charter was superior to it, by virtue of the fact that the central government was superior to those of the states. Wilson's "proof" was that "the act of independence was made before the articles of confederation. This act declares, that '*these United Colonies*,' (not enumerating them separately) 'are free and independent states; and that, as free and independent states, *they* have full power to do *all* acts and things which independent states may, of right, do.'" Congress had powers before there was a Confederation, and the Confederation was not intended to weaken or abridge them.[34] Thus by 1785 the theory of the sovereignty of the Continental Congress and the chief argument to sustain it had been developed in all its essentials. Justice Story, Daniel Webster, Herman Von Holst, and John W. Burgess did little more than to elaborate the basic formula used by James Wilson in defense of the Bank of North America.

But, according to the constitution which united the thirteen states from 1781 to 1789, the several states were *de facto* and *de jure* sovereign. No partisan treatises were able to eliminate that fact of American constitutional history, though in the guise of sober history they did much to obscure it and even to deny its existence.

[33] *The Federalist*, No. 15.
[34] James Wilson, "Considerations on the Power to Incorporate the Bank of North America," 1785, in Wilson, *Selected Political Essays*, 133. The genesis of the obligation of contract clause in the Constitution of 1787 is somewhat explained in this argument of Wilson's. It should be recalled that at this time John Marshall, like Wilson, was an attorney of Robert Morris's, who was closely connected with the Bank of North America.

VIII

The Completion of the Articles

LITTLE time was needed to finish the task of writing the first constitution of the United States once the major issues had been settled. Further changes were relatively minor, but on the whole they tended to shear from Congress powers granted to it in the Dickinson draft. This was especially marked in the provision dealing with the regulation of trade. The Dickinson draft had expressly prohibited the states from levying duties or imposts which might interfere with the provisions of treaties made by Congress.[1] On October 21 an amendment to this article was proposed, providing that a state might levy on foreign goods the same duties that its own citizens were required to pay when importing; that it might prohibit exportation and importation altogether; and that it might refuse privileges in its ports to the citizens of any foreign country which did not grant equal privileges to the citizens of that state.[2] This provision gave each state protection against any adverse regulatory action on the part of Congress. At first the states divided evenly on the amendment and it was lost,[3] but a second effort was successful. To the "sole and exclusive" power of Congress to enter into treaties and alliances with foreign states was added a provision that no treaty of commerce should be made whereby the legislative power of the respective states would be restrained from imposing such imposts and duties on foreigners as its own citizens were subject to, or restrained from prohibiting importation and exportation. All the

[1] *Journals*, 5:547–548.

[2] *Ibid.*, 9:826–827. This seems to have been the work of Richard Henry Lee. The Papers of the Continental Congress, No. 47, f. 109, contain the motion in his handwriting.

[3] *Journals*, 9:827–828. The votes were not recorded by states in this instance. Another amendment to this article was passed, however. It was moved to strike out "hereafter" and to insert "in pursuance of any treaties already proposed by Congress to the courts of France and Spain." The acceptance of this modification left the restriction rather ambiguous. *Ibid.*, 833, 911.

states except New Hampshire, Rhode Island, and Connecticut accepted this amendment. Even men so closely connected or allied with the merchant class as Robert Morris, James Duane, and William Duer supported it.[4] A possible explanation of their vote lies in the prevailing sentiment in their states at the time. The radicals in New York and Pennsylvania politics were distinctly anti-merchant, and the political life of congressional delegates depended on their reflection of state views in common affairs. The result of the amendment was to leave Congress with the power to regulate trade by treaties, but to provide no effective check upon practical regulation by the states.

A second significant change was made in the character of the body which Dickinson had called the "Council of State" and which the final draft called the "Committee of the States." The very titles selected are indicative of a wide divergence of opinion between those who drafted the one and those responsible for the other. Among the "sole and exclusive" powers of Congress in the Dickinson draft was that of appointing a "Council of State, and such committees and civil Officers as may be necessary for managing the general Affairs of the United States, under their Direction while assembled, and in their Recess, of the Council of State."[5]

This Council of State was apparently designed as the beginning of an executive organization, a permanent bureaucratic staff of the central government. In the final draft of the Articles the power to control committees and civil officers was not granted to the Committee of the States, which, instead of being a permanent body, was defined as "a committee to sit in the recess of Congress."[6] The Council of State, on the other hand, was to be appointed annually and was to be a permanent body functioning whether Congress was in session or not.[7]

The powers of the Council of State had been detailed in a separate article of the Dickinson draft. While it could make no agreements binding on the United States, the powers it did have were to be permanent, since they were embedded in a "perpetual" document relatively free from the danger of amendment.[8] No specific powers were delegated to it; it was to have only such

[4] *Journals*, 9:835.   [5] *Ibid.*, 5:551.   [6] *Ibid.*, 9:919–920.
[7] *Ibid.*, 5:551, 553.   [8] *Ibid.*, 553–554, Art. XIX.

powers as nine states in the Congress "shall from time to time, think expedient to vest them with." Furthermore, none of the really significant powers were ever to be delegated to it. The radical distrust of executive authority was manifest in the provision specifically restricting Congress from ever vesting the Committee of the States with the power to make war and peace, coin and regulate the value of money, or appoint a commander-in-chief, or with any other powers which under the Articles of Confederation required the assent of nine states.[9]

In only one respect was the power of Congress increased. In the Dickinson draft Congress had been given the power of "Coining Money and regulating the Value thereof."[10] This provision was stricken out and replaced by one which gave to Congress the power of "regulating the alloy and value of coin struck by their own authority, or by that of the respective states."[11] This extension of jurisdiction was at least a partial restriction upon the states, but the Articles of Confederation were not in effect long enough to demonstrate its significance.

Much more in harmony with the spirit of the writers of the final draft was the two-house legislature proposed by that arch-opponent of centralization, Dr. Thomas Burke of North Carolina. In May, 1777, he proposed that Congress be made up of two bodies of delegates: a "General Council" to be chosen by the several states and a "Council of State" to consist of one delegate from each state, also to be chosen by the states. All legislation was to be first moved in the General Council. When it had been read three times and passed, it had to be agreed to by a majority of the Council of State. Such legislation was to be binding on all the states, provided that it was within the powers expressly delegated to Congress. The sole exception to this procedure was that a declaration of war by the United States prior to a declaration by the enemy must be assented to by three-fourths of the General Council and by nine members of the Council of State. Even then, dissenting states were not to be bound by such legislation, except that they must refuse to give aid and protection to an enemy with whom the other states were at war.

[9] *Journals*, 9:923–924, Art. X. For the changes see *ibid.*, 848, 878–880.
[10] *Ibid.*, 5:550, Art. XVIII.
[11] *Ibid.*, 9:840–841; Papers of the Continental Congress, No. 47, ff. 71, 113–117.

In some ways the proposal resembles the organization of Congress under the Constitution of 1787. Burke may have intended it as a compromise between the large and the small states. However that may be, Congress refused to give the plan any consideration.[12] No reasons were recorded for its failure except some notations made by Burke on his copy of the document which might be taken as an indication of the attitude of the opposition. The first notation seems to indicate that Congress was looked upon as an executive body, and that such a plan would delay its work. The second, which is even more vague, refers to the "Idea of Distinctions resembling British Constitution." [13]

One of the main desires of the conservatives had been the creation of a central organization having power to settle disputes between individual states, especially those disputes arising over rival land claims. The Dickinson draft had given Congress "the sole and exclusive Right and Power" of "Settling all Disputes and Differences now subsisting, or that hereafter may arise between two or more Colonies concerning Boundaries, Jurisdictions, or any other Cause whatever." [14] However, no method of settling such disputes was provided for in the draft. This omission was not questioned until October, 1777, when the entire Dickinson provision was stricken out and replaced by a long clause setting forth in detail the method to be followed in settling all disputes that might arise.

This clause made the United States in Congress "the last resort on appeal," thus changing the intent of the Dickinson draft, which had made Congress the arbiter of all disputes whether the states wished it to act or not. The new procedure was seemingly calculated to delay congressional action, and certainly to insure as great a measure of impartiality as chance could make possible. On the petition of a state for a hearing in a disputed matter, Congress was to give notice to the other state involved in the controversy and to set a day for a hearing. The parties were then to be directed to appoint by joint consent judges or commissioners to act as a court. If the parties were unable to agree, Congress was

[12] *Journals*, 7:328–329.
[13] *Ibid.*, 329. The notations read: "1 Delays in Execution Congress Executive Body resembling King &c: 2. No Combination Except one or the other Idea of Distinctions resembling British Constitution."
[14] *Ibid.*, 5:550.

to name three persons from each of the United States. From this number each party would alternately strike out one until thirteen were left, of whom no fewer than seven nor more than nine were to be drawn by lot in the presence of Congress. Any five of these could finally decide the case. Should one party fail to appear without showing due cause, the secretary of Congress would act in its behalf. Should a state refuse to abide by the decision, the court was nevertheless to pronounce judgment and the proceedings were to be lodged among the acts of Congress "for the security of the parties concerned." At the end of this long section was the proviso, discussed above, "that no State shall be deprived of territory for the benefit of the United States." [15] This was a plain indication of the nature of the disputes that were expected to arise between the states. Thus provision was made for arbitration rather than judicial procedure. The Congress was to be a resort of last appeal, but even as such it was merely to prescribe the mode of solution rather than to make a decision or enforce a decision after it had been made.

By November 10, 1777, the Confederation was near enough to completion [16] to justify the appointment of Richard Law, Richard Henry Lee, and James Duane as a committee to report upon any additional articles which in their judgment ought to be added. They were definitely instructed not to alter or change any articles already agreed upon. [17] The next day this committee reported seven additional articles for the consideration of Congress. [18]

The first of these, which was accepted by Congress, declared that freedom of speech in Congress was not to be questioned or impeached in any court or place outside of Congress. [19] The second proposed that Congress be given the power to censure and fine its own members in order to enforce obedience to the rules and orders of the house. This amendment was rejected, and for it was substituted the provision that the members of Congress were to be protected from arrests and imprisonments while in attendance and while on the road to and from Congress, except for treason, felony, or breach of the peace. [20] Both the substitution

[15] *Journals*, 9:841–843.
[16] For consideration of other articles in which changes were largely verbal, or which involved no fundamental change in the document, see *ibid.*, 803–804, 805–806, 826, 833–835, 846, 848, 849, 879, 880.
[17] *Ibid.*, 885. [18] *Ibid.*, 887–890. [19] *Ibid.*, 887, 893. [20] *Ibid.*, 887, 894.

and the exceptions are indicative of a realistic appreciation of the facts of life and politics in the eighteenth century.

The third supplementary article offered, which was accepted in a somewhat altered form, dealt with the extradition of persons suspected of crime who had fled from one state to another. Upon the request of the governor or chief justice of the state from whence the suspect had fled, the governor or chief justice of the state in which refuge had been taken was to deliver him up.[21] The fourth proposed article provided that full faith was to be given in each state to the "Records, Acts, and Judicial Proceedings of the Courts and Magistrates of every other State." Congress agreed to this portion of the proposed article, but refused to accept the remainder, which provided that an action for debt might lie in the courts of law of any state for the recovery of a debt due on the judgment of the courts of law of any other state, provided that the judgment creditor would give sufficient bonds to the court before which the action was brought to answer damages to the debtor if the original judgment should be reversed and set aside. The votes were called for on this amendment. It received only the affirmative votes of Rhode Island and Connecticut. Strangely, every member of the committee which had proposed the article voted against it, for what reason is not recorded.[22]

The fifth proposed article was identical with one which had been in the Dickinson draft but which had been left out of the printed draft of August 20, 1776. It provided that persons removing from one state to another, except paupers, vagabonds, and fugitives from justice, should be accorded all the rights enjoyed by the citizens of the state to which they removed. The people of every state were to have, for their persons and their property, free ingress to and egress from every other state, except that on merchandise imported for sale they were to pay the same duties and imposts as the citizens of the state concerned. An attached clause provided that the property of the United States and of each of the states was to be accorded the same benefits as the property of an individual. The first portion was accepted as presented. The latter portion was so changed as to deny the states the right of levying duties or imposts on the property of the United States or on the property of the individual states.[23]

[21] *Journals*, 9:887, 895.   [22] *Ibid.*, 887, 895–896.   [23] *Ibid.*, 888–889, 899.

The sixth proposed article, which was accepted by Congress, provided that all the bills of credit emitted, monies borrowed, and debts contracted by the authority of Congress should be a charge against the United States.[24]

The seventh proposed a means for the settlement of disputes over private rights to soil claimed by two or more states under different grants made prior to any settlement of jurisdiction in such cases. The dispute between Connecticut and Pennsylvania over the Wyoming Valley was an example of this sort of situation, and another was the controversy between New York land speculators and the inhabitants of Vermont. James Duane, a leading New York speculator, was responsible for the inclusion of this clause among those presented by the committee. Apparently he hoped that it would provide a speedy means of satisfying the New Yorkers' claims. The amendment provided that if the rival parties petitioned Congress, the dispute was to be settled as nearly as possible in the manner provided for the settlement of territorial disputes between states. It was accepted by Congress.[25]

The consideration of the supplementary provisions was completed on November 13, and a second committee was appointed to arrange all the articles in their final order.[26] This was soon accomplished, and on November 15 the Articles of Confederation, as arranged by the committee, were agreed to. Three hundred copies were ordered printed and distributed to the various state delegations.[27]

The committee on arrangement of the articles had likewise been ordered to prepare a circular letter to the states to accompany the printed document. This letter, which was reported on November 17, was a realistic statement of the problems Congress had faced in writing a constitution for thirteen states. "To form a permanent union," it was pointed out, "accommodated to the opinion and wishes of the delegates of so many states, differing in habits, produce, commerce, and internal police, was found to be a work which nothing but time and reflection, conspiring with a disposi-

[24] *Journals*, 9:889, 900.

[25] *Ibid.*, 890, 900; Edward P. Alexander, *A Revolutionary Conservative, James Duane of New York* (New York, 1938), 110–111.

[26] *Journals*, 9:900. The committee consisted of Richard Henry Lee, James Duane, and James Lovell.

[27] *Ibid.*, 907, 928.

tion to conciliate, could mature and accomplish." No government which conformed to the wishes of only a single state could hope for a general ratification, and that, in the view of Congress, was extremely important. "More than any other consideration, it will confound our foreign enemies, defeat the flagitious practises of the disaffected, strengthen and confirm our friends, support our public credit, restore the value of our money, enable us to maintain our fleets and armies, and add weight and respect to our councils at home, and to our treaties abroad." This roseate picture of the future was heightened by a subsequent assertion that ratification was "essential to our very existence as a free people, and without it we may soon be constrained to bid adieu to independence, to liberty and safety." The letter closed with a plea that in states where the legislatures were not in session the executives should convene them at once so that ratification might be completed.[28]

Also indicative of the desire for prompt ratification is the fact that Congress was almost unanimous in rejecting May 1, 1778, and equally unanimous in fixing March 10, 1778, as the date upon which the states were to be prepared to ratify the Articles of Confederation.[29] Needless to say, neither the misty optimism nor the pessimism expressed in the congressional letter was borne out. Three and a half years were to pass before the Articles of Confederation became the first constitution of the United States.

[28] *Journals*, 9:932–934.
[29] *Ibid.*, 934–935. New Hampshire and Massachusetts were the only states wishing for delay.

IX

Early Reaction and Ratification

THE NATURE of the immediate reaction to the Articles of Confederation must be garnered largely from the official acts of the various legislatures empowering their delegates to ratify the document, or criticizing it and making further demands. Individual expressions of opinion are few, but these few are indicative of a continued divergence of ideas. Even before the Articles had been completed, Charles Carroll voiced the views of the conservatives when he wrote that he despaired of such a confederacy being created "as ought, and would take place, if little and partial interests could be laid aside." [1] Extreme radicals like Thomas Burke thought that a time of peace and tranquility was the time for drafting a constitution, for many were disposed to take advantage of the existing circumstances of the states, "which are supposed favorable for pressing them to a very close connection." [2]

Burke presented to the North Carolina legislature a lengthy analysis of the Articles of Confederation, which apparently caused the legislature to delay ratification for a time. In it he stated that Congress was a general council made necessary by the usurpations of Great Britain, and that its powers arose only from the necessity of war. That being the case, all idea of "coercive interpositions within the States respectively," except in the case of the army and navy, had been excluded, likewise any power to punish citizens of the states, "for that is not necessary for the end of their Institution, and every individual is to be tried and punished only by those laws to which he consents. The Congress for this reason can give no authority to any man or set of men to arrest or punish a Citizen, nor can it Lawfully be done but by the authority of the

[1] To Benjamin Franklin, Douhoregan, Maryland, August 12, 1777, in Burnett, *Letters*, 2:450–451.
[2] To Governor Richard Caswell, November 4, 1777, *ibid.*, 542.

particular states." Mention has already been made of Burke's belief
that the end of the war would end all necessity for the continuation of Congress. Finally, he thought, every state should have the
right to control the soldiers within its own territory.[3]

The effect of Burke's observations may be seen in the action of
the North Carolina legislature. In December a committee reported
that certain portions of the Articles should be ratified, but that
others, unnecessary to the success of the war and involving "what
may very materially affect the internal interests and Sovereign Independence" of the state, ought to be delayed for more leisurely
consideration.[4] Both houses agreed to this partial ratification.[5] Not
until April 25, 1778, did the North Carolina legislature agree to
ratify the Articles of Confederation as presented to it.[6]

In January, 1778, the Articles came before the South Carolina
Assembly. William Henry Drayton made a detailed criticism of
the document and finally offered an entirely new plan of confederation. He felt that in spite of the second article Congress had
been granted most of the important powers of government, and
that if one went through the restrictions upon the states, he
would find that "scarce the shadow of sovereignty remains to
any." He attacked what he declared to be the ambiguity of many
of the articles, and demanded more precision of statement and an
eradication of all that was doubtful. Accepting the axiom that
nothing was more dangerous than a consideration of "the spirit
of the laws," he insisted that there be a literal interpretation of
the bond, for while the present Congress might understand the
Confederation, future congresses would be sure to "look for the
spirit of the law." To make his point he quoted Beccaria's observation that when people begin to look for the "spirit," what
they find is " 'the result of their good or bad logic; and this will
depend on their good or bad digestion; on the violence of their
passions; on the rank and condition of the parties, or on their
connections with congress; and on all those little circumstances,
which change the appearance of objects in the fluctuating mind
of man.' " The aptness of this quotation was amply demonstrated

[3] To the General Assembly from the Hon. Thomas Burke [December,
1777], in *State Records of North Carolina*, 11:701–703.
[4] *Ibid.*, 12:228–229, December 19.
[5] *Ibid.*, 229, 263.
[6] *Ibid.*, 599, 608–609, 708–709, 717–718.

in the events of the next few years, when the conservatives attempted to "interpret" the Confederation according to their own views and desires.

Drayton prophesied also that a Northern and a Southern interest would inevitably arise "from the nature of the climate, soil and produce of the several states." He felt that the South was becoming more wealthy; moreover, it possessed more than half the territory; yet "the honor, interest and sovereignty of the south, are in effect delivered up to the care of the North." To remedy this inequality he proposed that the affirmative vote of eleven states be required for important decisions, rather than the nine votes stipulated in the Articles.[7]

The South Carolina Assembly offered no fewer than twenty-one amendments to the Articles. Most of them were verbal changes, but all tended toward increasing the power of the states and limiting that of Congress. Typical was the proposal that Congress be denied jurisdiction over disputes between one state and another. South Carolina was the only state to suggest that changes in the Articles be made by less than the unanimous vote of the thirteen states, eleven states being suggested as a sufficient number. Her delegates in Congress were not instructed to insist upon any of the amendments, however, but were empowered to ratify the Articles as presented to the states.[8]

In New Jersey the Assembly agreed upon a "Representation" which was the only measured criticism of the Articles from the conservative point of view. This "Representation" criticized the failure to require an oath of members of Congress. The states would require oaths of their delegates, "but as the United States,

[7] "The speech of the hon. William Henry Drayton, esq, chief Justice of South Carolina, delivered on the twentieth January, 1778, in the general assembly — resolved into the committee of the whole upon the articles of confederation of the United States of America," in Niles, *Principles and Acts of the Revolution*, 357–364. Drayton's plan of confederation is given on pages 364–374.

[8] *Journals*, 11:670. The South Carolina delegates were empowered to ratify on February 4–5, 1778. The amendments proposed by South Carolina are in the *Journals*, 11:652–656. The South Carolina conservatives soon deserted their extreme states'-rights position for one of nationalism. See Phillips, "South Carolina Federalists," in the *American Historical Review*, 14:529–543. Professor Phillips says that Drayton's attitude "seems to have been sporadic and to have made no lasting impression unless upon a few men like Rawlins Lowndes."

collectively considered, have interests as well as each particular State," it would be well that there be some binding oath on the delegates "to consult and pursue the former as well as the latter." It was predicted that the regulation of trade was so exclusively committed to the states as to involve difficulties and embarrassments, and even injustice to some states of the union. The sole power of regulating trade should be given to Congress and the revenues arising therefrom should be applied to building a navy and to such other purposes as seemed proper to Congress. Thus "a great security will by this means be derived to the union from the establishment of a common and mutual interest." A standing army in times of peace was strenuously objected to. Taxes should be apportioned at least once in every five years, since the value of property might increase more rapidly in some states than in others. The boundaries of the states ought to be fixed, to prevent jealousies and disputes. If it could not be done immediately, the principles for doing so ought to be established and the work carried out within five years after the ratification of the Articles. Doubt was expressed over the intention of the proviso attached to the ninth article, stipulating that no state was to be deprived of territory for the benefit of the United States. Did this mean the "crown lands?" The property of the common enemy, declared the New Jersey legislature, should belong to the United States for their common use. The jurisdiction over such lands should remain with the states within whose charter limits the lands might lie, but the property in the lands should belong to Congress. The apportionment of troops should be in proportion to total population, and the inhabitants ought to be counted once in every five years. Finally, as the states increased in number, the proportion of votes necessary for the passage of important measures should remain as nine to thirteen. Unlike the other states offering amendments, New Jersey did not empower her delegates to ratify if their recommendations failed of consideration.[9]

In New Hampshire the Articles received relatively democratic consideration, for the legislature ordered 250 copies to be printed and distributed to the towns. During the winter of 1777–78 New Hampshire town meetings considered the document and made returns to the legislature. In general, the towns were dissatisfied with the section apportioning taxes on the basis of surveyed and settled lands within a state. In New Hampshire wealth consisted mostly of real estate, and it was believed that the state would be forced to pay a greater proportion of taxes than states in which the bulk of wealth was in other than real property. Beyond this there were few common objections. Some towns wanted negroes to be included in estimating quotas of troops. Others believed that a declaration of war should represent the unanimous action of all the states rather than of nine, as provided for in the Articles.

Once this plebiscite had been concluded, the two houses of the legislature met in joint session. Those opposed to the Articles centered their attack on the eighth article, which dealt with the basis of taxation, but they were unable to delay ratification for very long, and on March 4, 1778, the Articles were agreed to by the legislature without qualification or suggested amendments.[10]

Massachusetts followed the procedure of New Hampshire. The General Court submitted the Articles to the towns for discussion and decision. Apparently the document was given thorough consideration, for many changes were suggested by the towns. Proposals were made that Congress should decide all matters by a vote of eleven states; that the power to offer amendments to the Articles should be retained by the states; that expenses should be shared among the states according to the value of income and personal property as well as of real property. Some towns urged that the matter of war and peace be left to the people, not to Congress. With these and other suggestions in hand, the General Court instructed the Massachusetts delegation to ratify the Articles as submitted to the states unless certain alterations desired by Massachusetts or proposed by the other states "can be received and adopted without endangering the Union proposed." [11]

Most of the states gave the Articles less consideration. The Virginia legislature had been the first to act. By a simple resolution the House of Delegates and the Senate signified their approval on

[10] Upton, *Revolutionary New Hampshire*, 73–75.
[11] Charles S. Lobingier, *The People's Law, or Popular Participation in Law-Making* (New York, 1909), 167–168; *Journals*, 11:663. Harlow, in his *Samuel Adams*, 288, says that Adams was anxious for the adoption of the Confederation. He served on the Boston committee which instructed the Boston representatives in the General Court to vote for the Articles.

December 15, 1777.[12] New York acted more formally and embodied its approval in a law, which included a provision that the Articles were not to become binding on the state until they had been ratified by all thirteen states.[13] Connecticut empowered its delegates to ratify "with such Amendments, if any be, as by them, in conjunction of the Delegates of the other States in Congress, shall be thought proper." [14] Rhode Island, which later acquired a reputation for obstructionism, gave even wider powers to its delegates. They were instructed to ratify if eight other states should do so, and in the event that any alterations in or additions to the Articles were proposed, they were empowered to accept whatever changes were agreed to by nine of the states. The state pledged itself to consider binding any changes agreed to by its delegation.[15]

On March 10, 1778, Virginia was the only state prepared to ratify without qualification or criticism. A Maryland delegate wrote with some truth and more venom that "Virginia ever desirous of taking the lead in this great Contest, was prepared and offered to ratify the Confederation. She stood single, and enjoyed a secret pride in having laid the corner stone of a confederated World." [16] One of the Massachusetts delegates wrote that he was mortified to hear other delegates assert that they had been instructed to ratify, "while the two Cyphers from Massachusetts could produce nothing. Our State is expected to be found in the Fore-front upon such Occasions." [17] The delegates from Maryland presented their instructions and objections, but so few states were present in Congress that only a short debate took place.[18]

In expressing these objections Maryland maintained the position she had taken while the Articles were being written. Once more she demanded that Congress be given the power to determine and fix the limits of all the states claiming territory to the South Sea,

[12] *Journals of the House of Delegates of the Commonwealth of Virginia* [1777–1780] (Richmond, 1827), 80.

[13] *Journals,* 11:665–668, January 29–February 6, 1778.

[14] *Ibid.,* 665, February 12.

[15] *Ibid.,* 663–665, February 18.

[16] John Henry, Jr., to the Speaker of the Maryland House of Delegates, March 17, in Burnett, *Letters,* 3:132.

[17] James Lovell to Samuel Adams, March 10, *ibid.,* 121.

[18] John Henry, Jr., to Governor Thomas Johnson, March 10, and to the Speaker of the Maryland House of Delegates, March 17, *ibid.,* 123, 132–133.

and that Congress recognize Maryland's claim to a share of the country lying "Westward of the frontiers of the United States, *the property of which was not vested in Individuals at the commencement of the present war.*" The Maryland delegates were not optimistic about the success of their demands. They wrote to the Maryland legislature that "the Argument may be renewed but the Decision will be the same. The bare mentioning of this subject rouses Virginia, and conscious of her own importance, she views her vast Dominion with the surest expectations of holding it unimpaired." [19]

The discussion of ratification was delayed from time to time until June 20,[20] when it was decided that the delegates of the states, beginning with New Hampshire, should deliver the reports of their constituents. It was agreed that no amendments would be accepted except those from states.[21]

When Congress took up the question of ratification on June 22, the Maryland delegates at once read their instructions and demanded that the objections raised by their state be considered first, contrary to the order agreed upon. Congress consented, and the Maryland delegates proceeded to offer amendments. The first declared that no state should be burdened with the care of the poor removing to it from other states. The second gave Congress jurisdiction in disputes over land which might be granted in the future, as well as in disputes over land already granted. Both amendments were rejected by Congress.[22]

---

[19] John Henry, Jr., to the Speaker of the Maryland House of Delegates, March 17, *ibid.*, 132–133; Thomas Burke to Governor Richard Caswell, March 12, *ibid.*, 128. The italics are mine. That one statement, the first expression of this principle, is really the issue around which the entire cession of land claims centered. A number of Marylanders, Governor Johnson for one, were members of the Illinois-Wabash Company, which in 1773 and 1775 had bought lands from the Indians northwest of the Ohio. They maintained that Indian nations were sovereign, and that the grants were valid. They insisted that all of Virginia's claims should become the property of the whole — except the lands which they had bought. Virginia, when she was ready to cede the Old Northwest, made it a condition that none of these purchases from Indians should be considered valid, and that *all* the territory to be ceded should become common property. Maryland and the other states insisted upon the cession, of course, if for no other reason than that they could never hope to get anything out of their land purchase if the territory remained in the hands of Virginia.

[20] *Journals*, 11:485, 556, 625.   [21] *Ibid.*, 628.   [22] *Ibid.*, 631.

The Maryland delegates then offered a third amendment. They proposed that in Article IX, after the words "shall be deprived of territory for the benefit of the United States," there be inserted the words, "the United States in Congress assembled, shall have the power to appoint commissioners, who shall be fully authorized and empowered to ascertain and restrict the boundaries of such of the confederated states which claim to extend to the river Mississippi or South Sea."[23] This was of course the same demand which the landless states had voiced when the Articles were being written.

The amendment was debated and deferred to the next day, when it was to be voted on without further debate. Its significance is indicated by the fact that, of all the amendments presented, it was the only one for which a record of the votes was entered in the Journals. The landless states, Rhode Island, New Jersey, Pennsylvania, Delaware, and Maryland, voted for it. New Hampshire, Massachusetts, Connecticut, Virginia, South Carolina, and Georgia voted against it. The two New York delegates were divided.[24]

A fourth objective of the Maryland delegation was not broached at this time. Three months earlier, when the state's instructions had first been read to Congress, John Henry, Jr., had prophesied the failure of attempts to vest in Congress the power to determine and fix state boundaries. He had also prophesied that "equally unsuccessful will prove the Efforts made to obtain a right in common to that extensive Country which lies to the Westward of the frontiers of the United States, the property of which was not vested in Individuals at the commencement of the present war."[25] Maryland did not make this demand in the form of an amendment to the Articles of Confederation, but both Rhode Island and New Jersey did so. Rhode Island moved that in Article IX, after the words "provided also that no state shall be deprived of territory for the benefit of the United States," an amendment be added that all lands within the states which had been crown lands before the war or upon which quit-rents had been paid should become the property of the United States, to be disposed of by Congress for the benefit of the confederacy. This proposal was much more

[23] *Journals*, 11:631–632. [24] *Ibid.*, 636–637.
[25] John Henry, Jr., to the Speaker of the Maryland House of Delegates, March 17, in Burnett, *Letters*, 3:132–133.

moderate than that of Maryland, since it conceded that there was no land lying outside the bounds of the individual states. It also provided that the states within which the crown lands lay might retain complete jurisdiction over them.[26]

Even thus soon after the struggle of the previous autumn there seems to have been some uncertainty as to the real purpose of the clause guaranteeing the lands of the states. In answer to a query of George Read's, Thomas McKean of Delaware gave it as his opinion that the purpose was to insure that in a boundary dispute between two states the territory of one state should be added to the other and not awarded to the United States. He said, however, that the clause might later be construed as a guarantee of the claims of the landed states. But he did not believe that Delaware would be injured even if Virginia did extend to the South Sea. He felt that Delaware had a right to apply for townships in Virginia for the purpose of giving land bounties to the Delaware troops. Furthermore, he was not alarmed, as so many were, at the prospect of the future growth of Virginia. If Virginia grew more rapidly than the other states, it would have to bear a larger proportion of the costs of the union. If it grew too large, the people themselves would insist on the erection of new states.[27] But this temperate attitude was not to prevail. Very rapidly the control of the West became the sole issue, which was to delay ratification of the Articles of Confederation for three years.

Other issues which had been the cause of controversy when the Articles were being written once more arose in the form of amendments offered during the early stages of ratification. The New Englanders again objected to the apportionment of common expenses upon the basis of lands granted and surveyed and the improvements thereon. Connecticut moved that the basis be changed to population,[28] as it had been in the Dickinson draft. Massachusetts proposed that the rule of apportionment be varied from time to time until experience had shown which was the most equitable basis for taxation.[29] South Carolina disliked the provision in the Articles for estimating the value of lands and im-

---

[26] *Journals*, 11:639; Maryland Delegates to the Governor and Assembly of Maryland, June 22, in Burnett, *Letters*, 3:314–315.

[27] Thomas McKean to George Read, April 3, *ibid.*, 149.

[28] *Journals*, 11:639.   [29] *Ibid.*, 638.

provements "according to such mode as the United States . . . shall, from time to time, direct and appoint." She asked that this be stricken from the Articles and a provision substituted giving the power of estimating values to persons appointed by state legislatures.[30]

The all-prevailing distrust of standing armies in times of peace was voiced by some of the states. New Jersey commented upon the wisdom of forbidding the states to maintain an active body of troops in times of peace and felt that there should be a similar restriction upon the United States, unless the maintenance of a body of troops should be approved by nine states. "A standing army, a military establishment, and every appendage thereof, in time of peace, is totally abhorrent from the ideas and principles of this State. In the memorable act of Congress, declaring the United Colonies free and independent states, it is emphatically mentioned, as one of the causes of separation from Great Britain, that the sovereign thereof had kept up among us, in time of peace, standing armies without the consent of the legislatures."[31] Connecticut also offered an amendment to Article IX, providing that no land army be maintained in time of peace nor any officers kept in pay by Congress who were not in actual service, except such as were unable to support themselves because of injuries received while in the army.[32]

The division between the Northern and Southern states over the apportionment of the troops to be furnished in time of war — a dispute which had been coupled with the dispute over the basis of taxation — also appeared once more in the amendments offered. Pennsylvania asked that the word "white" be stricken from the clause providing for the apportionment of troops on the basis of the white population in each of the states. Massachusetts likewise requested reconsideration of this portion of the Articles.[33]

All the proposed amendments were rejected with monotonous regularity. The attitude of Congress was that the Articles of Confederation must be completed first, and that nothing must stand in the way; "a great majority are resolved to reject the amendments from every State, not so much from an opinion that *all* amendments are improper, as from the conviction, that if *any*

[30] *Journals*, 11:654.   [31] *Ibid.*, 649.   [32] *Ibid.*, 640.   [33] *Ibid.*, 638, 652.

should be adopted, no Confederation will take place, at least for some months, perhaps years; and in that case, many apprehend none will ever be entered into by all of the present United States." [34]

At this time Delaware and North Carolina were not represented in Congress, although a letter from Governor Caswell of the latter state indicated that the legislature had ratified the Articles. The Georgia delegate had received no instructions, but assured Congress that his state would ratify. A committee was appointed to prepare a form of ratification. [35] This form was laid before Congress on July 9, 1778, and was that day signed by the delegations from New Hampshire, Massachusetts Bay, Rhode Island and Providence Plantations, Connecticut, New York, Pennsylvania, Virginia, and South Carolina. North Carolina and Georgia were not present in Congress. The Maryland, Delaware, and New Jersey delegates said they were not authorized to sign. [36]

A committee was now appointed to prepare a circular letter to the three states which had failed to instruct their delegates. This letter urged that a confederacy could "alone establish the liberty of America and exclude for ever the hopes of its enemies." It had been difficult to devise a plan conforming to the wishes of so many states "differing essentially in various points," and so Congress had agreed to adopt the Articles of Confederation as submitted to the states. The states were asked to ratify, "trusting to future deliberation to make such alterations and amendments as experience may shew to be expedient and just." [37]

Shortly after this appeal both North Carolina and Georgia signed. [38] But the optimism with regard to early ratification which many of the members had shown in June had been shattered. [39]

[34] Maryland Delegates to the Governor and Assembly of Maryland, June 22, in Burnett, *Letters*, 3:314–315.

[35] *Journals*, 11:656. Richard Henry Lee, Francis Dana, and Gouverneur Morris constituted the committee.

[36] *Ibid.*, 657–658, 677.

[37] *Ibid.*, 678, 681.

[38] *Ibid.*, 709, 716. North Carolina ratified on July 21, Georgia on July 24.

[39] See Rhode Island Delegates to the Governor of Rhode Island, June 20, in Burnett, *Letters*, 3:311; Richard Henry Lee to John Adams, June 20, *ibid.*, 308; Henry Laurens to the President of South Carolina, June 23, *ibid.*, 316. Laurens expected ratification within a week. He said that if all the amendments were discussed and alterations made, he would never live to see the ratification.

John Matthews wrote: "This I am clear in, from what I have seen, and know, since I have been in Congress, that if we are to have no Confederation until the Legislatures of the Thirteen States agree to one, that we shall never have one." [40] It was predicted that "Maryland will take airs and plague us, but upon our determination to confederate with 12 will do as she has always before done — come in without grace." [41]

The Maryland legislature, however, adjourned until November and thus defeated hopes that a new Congress under the Confederation might convene in 1778.[42]

New Jersey was the first of the three recalcitrant states to ratify. Her attitude had never been extreme, although she had voiced the viewpoint of the landless states. Nathaniel Scudder, one of her delegates, urged the state to ratify, saying that Samuel Chase of Maryland "imagined" that the determination of Maryland would depend much on that of New Jersey. As to "the grand and capital Objection respecting the Lands," Scudder wrote that even if the state of New Jersey never did get its full quota, it would never lose much, and that really the smaller states would be benefited by the growth of the larger, for in proportion as the latter increased in area and population, their debt also would increase. "What avails it therefore to us, whether five Pounds of our national Debt be paid by the Accession of a Subject to this State, or whether our Quota be really lessened Five pounds by the Settlement of a Person in the State of Virginia at a Distance of a thousand Miles from the Atlantic?" [43] Whether or not this reasoning was instrumental, the New Jersey Assembly empowered its delegates to ratify the Articles, and on November 25 John Witherspoon laid these instructions before Congress. The Assembly protested that it still considered the Articles unequal in many respects, but that the conviction of the necessity of union, and the

[40] John Matthews to John Rutledge, July 7, *ibid.*, 332. Matthews was afraid that if the confederation was not ratified, "we shall be literally a rope of sand, and I shall tremble for the consequences that will follow at the end of this War."

[41] James Lovell to William Whipple, July 14, *ibid.*, 329.

[42] Richard Henry Lee to Thomas Jefferson, August 10, in *Letters*, 1:430.

[43] Nathaniel Scudder to the Speaker of the New Jersey Assembly, July 13, in Burnett, *Letters*, 3:326–328.

hope that the candor and justice of the other states would remove inequalities, had led it to authorize ratification.[44]

In January, 1779, Delaware empowered its delegates to ratify, protesting in the language of the New Jersey act that the state was not satisfied, but that it trusted to the candor and justice of the other states. On February 22 Thomas McKean signed for Delaware.[45] As one New Hampshire delegate wrote, "there now only remains Maryland who you know has seldom done anything with a good Grace. she has always been a froward hussey." [46] The question was now "whether we shall send to all the States for their consent to a Confederation of twelve, or wait for Maryland to consider better of it and accede." [47]

But Maryland refused to "consider better of it and accede." The landless states continued to demand that, for "the good of the whole," the West be given up, with the significant exception of those lands within Virginia's charter bounds to which their prominent citizens laid dubious claims. The driving force of desperation was added to their determination as the state of Virginia took step after step to nullify the claims of the Pennsylvania, Maryland, and New Jersey speculators. Ultimately the land companies, as well as their representatives, who were often members of Congress, appealed to Congress for help. It was an appeal that failed, possibly because of its very openness, for it enabled the landed states to draw about them the cloak of disinterested patriotism and to blacken their opponents, whose interest in the West, be it said, was no less mercenary than that of their detractors.

[44] *Journals,* 12:1162–1163, 1164. New Jersey ratified on November 26.

[45] *Ibid.,* 13:150, 186–188, 236. Delaware's slowness seems to have been the fault of Congress. Caesar Rodney wrote on June 11, 1778, that so far as he knew, Delaware had received neither a recommendation to ratify nor a copy of the Confederation. On July 31 he wrote to Henry Laurens, president of Congress, that the receipt of the letter from Congress (to the three states of Maryland, New Jersey, and Delaware) was the first request for ratification received from Congress, and that members of the Assembly had given this as their reason for not taking it into consideration before. *Letters to and from Caesar Rodney,* pp. 272, 278, 283, 285, 287, note 1, 288–289.

[46] William Whipple to Josiah Bartlett, February 7, 1779, in Burnett, *Letters,* 4:60.

[47] Connecticut Delegates to the Governor of Connecticut, February 11, 1779, *ibid.,* 63.

X

Virginia and the Western Problem
1778–1779

IN THE autumn of 1778 the Virginia Assembly continued the policy toward the West which had been inaugurated by the Convention in the summer of 1776. Since that time counties had been set up west of the Alleghenies,[1] a commission had been at work gathering evidence against those claiming land under grants from Indian nations,[2] and George Rogers Clark had been sent to the Ohio to subdue the enemy posts there.[3] Such activity forecast what was to be done by the Assembly between October and December, 1778, in spite of the fact that the land question had now become a definite issue between the two strong groups contending for leadership in the state. Thomas Jefferson, Richard Henry Lee, and George Mason were leaders of the radical party, which opposed the schemes of the land companies of the Middle states. The conservative party was led by such men as Benjamin Harrison, Edmund Pendleton, and Carter Braxton. Many of its leaders had commercial connections with Robert Morris, the Whartons, and the Gratzes, and hence supported the claims of the speculators from the Middle states both within and outside the halls of the Assembly.[4]

Nevertheless the radical-expansionist element was able to continue with the policy initiated by earlier measures. On November 4 the House of Delegates declared void all purchases from Indians within the state's charter bounds. Thus, in general terms, the

---

[1] See Frederick J. Turner, "Western State-Making in the Revolutionary Era," in the *American Historical Review*, 1:70-87, 251–269 (October, 1895).

[2] See *Calendar of Virginia State Papers*, 1:277–282, for the type of investigation that was carried on; also the opinion of George Morgan, leader of the Indiana Company, concerning the investigations, in a letter to Thomas Wharton, Fort Pitt, February 25, 1777, in the George Morgan Letter Books, 1:55, in the Wisconsin Historical Society.

[3] James A. James, *Life of George Rogers Clark* (Chicago, 1928), chs. 6–8.

[4] Abernethy, *Western Lands and the American Revolution*, 217–221.

claims of four important groups of speculators in neighboring states were declared to have no validity so far as Virginia was concerned.[5] The first of these was the Transylvania Company, which had been organized by Judge Henderson of North Carolina. His claim was not without influence, however, for on the same day that the above act was passed, the House of Delegates, while declaring the Henderson grant void, recommended that the company be given some compensation, since Virginia was receiving advantages from it in frontier defense and increased population.[6] In accordance with this recommendation, Henderson's company was given a grant of land between the Green and Ohio rivers.[7]

The claims of the three other companies, whose membership centered chiefly in Pennsylvania and Maryland, were voided. The most important of these was the Indiana Company, most of whose members resided in Pennsylvania and particularly in Philadelphia. The grant it had obtained from the Six Nations at the Treaty of Fort Stanwix in 1768 covered a large region to the south of Pittsburgh in what is now West Virginia. It was almost exactly the same area as had been granted to the Ohio Company of Virginia in 1749. The action of Virginia also voided the claims of the two land companies north of the Ohio River, the Illinois and Wabash companies. Their membership likewise centered largely in Pennsylvania, but it included also a number of Marylanders, not the least important of whom was Thomas Johnson, governor of Maryland during a part of the time when the struggle over the control of the West was most bitter.[8]

Meanwhile some officers and soldiers of the Virginia line were apparently more interested in the prospect of a land office in Virginia than in fighting the battles of the American Revolution; Colonel William Russell was even ready to resign from the army rather than have his hopes of a fortune in Western lands thwarted

[5] *Journal, House of Delegates* [October–December, 1778], *1777–1780*, 42.
[6] *Ibid.*
[7] William Hening, *The Statutes at Large, Being a Collection of All the Laws of Virginia from . . . 1619* [*to 1792*], 9:571 (Richmond, 1821).
[8] The original members of both companies are listed in *American State Papers: Public Lands* (Washington, 1832–1861), 2:117–118, 119. The Wabash Company of 1775 included Lord Dunmore and his son; John Murray, Moses and Jacob Franks of London; Thomas Johnson of Annapolis; John Davidson, William Russell, Matthew Ridley, Robert Christie, Sr., and Robert Christie,

by the opening of such an office in his absence.[9] These Virginia officers and soldiers, who were with Washington's army in New York, sent Colonel William Wood with a petition to the Virginia Assembly. The result of this petition was an act of the Assembly reserving for the officers a tract in the same area as that granted to the Henderson Company.[10] The news of Clark's success on the Ohio River was followed by the establishment of the County of Illinois in the region north of the river.[11] Finally, the Assembly took notice of Maryland's attitude toward the Articles of Confederation.

At this time Maryland, Delaware, and New Jersey had not yet ratified. Their official reasons for delaying ratification were well expressed in a letter of the Connecticut delegates. "These and some other of the States are dissatisfied that the western ungranted lands should be claimed by particular States, which, they think, ought to be the common interest of the United States, they being defended at the common expense. They further say that if some provision is not now made for securing lands for the troops who serve during the war, they shall have to pay large sums to the

Jr., merchants of Baltimore; Peter Campbell, a merchant of Piscataway, Maryland; William Geddes, a collector of customs at Newtown Chester, Maryland; David Franks and Moses Franks of Philadelphia; Louis Viviat, William Murray, and Daniel Murray, merchants of the Illinois Country; and Nicholas St. Martin, Joseph Page, and Francis Perthius, gentlemen of the Illinois Country. In the Illinois purchase of 1773 Bernard and Michael Gratz of Philadelphia had been concerned, as were the lesser merchants of York, Lancaster, and Pittsburgh.

[9] Colonel William Russell to Colonel William Fleming, October 7, 1778, in the Draper MSS., 2U47, in the Wisconsin Historical Society.

[10] *Journal, House of Delegates* [October–December, 1778], *1777–1780*, 126. Russell to Fleming in the Draper MSS., 2U47, in which he makes it plain that Colonel Wood was sent with a petition specifically asking for consideration of the Virginia soldiers' land claims. In Kate M. Rowland, *The Life of George Mason, 1725–1792* (2 vols., New York, 1892), 1:306, is printed a letter from Wood to Washington giving his opinion of the legislators. It is doubtful whether Washington's military duties caused him to forget the major activity of his pre-Revolutionary days, especially since he probably had as much at stake in this case as any other Virginian.

[11] *Journal, House of Delegates* [October–December, 1778], *1777–1780*, 72; Rowland, *George Mason*, 1:307; Hening, *Statutes of Virginia*, 9:552–555. The day after the news of Clark's conquest arrived, the Ohio Company of Virginia presented a petition asking that it might receive patents as soon as the land office was opened. *Journals, House of Delegates* [October–December, 1778], *1777–1780*, 74.

States who claim the vacant lands to supply their quota of the troops." [12]

In December, after New Jersey had ratified, Congress dallied with the idea of appointing a committee to go to Maryland to "hold out the grant of the bounty lands" to induce that state to ratify, since, as James Duane said, "the want of ability to gratify their soldiery is a capital if not the material objection." [13]

The ostensible reason for Maryland's recalcitrancy had been this presumed inability to provide bounty lands for its soldiers. The knowledge of it must have been fairly prevalent, for it had been stated by Maryland as early as the autumn of 1776, and re-stated many times thereafter. It was to remove this, "a capital if not the material objection" of Maryland, that the Virginia Assembly now offered to furnish bounty lands out of its territory, without purchase price, to those of the United States which had no lands for that purpose and which had ratified or would ratify the Articles of Confederation. This was to be done in conjunction with the other states having claims, the share to be assumed by each state being left to Congress. [14]

Maryland's official position was thus undermined, but Virginia made an even more direct attack. On December 3 the Virginia delegates in Congress were authorized to confederate with as many of the states as were willing to do so. A few days later Virginia specifically instructed her delegates to urge Congress to recommend to each state that it authorize ratification with as many of the others as would do so, allowing either a definite or an indefinite time for the rest to ratify. [15] This was a drastic step designed to force the recalcitrant states to join the union.

Thus, by her action in the autumn of 1778, Virginia made it plain that she meant to maintain her claims to all that lay within her charter bounds. She likewise made it plain that she had no intention of yielding to any of the speculative companies claiming lands through purchase from Indian nations. Finally, instead of

[12] The Connecticut Delegates to Governor Jonathan Trumbull, October 15, 1778, in Burnett, *Letters*, 3:449–450.

[13] James Duane to Governor George Clinton, December 10, 1778, *ibid.*, 3:530.

[14] *Journal, House of Delegates* [October–December, 1778], *1777–1780*, 124–125, December 18.

[15] *Ibid.*, 98, 124, December 18.

showing any desire to compromise with Maryland, Virginia took action to remove the ostensible reason for that state's delay, and then ordered her delegates in Congress to urge confederation without Maryland if the latter still refused to confederate after the apparent obstruction had been removed. Thus the struggle was shifted to Congress, where both Virginia and Maryland assumed an attitude that left little grounds for hope of compromise.

*　　*　　*

At the beginning of 1779 Congress was reported by one delegate to be "fuller than I ever knew it at this time of Year." All the states were represented and all were confederated except "our Froward Sister M—— and her little Crooked Neighbor." [16] "Froward Sister M——" soon made it plain that she would continue to prevent the completion of the Articles of Confederation until she had her own way with regard to the control of the West.

On January 6 the Maryland delegates laid before Congress a "Declaration" of the Maryland Assembly. In this document it was announced flatly that Maryland considered herself entitled to a right in common with the other states to the country lying west of the frontiers of the United States "the property of which was not vested in, or granted to individuals at the commencement of the present war." Maryland would never ratify the Articles of Confederation unless they were amended to give Congress full power to fix the bounds of all states claiming to the Mississippi or the South Sea, and to expressly secure to the United States a right in common to all the lands lying west of such frontiers, with the significant exception of the lands not granted to, surveyed for, or purchased by individuals at the beginning of the war. [17] After a debate in Congress, consideration of this declaration was postponed indefinitely. [18] On January 26 Meriwether Smith of Virginia laid before Congress his state's offer of bounty lands, free of cost. [19] Delaware ratified on February 22, and Maryland was left alone outside the Confederation.

[16] William Whipple to Josiah Bartlett, January 3, 1779, in Burnett, *Letters*, 4:6.
[17] Papers of the Continental Congress, No. 70, ff. 293–299. The "Declaration" was agreed upon on December 15, 1778. Most of the emphasis in the document was on the fear of "oppression" and the apprehension that Maryland would be impoverished by having to buy lands for her soldiers.
[18] *Journals*, 13:29–30.　　[19] *Ibid.*, 116.

Early in May, Daniel of St. Thomas Jenifer wrote to Governor Thomas Johnson of Maryland that the Congress was "now more disposed to explain the Confederation than it was sometime ago." [20] The extent of his misjudgment was demonstrated on May 20, when the Virginia delegates laid before Congress their instructions to confederate with as many of the states as would be willing to do so and made a motion to that effect. [21] That this proposal to force Maryland's hand caused some excitement is indicated by the haste with which the North Carolina delegates wrote to their governor for instructions in the new turn of affairs. [22] The Maryland delegation was equal to the occasion, for it had one last weapon at hand. Accompanying the Maryland "Declaration," presented to Congress in January, had been a set of "Instructions" which the Maryland delegates had been advised to hold in readiness to present to Congress whenever they saw fit. [23] The move by Virginia was deemed a fitting occasion.

The professed purpose of these instructions was to make it plain that the Maryland delegation was expressing the attitude of the state as a whole and not merely that of certain individuals in the state. Maryland feared, so the instructions stated, that many of the states had acceded to the Confederation against their best judgment and that as soon as the need for union disappeared, they would again assert their independence. "Is it possible that those states, who are ambitiously grasping at territories, to which in our judgment they have not the least shadow of exclusive right" will use with greater moderation the increase of wealth and power deriving from these territories? Maryland thought not and expressed a fear that they would become the oppressors of the small states. Even if they did not, Maryland would become impoverished and depopulated. Suppose Virginia did own the lands she claimed. She would sell those lands cheaply, draw vast sums of money into her treasury, reduce her taxes, and thus draw the best and wealthiest inhabitants from Maryland and other states, which would then descend to a minor position in the Confederation.

It had been reported that the delegates of a "neighboring state" had said that so large a territory could not be governed easily and that hence it should be split up into independent governments.

[20] May 9, 1779, in Burnett, *Letters*, 4:203. [21] *Journals*, 14:617–618.
[22] May 20, in Burnett, *Letters*, 4:221. [23] *Journals*, 14:619–622.

Such governments, Maryland declared, would be under the influence of the parent state, and that would be quite foreign to the "spirit" of the Confederation. There could be only two possible motives for claiming those lands and for promising to give them up some day. Both were decidedly ulterior motives, according to the Marylanders. Either such statements were made to "lull suspicion asleep, and to cover the designs of a secret ambition," or "the lands are now claimed to reap an immediate profit from the sale." Most startling of all was Maryland's flat denial of the validity of charter claims. Claims to more than half the United States, she said, should be supported by the clearest evidence of right, yet no arguments worthy of serious refutation had been submitted in favor of those rights. This land should be common property, since it was being taken from the British government at the cost of the blood and treasure of the thirteen states, and it should be parcelled out by Congress into free and independent governments. Being so convinced, Maryland refused to ratify the Articles of Confederation until they had been amended to conform to the "Declaration" of January 6.[24]

The obvious intention of this lengthy reiteration of the Maryland case was to cast the onus of selfish motives entirely upon Virginia. William Fleming of Virginia considered the Maryland instructions "a very extraordinary, indecent performance," [25] and the Virginia delegates, in their report of the matter, termed it an "intemperate paper." [26] The Maryland delegates were pleased to have their instructions entered upon the Journals. They felt hopeful too that their claims would be recognized, because Connecticut was thought to be willing to allow Congress to dispose of the backlands.[27] But Connecticut veered over to the Virginia side when her delegation presented its instructions to confederate with the other states, although they specified that Maryland should not be excluded should she wish to enter the union later.[28] On the other hand, New York and Virginia, particularly, were said to be "inflexible" in the matter. Nevertheless, the Maryland delegation

[24] *Journals*, 14:619–622.
[25] William Fleming to Thomas Jefferson, May 22, in Burnett, *Letters*, 4:226.
[26] Virginia Delegates to the Speaker of the House of Delegates, May 22, *ibid.*, 224–225.
[27] Daniel of St. Thomas Jenifer to Governor Thomas Johnson, Jr., May 24, *ibid.*, 232.
[28] *Journals*, 14:624.

was determined to block confederation until justice, as they conceived it, had been done.[29]

It appeared that there was no room for compromise between Maryland, who was determined not to confederate unless Congress was given control of the West, and Virginia, who so far had shown no disposition to renounce her Western claims. It is significant that Maryland completely ignored the Virginia offer of bounty lands, for it indicates that such lands were not her real objective. The land speculators had not yet appeared in the open.

It was the action of the Virginia Assembly in May and June of 1779 that gave the controversy a new twist and brought into the open what had hitherto been concealed in official pronouncements such as the Maryland "Declaration." George Mason of Virginia, who was content to stay in Virginia and exercise his great abilities there, and who was the chief backer of the Ohio Company of Virginia, which had a prior grant to the same area claimed by the Indiana Company, peered into the froth of arguments and saw certain glimmerings of reality. To him the Maryland "Declaration" confirmed certain suspicions he had long entertained. In his opinion "the secret and true cause of the great opposition to Virginia's title to her chartered territory" was the great Indian purchase between the Illinois and Wabash rivers, "in which Governor Johnston [*sic*] and several of the leading men in Maryland are concerned" with Lord Dunmore, Governor Tryon, and others. Mason wrote, "Do you observe the care Governor Johnston . . . has taken to save this Indian purchase." Mason pointed to the exception that was made of lands not granted to, surveyed for, or purchased by individuals at the beginning of the war. He said that if Congress would declare void all purchases from Indians already made or to be made, except those made by public authority, it would be more effectual than all the argument in the world.[30]

---

[29] Daniel of St. Thomas Jenifer to Governor Thomas Johnson, June 8, in Burnett, *Letters*, 4:253. Jenifer said that while Maryland retained its negative on the present plan of Confederation, "the Door will be open for Justice to be done us, the moment it is turned into an affirmative, it will not only be shut, but locked against us." He promised to make use of hints which the governor had let fall; "they shall be extended to take in those objects for which they were designed." See also Charles Carroll to William Carmichael, May 31, *ibid.*, 239.

[30] George Mason to Richard Henry Lee, April 12, 1779, in Rowland, *George Mason*, 1:321–322. Mason pointed out the obvious fact that there

The action of the Virginia Assembly in May and June, 1779, is readily understood when one considers that Mason was one of the more influential men in the state.

*   *   *

Virginia had been receiving petitions from the Indiana, Illinois, and Wabash companies ever since the fall of 1776, but had never given them official recognition. In 1776 Thomas Wharton had sent to the Virginia Assembly on behalf of the Indiana Company a petition protesting against the resolution of the Virginia Convention calling into question the validity of land titles granted by Indians.[31] In March, 1777, George Morgan sent a memorial for the Indiana Company protesting that the resolution of the convention was an *ex post facto* action and a violation of the rights of private property. The company was ready to defend its title in a proper court but refused to defend it before the commissioners appointed by Virginia to investigate it.[32]

In December, 1778, after the Virginia legislature had declared void all purchases from Indians, William Murray, acting for the Wabash Company, presented to the Assembly a memorial declaring that since the freedom of Virginia and her sister states was now "gloriously and fully established," the company thought it necessary to notify the governor and legislature of the state of their purchase, "upon a supposition that the said Lands may be within the Limits and Boundarys claimed as within the States and Dominion of Virginia." Noncommittally the memorial declared that it was not the intention of the company to dispute the jurisdiction of Virginia or of any other state "rightly claiming Jurisdiction over any part of the Land purchase in Question, provided they chose to exercise the same." [33]

The Virginia Assembly finally invited all the claimants to ap-

was no claim to the region northwest of the Ohio except charter claims, and that if these were void, the region belonged to Canada.

[31] Memorial to the Virginia Assembly from the Proprietors of the Indiana Company, October 1, 1776, in *Calendar of Virginia State Papers*, 1:273–274.

[32] "The Memorial of the Proprietors of a Tract of Land on the Ohio Called Indiana," Pittsburgh, March 12, 1777. Copy in the Draper MSS., 1CC140–146.

[33] "Memorial of William Murray et al, Purchasers and Proprietors of lands on the Oubache River in the Illinois Country, to the Governor, the Council, the Senate, and Burgesses of Virginia," December 26, 1778, in *Calendar of Virginia State Papers*, 1:314.

pear before it during the spring session of 1779.[34] The land companies immediately made preparations to present their case. The wise men in charge did not place all their faith in the justice and supposed legality of their case. Land company shares were sold to Virginians. William Trent, for instance, sold nine hundred shares of the Indiana Company to William Grayson of Prince William County, for twelve hundred pounds "lawfull money" of Pennsylvania.[35] Edmund Randolph seems to have accepted the validity of the Indiana grant, though whether it was because of a disinterested conviction, a retainer fee, or a share in the company is not certain.[36] Likewise, pamphlets stating the case of the Indiana Company were arranged for, though none of them seem to have been completed before the meeting of the legislature.[37] William Trent was chosen to present the company's case at Williamsburgh.

George Morgan, who was both an Indian agent in the Middle Department and an agent for the Indiana Company, apparently

[34] William Trent to George Morgan, Philadelphia, January 23, 1779, in the Ohio Company Papers, vol. 2, f. 37, in the Pennsylvania Historical Society; *Journal, House of Delegates* [October–December, 1778] *1777–1780*, 108, December 10.

[35] Bill of Sale from William Trent to William Grayson, May 1, 1779, in the Ohio Company Papers, vol. 2, f. 37.

[36] William Trent to Edmund Randolph, Trenton, November 9, 1779, in the Ohio Company Papers, vol. 2, f. 47. The letter was one introducing George Morgan. The Indiana Company, while it appealed to Congress, still had hopes in Virginia. Morgan tried to induce the Virginia Assembly to repeal the acts passed in June. Trent wrote: "when I consider what a respectable number there were in the Senate as well as in the Assembly for making us a full restitution; That many who voted on the other Side, some from Conviction, and others from a Knowledge that all most every man in Congress, as well as out of Doors reprobate their Conduct, will probably alter their Sentiments." Morgan was to appeal to Randolph if he needed advice. If the matter came before the high court of appeals, Trent hoped Randolph would be the advocate for the Indiana Company. "The fresh Matter He [*Morgan*] will supply you with added to those Arguments you have already made so masterly a use of . . . will put it in your Power to convert the Infidels if there are any respecting the Indiana Title." Patrick Henry seems to have been connected in some manner with the Illinois-Wabash group, and Clarence W. Alvord suggests that Clark's "conquest" of the Old Northwest had something to do with a connection between Henry, who was governor of Virginia at the time, and the two companies. See Alvord's Introduction to *The Illinois-Wabash Land Company Manuscript* (facsimile, Chicago, 1915), 20–21; Abernethy, *Western Lands*, 227.

[37] George Morgan to William Trent, September 27, 1778, in the Ohio Company Papers, vol. 2, f. 28; Trent to Morgan, January 23, 1779, *ibid.*, vol. 2, f. 33.

did not place all his hopes on the Virginia Assembly. In the middle of May, Richard Henry Lee and Meriwether Smith reported that they suspected that Morgan was bringing the claims of the companies before Congress. Lee and Smith urged the Assembly to declare the land claims invalid in order to prevent any such action.[38]

At the appointed time there appeared before the Assembly the representatives of the Indiana Company, of the now united Illinois and Wabash companies, of the Ohio Company of Virginia, and of George Croghan, who had large private grants from the Indians.[39] The Indiana claim was taken up first, before a joint session of the House of Delegates and the Senate. The matter was debated for several days, during which time strenuous efforts were made both within and outside the Assembly to gain support for the claim of the company.[40]

The House finally passed a series of general resolutions applying to all land purchases. The first of these declared that Virginia had the exclusive right to purchase land from the Indians within her chartered territory and that no one else had ever had that right. The second stated that all purchases made by the British crown in Virginia should now belong to the state. As a consequence of these two resolutions the deed of the Six Nations to the Indiana Company at Fort Stanwix in 1768 was declared to be null and void.[41] So far as legislative action by Virginia was concerned, this disposed of the Indiana Company and all other companies and individuals claiming lands on a similar basis. A futile attempt was made to give the company a consolation grant as had been done in the case of the Henderson Company.[42] In spite of George Mason's best efforts even Virginia's own Ohio Company failed to get a hearing.[43]

Practically, of course, the action of the Assembly meant that

[38] To Governor Patrick Henry, May 17, 1779, in Burnett, *Letters*, 4:216.

[39] Volwiler, *George Croghan*, 310–311.

[40] *Journal, House of Delegates* [May–June, 1779], *1777–1780*, 12, 18, 25, 31, 38; George Mason to Richard Henry Lee, June 19, in Rowland, *George Mason*, 1:333–334; Abernethy, *Western Lands*, 225–226.

[41] *Journal, House of Delegates* [May–June, 1779], *1777–1780*, 39–40, June 9; Hening, *Statutes of Virginia*, 10:97–98.

[42] *Journal, House of Delegates* [May–June, 1779], *1777–1780*, 56, June 18.

[43] George Mason to Richard Henry Lee, June 19, in Rowland, *George Mason*, 1:334.

areas not already granted or settled in the West were to be open to settlement. On June 16 an act was passed for settling the titles to all unpatented lands in Virginia. This measure was designed in part to take care of all the Virginia speculators whose claims were based upon the Dinwiddie Proclamation, upon the Proclamation of 1763, and upon grants by various colonial governors. Thus before Western lands were thrown open to public sale, speculators like George Washington were guaranteed their claims, however shaky the foundation upon which they rested. Actual settlers before January 1, 1778, were granted four hundred acres at a nominal price and given pre-emption rights to an additional thousand acres at the regular price.[44] The next day an act was passed setting up a land office to dispose of all ungranted lands in the West.[45]

This action of Virginia alarmed two widely different groups of people. Marylanders were immediately aroused. One of the Maryland delegates in Congress wrote that emigrations from the frontier counties of his state were alarming and that Virginia's measures to dispose of her lands ought to cease. Congress, the only possible brake upon Virginia, did not seem inclined to stop her.[46]

The Virginia soldiers in Washington's army in New York were more than sorry to hear of the proposed opening of the land office. William Russell wrote that it would "undoubtedly rob our army this fall of many valuable soldiers; who will prefer the present chance to the future one." He himself was glad that since the land office was to be opened, Colonel Fleming had made provision for all the unlocated warrants, which would thus take care of Russell's warrant for three thousand acres.[47]

---

[44] *Journal, House of Delegates* [May–June, 1779], *1777–1780*, 51; George Mason to George Mercer, February 6, 1778, in Rowland, *George Mason*, 1:291; Abernethy, *Western Lands*, 224–225.

[45] *Journal, House of Delegates* [May–June, 1779], *1777–1780*, 53, June 17.

[46] James Forbes to Thomas Sim Lee, September 21, in Burnett, *Letters*, 4:428; William Trent to Edmund Randolph, November 9, 1779, in the Ohio Company Papers, vol. 2, f. 47. "Everything prophesied respecting your State opening an office for the Sale of the back Lands has come to pass. It has depopulated a great Part of the interior Counties, lowered your Estates in Value, put it out of your power to furnish your Quota of Troops." Trent's statement must be viewed in the light of his relations with the land companies.

[47] Colonel William Russell to Colonel William Fleming, Smith's Clove [N. Y.], July 25, 1779, in the Draper MSS., 2U65, in the Wisconsin Historical Society.

The land companies were now forced to take new steps to protect their interests. The proposed opening of a Virginia land office in October meant that the choicest lots within the areas they claimed would be lost to them forever — provided of course that the Virginia speculators had left any choice lots to be sold. The only hope of the land companies was Congress. They had appealed to Congress in a most indirect fashion in 1776; they now petitioned openly. They agreed with Maryland that Congress should have control of the West and supplied "constitutional" theories to justify a control which was now their only hope for profit.

XI

Congress and the Western Problem: Land Speculation and the Spanish Alliance

THE RELATIONSHIP between the land companies and the conservative politicians of the Middle states was a very close one, and it throws much light on the attitude of those states toward the Articles of Confederation and on their demand for congressional control of the West. The Illinois and Wabash companies formally joined forces in the spring of 1779, before the denial of their claims by the Virginia legislature.[1] Some of the original members remained in the united company, the most notable being Thomas Johnson of Maryland. The company was of course speculative in character, shares being bought, sold, and subdivided, and hence the number interested in its success was far greater than the official membership. Charles Carroll of Carrolton, William Paca, and Samuel Chase owned shares. The list of shareholders residing in Pennsylvania was even more imposing. Leading it was Robert Morris, and next came James Wilson, a leader of the conservative forces in the state and one of the most ardent land speculators of the period. Others were George Ross, another important conservative politician, the Reverend Dr. Smith, a prominent conservative clergyman of Philadelphia, and the Franks and Gratzes, also of Philadelphia. The company likewise numbered among its members Silas Deane of Connecticut, an enemy of the Lees of Virginia, Conrad Gerard, French minister to the United States, and John Holker, French consul in Philadelphia. Gerard and Holker were involved in the shady commercial activities of Silas Deane, Robert Morris, and the French businessmen engaged in making money out of the American Revolution.[2]

The Indiana Company was more exclusively a Pennsylvania or-

[1] Alvord, *Illinois-Wabash Land Company Manuscript*, Proceedings of March 13, 26, 1779; Abernethy, *Western Lands*, 234–235.

[2] The Papers of the Continental Congress, No. 41, vol. 10, f. 32, contains the list of the company's members. Another list may be found in the James Wilson

ganization, although when it broadened out into the Vandalia scheme before the Revolution it added many Englishmen to the number interested in its fate. The firm of Baynton, Wharton, and Morgan was extinct, but all its creditors were exceedingly active and hopeful of profiting from the partnership's interest in the Indiana Company. George Morgan and Samuel Wharton were still active. Benjamin Franklin and his son William were both interested, and Franklin found time to support the company even while he was busy in France. Joseph Galloway was also a member and had been elected president in the spring of 1776. Of the many other members some were original partners and some were persons who had bought shares or parts of shares as a matter of speculation. The ramifications of the company are indicated by its statement that there were independent grants "from several proprietors to several Persons residing in different States." [3]

The Virginia acts nullifying their claims and setting up a land office forced these companies to take drastic steps. They appealed openly to Congress to stay Virginia from beginning land sales. On September 14 George Morgan presented to Congress a memorial from the Indiana Company [4] and William Trent one on behalf of the more or less extinct Vandalia-Walpole Company,[5] which had grown out of the original Indiana Company and had then collapsed. The two memorials were intimately related, for the grounds upon which the Indiana Company demanded redress were based in part on the Vandalia claim. This was a new tack on the part of Morgan, who had bitterly opposed the inclusion of the Indiana Company in the Vandalia Company scheme.[6] The memorial which he presented held that because the Indiana Com-

---

Papers, 10:100, in the Pennsylvania Historical Society Manuscripts. The latter list is dated at Philadelphia, May 4, 1781. By this time at least, James Wilson was the head of the company. On February 19, 1781, at a meeting of the company, Wilson was asked to accept one of the unappropriated shares of the company's lands, as a consideration for the trouble he "must unavoidably be at, in managing their affairs." James Wilson Papers, 10:100; Abernethy, *Western Lands*, 231–232. See also Thomas P. Abernethy, "Commercial Activities of Silas Deane in France," in the *American Historical Review*, 39:477–485 (April, 1934).

[3] A list of the proprietors of the Indiana Company is in the Papers of the Continental Congress, No. 41, vol. 10, ff. 524–527.

[4] *Journals*, 15:1063.   [5] *Ibid.*, 1064.

[6] Morris K. Turner, "The Baynton, Wharton, and Morgan Manuscripts," in the *Mississippi Valley Historical Review*, 9:236–241 (December, 1922).

pany had been a part of the Vandalia project, and because Vandalia had been separated from Virginia, the Indiana claim could no longer be under the jurisdiction of that state or of any particular state, and it must therefore belong to the United States as a whole.

The Virginia act authorizing the beginning of land sales in October "for the particular benefit of that state" was denounced as a maneuver to defeat the interposition of Congress. Morgan demanded that Congress order Virginia to stop the sale of lands until both the state and the Indiana Company could be heard before Congress, and until the right to Vandalia, of which Indiana was a part, "shall be ascertained in such a manner as may tend to support the sovereignty of the United States and the just rights of the individuals therein." [7]

The petition presented by Trent began with an outline of the Indiana Company's history, its enlargement into the Vandalia project, and its negotiations with the British government until the outbreak of the Revolution. The memorial did not insist that the grant had been formally completed. It stated that in August, 1774, Thomas Walpole and his associates had presented a petition to the king asking that the grant be no longer delayed. This remained the status of the company until the Declaration of Independence, when the memorialists "apprehend, *that all the Rights and all the obligations of the Crown of Great Britain* respecting the lands and governments herein before mentioned devolve upon the *United States* and are to be claimed, exercised and discharged by the United States in Congress Assembled." The doctrine of the "devolution" of sovereignty was thus utilized by the land companies in support of their interest. Maryland had insisted that the Western lands had been won by an expenditure of the blood and treasure of all, and hence should be common property, but she had never urged the metaphysical doctrine of "devolution." [8] Like the Indi-

[7] Papers of the Continental Congress, No. 77, ff. 234–236.

[8] The argument in the Vandalia memorial with respect to the nature of the powers of Congress is strikingly like that of the conservatives in 1776. It is even more akin to James Wilson's arguments for the Bank of North America in 1785, and considering his close connection with the Illinois-Wabash Company, which stood to gain by the adoption of the principle of the sovereignty of Congress, it is worthy of even closer examination. It might be said with some justice that the origin, or at least the effective support, of the doctrine of the sovereignty of Congress came first from the eighteenth-

ana memorial, the Vandalia memorial requested Congress to stay the sale of lands by Virginia. Both memorialists pleaded to be heard before Congress in defense of their claims.[9]

As soon as the petitions had been read, the New Jersey delegates moved that they be submitted to a committee.[10] The motion was significant aside from the dispute between the landed and the landless states. Its adoption was an assumption by Congress of prerogatives which it had been the design of the Articles of Confederation to withhold from Congress forever. The appeal of the Vandalia memorial to the sovereignty of Congress was aptly designed to meet not only the needs of the land companies but of the conservatives in the United States who wanted the creation of a centralized government.

New Hampshire, Massachusetts, Virginia, and both the Carolinas voted against the motion; Rhode Island, Connecticut, New Jersey, Pennsylvania, Delaware, and Maryland in favor of it. The New York delegation was divided.[11] Virginia, having failed to prevent a vote by her long and bitter opposition, now moved that Congress had no jurisdiction in disputes between a state and private land companies, and hence had no right to appoint a committee. This motion occasioned even more debate, but a vote on it was evaded on a point of order.[12]

On October 8 a committee was appointed consisting of John Witherspoon of New Jersey, Daniel of St. Thomas Jenifer of Maryland, Samuel Atlee of Pennsylvania, Roger Sherman of Connecticut, and Nathaniel Peabody of New Hampshire.[13] The selection of this committee was thus a victory for the landless states. After it had been appointed, Virginia moved that it be instructed to inquire into her objection to congressional jurisdiction in the matter, and to report on that question before taking up the petitions of the land companies. Congress agreed to this demand.[14]

century land speculators, whose hopes were thwarted by Virginia. The connection of Robert Morris and James Wilson with these companies, and their later use of the doctrine in the Convention of 1787, is hardly accidental.

[9] *Papers of the Continental Congress,* No. 41, vol. 10, ff. 79–86.

[10] *Journals,* 15:1064. The motion was made and seconded by the New Jersey delegates.

[11] *Ibid.,* 1064–1065.

[12] John Fell, Diary, September 14, in Burnett, *Letters,* 4:418.

[13] *Journals,* 15:1155.

[14] *Ibid.*

The treatment accorded the Virginia delegates in their first meeting with the committee indicates how partial its members were. The Virginians were ordered to put all their objections in writing, and they were forbidden to make mention of the treaties and charters upon which their state based her claims to the West. The Virginia delegates acquiesced in this in the hope that by so doing they could keep the committee from going into the question of the Treaty of Fort Stanwix, upon which the Indiana Company based its claim.[15]

At about this time Jenifer of Maryland expressed to Governor Johnson his hope that a large part of the backlands would be placed at the disposal of Congress.[16] A few days later the committee, of which he was a member, reported that after considering all the facts presented by the Virginia delegates it saw no "such distinction between the question of the jurisdiction of Congress, and the merits of the cause, as to recommend any decision upon the first separately from the last."[17] This was a mere quibble. Then, contrary to congressional orders, the committee presented to Congress a resolution recommending that Virginia and other states with Western claims suspend the sale, grant, or settlement of lands "unappropriated at the time of the declaration of independence, until the conclusion of the war."[18]

The Virginia delegates failed to get the report sent back to the committee.[19] Congress adopted it after a somewhat acrid discussion over the preamble to be affixed to it. The Marylanders moved the adoption of a preamble charging that the United States were being weakened by emigrations resulting from Virginia's decision to open a land office.[20] It was finally agreed, however, that it would be unwise to have the country know that this was the opinion of Congress on a matter of general concern. Gouverneur Morris proposed a more general statement to the effect that the appropriation of vacant lands would be "attended with great mischiefs," and that it was therefore to be recommended that Vir-

[15] Virginia Delegates to the Speaker of the Virginia House of Delegates, November 2, in Burnett, *Letters*, 4:506.

[16] October 25, *ibid.*, 497.

[17] *Journals*, 15:1223–1224.   [18] *Ibid.*, 1224.

[19] *Ibid.*, 1223–1224; John Fell, Diary, in Burnett, *Letters*, 4:500.

[20] *Journals*, 15:1226; Virginia Delegates to the Speaker of the Virginia House of Delegates, November 2, in Burnett, *Letters*, 4:504.

ginia and other states suspend land sales during the remainder of the war.[21]

Cornelius Harnett explained to the governor of North Carolina that the real object of the resolution was to enable the states to appropriate the vacant lands at the end of the war for the payment of the public debt, and not at all to stop emigration of people to the West.[22] In their official report the North Carolina delegates urged that it be noticed how cautiously the question of the jurisdiction of Congress had been evaded. "On the whole it appears to us that there are great jealousies particularly respecting Virginia's extensive claim of Territory and generally of the other States under similar circumstances." The North Carolina delegates felt that with many of the delegates it was less a question of the justice or injustice of the Indiana and Vandalia claims than of "laying down some principle or pursuing such a line of conduct as may be most likely to obtain the main object, namely, that Congress shall have the disposal of all the unapropriated lands on the Western frontiers of these States and that such lands may become the common property of the whole." [23]

The Virginia delegates reported that they had been vigorous in defending the rights of their state and in preventing Congress from establishing a precedent dangerous to the common rights of the United States. It was understood, they said, that the real motives behind the words "much Mischiefs" in the preamble of the recommendation that Virginia suspend land sales were "the Clamours of Maryland and the discontented States of Jersey and Delaware" and the general inconvenience of weakening the United States by emigrations to the West.[24]

As the North Carolina delegates pointed out, the Indiana claim was based on a principle that involved a basic constitutional issue of the time: "The principle on which the Indiana company found their memorial *is*, that the Territory which they claim is not

[21] *Journals*, 15:1227, 1228, 1229–1230. New Hampshire, Massachusetts, Rhode Island, Connecticut, New Jersey, Pennsylvania, Maryland, and South Carolina voted for the motion. Virginia and North Carolina voted against it. New York was divided, Gouverneur Morris being opposed to the recommendation.

[22] November 2, in Burnett, *Letters*, 4:503.

[23] North Carolina Delegates to the Governor of North Carolina, November 4, *ibid.*, 507–508.

[24] Virginia Delegates to the Speaker of the Virginia House of Delegates, November 2, *ibid.*, 504.

within nor subject to the Jurisdiction of either of the States, but to the whole United States in Congress Assembled." This principle the North Carolina delegates refused to accept, "it being against one of the principles of the general union." They pointed out that it was a controversy not between two states but between one state and individuals.[25]

So far as the land companies were concerned, they had gained a temporary objective, open support of their claims in Congress. But they wanted permanent recognition of their claims and they now set about to get it with the most substantial means within their power. Cyrus Griffin of Virginia charged that the Indiana Company had offered Congress ten thousand pounds to confirm its grant, but that it was still anxious to secure the recognition of Virginia. If it could receive some compensation from that state, it was ready and willing to defend Virginia against all opposition.[26] It seems to have been with this in mind that the Indiana Company sent George Morgan to Williamsburgh in the winter of 1779 to urge the Virginia legislature to revoke its action of the past summer. The company felt that it still had a chance, since it had a great deal of support in the Virginia Assembly from the conservative allies of the speculators of the Middle states.[27]

The hope was quite unfounded. From the point of view of Virginia, congressional consideration of the land company claims was a direct infringement of the rights of Virginia as a sovereign state. The result was the adoption of a remonstrance against the action of Congress in hearing the land company petitions.[28] This document reflected the ideas of George Mason, who wrote it. He

[25] To the Governor of North Carolina, November 4, *ibid.*, 507. Cyrus Griffin was aware of the significance. He wrote, "When Virginia instructed her delegates in Congress to sign the declaration of Independency what did she mean by reserving the sovereignty and internal Government of the state?" To the Speaker of the Virginia House of Delegates, November 9, *ibid.*, 513.

[26] Cyrus Griffin to the Speaker of the Virginia House of Delegates, November 9, *ibid.*, 513.

[27] William Trent to Edmund Randolph, Trenton, November 9, 1779, in the Ohio Company Papers, vol. 2, f. 47. Trent wrote, "We have stopped every kind of Publication on our Part in hopes that Virginia will see Her Interest in doing us Justice." He expressed regret over what had been done, but said that it had been done to procure justice, which had been withheld by the artifices of a few designing men. Abernethy, *Western Lands*, 226.

[28] *Journal, House of Delegates* [October–December, 1779], *1777–1780*, 55, November 13, 1779.

pointed out that the Indiana and Vandalia companies included several men of great influence in the neighboring states, that under color of creating a common fund these companies had made propositions to Congress which were calculated to guarantee their claims, and that if these claims were to be confirmed, the greater part of the unappropriated lands would be converted to private use.

The remonstrance argued that the United States held no land except by virtue of the claims of the individual states, and that if the lands northwest of the Ohio River did not belong to Virginia, they were a part of Canada. It was pointed out that Virginia had offered to furnish lands out of her own territory northwest of the Ohio, free of purchase price, for the continental troops of such states as had no vacant lands; she was ready to make a sacrifice in the common interest of America, as she had already done with respect to representation. She would be ready to listen "to any just and reasonable propositions for removing the *ostensible* causes of delay to the complete ratification of the Confederation," but she protested against any assumption of jurisdiction by Congress in the matter of the Indiana and Vandalia petitions, or in anything else "subversive of the internal policy, civil government, or sovereignty of this or any other of the United American States, or unwarranted by the Articles of Confederation." [29] Thus Virginia denied the right of Congress to take the land company claims into consideration, but indicated a willingness to listen to suggestions from Congress as to how the completion of the Articles of Confederation could be hastened.

In the meantime another struggle over the West had been going on since the summer of 1778, when the Articles of Confederation had first come up for ratification. The principals in the struggle were the same, but the program of the landless states in relation to the Spanish alliance was of such illuminating inconsistency that it is worthy of some consideration.

*   *   *

The alliance with France brought the Western problem into prominence in quite another way than did the struggle over the ratification of the Articles of Confederation. During the early

[29] Rowland, *George Mason*, 1:341–343.

years of the Revolution Congress had pretty much ignored the western phase of the conflict. The burden of defense in the West had fallen on Virginia's not unwilling shoulders and she had been busy setting up counties and organizing militia forces, and had finally supported George Rogers Clark in his campaign across the Ohio. But the alliance with France forced Congress to take a positive stand, for France's ally, Spain, soon claimed most of the Mississippi Valley, and France herself was not without ambitions in that area. The immediate aim of both France and the United States was to bring Spain into the war against Great Britain.[30]

Spain, however, was not at all eager to enter into a contest whose outcome was so dubious. Her far-flung territories would be prey to the English navy. The revolting American colonies set a dangerous example to her own dissatisfied colonies. Moreover, if they became independent they might become aggressive, and Spain had no desire for aggressive neighbors so near to her possessions. Florida Blanca, the Spanish minister of state, well expressed the dilemma of Spain when he said that as between England and her rebellious colonies, there was "a sort of equality of enmity which makes it difficult to prefer either of them." [31]

On the other hand, the Spanish realized that it was impossible to maintain a purely negative attitude throughout the war. Florida Blanca concluded that if Spain was to maintain her position in the New World, she would need to be insured against the potential danger of powerful American states as near neighbors. Hence if she were to come to their aid now, it would be only in return for adequate guarantees of her future security. Spain must have the Floridas, the Gulf of Mexico, the Mississippi River, and the Mississippi Valley as far east as the Alleghenies. Florida Blanca suggested that Nova Scotia and Canada should be guaranteed to Great Britain, and even that she keep such strategic ports as New York and Boston.[32]

[30] Frederick J. Turner, "The Policy of France toward the Mississippi Valley in the Period of Washington and Adams," in the *American Historical Review*, 10:249–253 (January, 1905); Samuel F. Bemis, *The Diplomacy of the American Revolution* (New York, 1935), ch. 8, "Spain's American Policy."

[31] Paul C. Phillips, *The West in the Diplomacy of the American Revolution* (*University of Illinois Studies in the Social Sciences*, vol. 11, no. 7, Urbana, 1913), 92–93.

[32] *Ibid.*, 89–90, 100.

With the completion of the Franco-American alliance, Conrad-Alexandre Gérard was sent to Philadelphia as the envoy of the French government to the Congress of the United States. He arrived in July, 1778, at the time when the Articles of Confederation were up for formal ratification. He had no specific instructions with regard to Spanish claims, but he knew that France wanted Spain to enter the war, and he had general instructions to look out for Spain's interests. He soon became aware that the members of Congress from the Middle states were jealous of the states with Western claims. Moreover, he became a shareholder in the Illinois-Wabash Company, so his association with those members was something more than a purely diplomatic gesture.[33]

He began early to urge Congress to give Spain assurance that the United States had no desire for an empire in the West. He asked Congress to pass a resolution declaring any state that attempted to extend its boundaries beyond specified limits to be an enemy of the Confederation. This met with the favor of several members of Congress, particularly those from the landless Middle states.[34] Those who opposed the claims of Virginia and the representatives of the mercantile interests of Philadelphia and New York swung very early to the support of Gérard's program. The leaders of this group were John Jay, Robert Morris, Gouverneur Morris, and Daniel of St. Thomas Jenifer.[35] Their attitude was a compound of various inconsistent elements. In it there was much of the timidity which the conservatives had shown in 1776 when they opposed a declaration of independence on the ground, among others, that it was first necessary to secure foreign aid. They continued to be frightened of the possible consequences of failure, and hence spared no effort to bring Spain into the war. Another factor was the fear with which the conservatives of the seaboard

[33] Excerpts from Gérard's dispatches, upon which Phillips' work is largely based, are to be found in the *Records of the American Catholic Historical Society of Philadelphia*, 31:215–228 (September, 1920); 32:274–289 (September, 1921); 33:54–91 (March, 1922).

[34] Phillips, *West in the Diplomacy of the Revolution*, 109.

[35] *Ibid.*, 110, 114–115. See also Kathryn Sullivan, *Maryland and France, 1774–1789* (Philadelphia, 1936), ch. 4, "Maryland and the French Ministers," for a concise account of the activity of Gérard, La Luzerne, and Marbois and of the Maryland delegates in Congress.

viewed the future growth of the West, for they realized that eventually they would be outweighed and outvoted as a result of western expansion. Furthermore, they wanted to control the trade of the West, and this would be denied them, they felt, if the Mississippi were open to Western trade. They believed that only by closing the river could Western commerce be forced eastward across the mountains to the cities of the seaboard. Moreover, many Easterners were afraid that the West would develop rapidly, draw off the laboring population of the East, and thus raise the price of labor.[36]

Western expansion, being primarily agrarian in its political and economic implications, was opposed by the mercantile interests of the East, which feared the usurpation of their political and economic control. True, the opposition to Western expansion was inconsistent with the larger interests of that class and section, but then economic vision is usually limited to the immediate future. The merchants and their associates faced across the Atlantic with their backs to the West, and they opposed the agrarian interests which threatened to displace them in power. The rise of agrarianism made the years of the American Revolution unpleasant for more than one merchant. The plaint of Samuel and Robert Purviance illustrates the feeling of the mercantile element. As they wrote to Robert Morris (who was engaged in privateering), they were trying to formulate a plan to check privateers, for the matter had been utterly neglected by the various assemblies, especially that of Virginia. This neglect, they said, must be attributed to "the small Representation of the Mercantile Interest in the respective Assemblies" and "the unaccountable the universally prevailing Prejudice of the Planters & Farmers against the Trading Interest." Matters were no better in Pennsylvania, "where the Interests of trade have ever been the principal care of Government, we are sensible how little can be expected from them in the present State of things."[37]

[36] Paul C. Phillips, "American Opinions Regarding the West, 1778–1783," in the *Proceedings of the Mississippi Valley Historical Association*, 7:286–305 (1913–14).

[37] Samuel and Robert Purviance to Robert Morris, Baltimore, December 8, 1778, in the Robert Morris Papers, in the Library of Congress. See also Rufus King to Elbridge Gerry, June 4, 1786, in the *Proceedings of the Massachusetts Historical Society*, 9:9–12 (1866–67).

Gouverneur Morris told Gérard that he and some of his colleagues were impressed with the necessity of preventing any additions to the states already in the union. He believed that if Spain were given control of the Mississippi, the immense population which would form along the river could be held in subjection by the Eastern states. But if the population of the West were in control of the Mississippi and the St. Lawrence, then it would dominate the Eastern states.[38]

Thus there formed around Gérard a party composed of the Easterners opposed to the growth of the West and the land speculators interested in exploiting it. Opposing them was a party which was in reality a continuation of the old radical party which had helped to bring on the Revolution. It was led by Sam and John Adams and by the Lees of Virginia, and was known as "the Junto" or the "Anti-Gallican" party. Antagonism to Gérard's policy and the furtherance of the somewhat divergent aims of Massachusetts and Virginia were the cohesive forces which held it together. A less tangible though no less important factor was that many, Virginians particularly, were expansionists who had a vision of the growth of new states to the westward.

Gérard's policy involved surrender to Spain of the right to navigate the Mississippi River and cession of most of the territory in the Mississippi Valley as the price of her entry into the war against Great Britain. Thus while the land company politicians from the landless states and their allies from other states were insisting that Virginia's charter claims should become the common property of all the states, many of them were at the same time trying to force Congress to concede to Spain much of what she demanded in the Mississippi Valley. Not all of Gérard's supporters, of course, were motivated by the same considerations. John Jay and Gouverneur Morris of New York, a state with Western claims, approved of surrendering the right to navigate the Mississippi, but they did not support Spain's claims to territory west of the Alleghenies. Neither did the land company speculators demand a restricted boundary for the United States. The sincerity of these demands of Gérard's on behalf of Spain is open to question, since he was a member of the Illinois-Wabash

[38] Phillips, *West in the Diplomacy of the Revolution,* 110.

Company. It is significant that the western boundary caused much less discussion than the navigation of the Mississippi.[39]

The proposed treaty between the United States and Spain was the center about which the conflict revolved. The first report of the committee on foreign affairs was a victory for "the Junto," since it declared that the United States should demand Canada, the Mississippi, and Florida as boundaries; freedom of navigation of the Mississippi; the use of the Newfoundland fisheries; and absolute evacuation by the British.[40] Gérard fought these terms in Congress and out, with the result that when the report came to a vote, only Virginia voted that the right to navigate the Mississippi should be insisted upon. Gérard and his party erred, however, in delaying a final vote on the terms of the treaty until it was supposed that they could absolutely overwhelm the Junto and until Richard Henry Lee should find himself alone in opposition. John Jay promised that even if the Junto did win, he would attack the validity of the terms on the ground that under the Articles of Confederation every state had to ratify the treaty. Gérard's party delayed so long, however, that the weakened Junto again revived and was able to carry on the fight.[41]

Spain finally entered the war without making a treaty with the United States, but the question of Western policy remained a source of continued dispute. When the news came that Britain might seek peace, the Junto was able to elect John Adams as treaty commissioner, over the opposition of Gérard and his party, who tried to elect John Jay. Congress gave Jay a consolation prize by electing him to make a treaty with Spain, but his final instructions were to demand the navigation of the Mississippi and the recognition of that river as the western boundary of the United States.[42]

Gérard was recalled and replaced by La Luzerne, who continued to argue with Congress. Although Gérard had begun to lose the more important supporters of the French policy, Jenifer of Maryland supported La Luzerne; indeed, he went so far as to declare that Spain could have all she could conquer, even includ-

[39] *Ibid.*, 115–120; Abernethy, *Western Lands*, 235–238.

[40] *Journals*, 13:239–244, February 23, 1779.

[41] Phillips, *West in the Diplomacy of the Revolution*, 122–129.

[42] *Journals*, 15:1042–1043, 1046–1047, 1116, 1168; Phillips, *West in the Diplomacy of the Revolution*, 127–128.

ing the states then in possession of the British. Jenifer wrote the ablest defense of Spain's demands that was made at the time. He denied the charter rights to the West and the territorial gains of the Treaty of 1763. He said that Spain was victorious on the Mississippi and that the United States must have Spain's help to win the war.[43] New England and Virginia continued to insist on the right to navigate the Mississippi. Toward the end of 1780 the military situation finally forced concessions to Spain. Although Virginia and New England refused to give up the region between the Mississippi and the Alleghenies, they did concede the right of navigation south of the thirty-first parallel, if the right of the United States north of that line would be recognized.[44] But Jay's mission to Spain was a failure, and the ultimate solution of the controversy between Spain and the United States was delayed until long after the ratification of the Articles of Confederation.[45]

In this long and confusing struggle over the concessions to be made to Spain in return for a treaty, certain things are evident. The Middle states, or rather their mercantile and land speculator elements, favored surrendering to Spain everything west of the Alleghenies and especially the right to navigate the Mississippi. At the same time they urged that the trans-Allegheny region be given to the United States as a common fund for the payment of debts and bounty lands to soldiers — always excepting the lands not granted to, surveyed for, or purchased by individuals before the beginning of the war. It was, to say the least, a program of great inconsistency. One might guess at all sorts of connivings in addition to those about which no guesswork is necessary. Suffice it to say that, so far as the ratification of the Articles of Confederation was concerned, the whole controversy did tend to point the issue and to draw the party lines more clearly. The solution, however, came from another source than the combined pressure of land speculators, the landless states, and the representatives of French and Spanish interests.

[43] Phillips, *West in the Diplomacy of the Revolution*, 182–184. This memoir of Jenifer's was sent to France by Marbois in a letter of October 17, 1780.

[44] *Journals*, 18:1120–1121; James Madison, Instructions to John Jay, October 17, 1780, in *The Writings of James Madison*, edited by Gaillard Hunt (9 vols., New York, 1900–10), 1:82–86; Madison to Joseph Jones, December 5, 1780, *ibid.*, 1:111–112; *ibid.*, pp. 102–103, note 1; *Journals*, 19:151–152.

[45] Bemis, *Diplomacy of the Revolution*, 101–104.

XII

The Completion of the Confederation

PROBABLY the first expression of the idea of creating independent states in the West was contained in Jefferson's proposed constitution for Virginia in 1776. The idea remained alive among that group of Virginia politicians of which Jefferson eventually became the recognized leader. In November, 1778, before Maryland finally refused to ratify the Confederation, Richard Henry Lee suggested that Virginia should voluntarily limit her size, and proposed that the Ohio River be made the western boundary of the state. In support of his proposal he urged that the completion of the Confederation was necessary; that it was difficult to govern by republican laws a country so far distant; that the creation of a buffer state against the Indians would be an economical move for Virginia; and that, lastly, it would unmask those who based their opposition to the Confederation upon the extensiveness of Virginia's claims.[1] The Virginia remonstrance in the fall of 1779 made it plain that at least a majority of the Virginia Assembly was willing to make a cession of some of Virginia's claims to the West. At the same time it denounced the claims of the land company speculators from the Middle states and suggested that Congress should take the first step by approaching Virginia.

While there was thus a body of sentiment in Virginia favorable to the idea of a cession, the first state to cede her Western claims to Congress was New York. During the year 1779 various New York leaders came to look with favor upon the idea of such a cession. John Jay, like Richard Henry Lee in Virginia, believed that the West was too extensive a territory to be governed adequately and looked upon it as a possible source of trouble. Robert R. Livingston, who believed that the weight of taxation would

---

[1] To Governor Patrick Henry, November 15, in Lee, *Letters*, 1:452-453; Abernethy, *Western Lands*, 223-224.

drive the other states to seize all the Western lands as a means of paying their debts, felt that it might be well for New York to cede some of her claims in order to preserve the remainder. Governor Clinton too was in favor of a cession; he agreed that the states would be likely to claim the Western lands, and even believed that the confiscated Loyalist estates might be seized as common property. Moreover, New Yorkers generally were anxious to secure the support of Congress in the bitter dispute between their state and the inhabitants of Vermont, and it was recognized that a cession of New York's claims might win for her the support of the landless states and their allies in Congress, even though it alienated Virginia and North Carolina, the chief claimant states. Thus New York leaders had come to the conclusion that a cession should be made before the landless states renewed their fight upon the landed states in the fall of 1779. Pressure from Maryland seems to have been the least of the influences acting upon the New York politicians.[2]

During the fall of 1779 General Philip Schuyler was sent to Congress as a delegate from New York. He soon induced Congress to take up the business of making peace with the Six Nations. On November 27 a committee reported on the terms which Congress should demand as a condition of a peace with the Indians. Among other things it was recommended that the Six Nations should make considerable offers of territory "as the most pointed marks of their contrition." The commissioners from Congress, however, should decline this offer in order to demonstrate "the superior Generosity of America, compared with their Experience of others."

The submission of this report to Congress proved to be a point of departure for a new attack by the landless states. Forbes of Maryland at once proposed that Congress should accept any cession the Six Nations might make, reserving to the states their prior claims to the territory. A New York delegate countered this proposal with another to the effect that any such cession should be negotiated for the benefit of the state with such prior rights. Both these motions were set aside. Marchant of Rhode Island then proposed as one of the conditions of peace with the Six Nations

[2] Thomas C. Cochran, *New York in the Confederation* (Philadelphia, 1932), 74–77.

that no land could be sold or ceded by the Indians, either as nations or as individuals, "unless to the United States of America or by the consent of Congress." [3]

The New York delegates objected vigorously to motions so widesweeping in their implications. Proponents of the motions repeated the time-worn argument that lands won by common expense should become common property. They argued that while the lands in question might be within New York's charter limits, they were not the property of New York but of the Six Nations. If the lands didn't belong to the Six Nations, then by right of conquest they belonged to the United States. Such arguments were largely hypothetical, since the Six Nations were as yet unconquered by either New York or the United States. The Rhode Island motion was dropped from consideration, but a few days later Schuyler was given what he considered "convincing proof that an Idea prevailed that this [*New York*] and some other States ought to be divested of part of their Territory for the Benefit of the United States." One member of Congress took the New York delegates aside and allowed them to read a resolution, which he said would be introduced in Congress, to the effect that all the lands which had been grantable by the British crown before the war, and which had not been granted to individuals, should be considered the property of the United States. Schuyler was told that if the states would consent to a reasonable limitation, Congress would not interfere except to fix permanent boundaries. Thus the obstacle to confederation would be removed.

Schuyler was alarmed, since New York would be "eminently affected" by such a measure. He showed a certain amount of guile, however, for he determined "as fully to investigate their Intentions as could be done consistent with that Delicacy and prudence to be observed on so interesting an Occasion." Accordingly he expressed a wish, which he said arose from mere curiosity, to know what a reasonable limitation would amount to. The New York delegates were then shown a map on which a line was drawn from the northwest corner of Pennsylvania through Lake Ontario and down the St. Lawrence to the forty-fifth parallel. The boundaries of Virginia, the Carolinas, and Georgia were to be restricted to the Alleghenies or, at the farthest, to the Ohio and the Mississippi. All west of the line to be drawn was to belong to the Confederation.[4]

This information moved Schuyler to get a leave of absence immediately and return to New York, where the legislature was in session. He wrote out a lengthy report of the situation in Congress, possibly at the suggestion of Governor Clinton for the purpose of hastening the action of the legislature. In any event, within a few days of Schuyler's return the legislature passed its act of cession with relatively little debate. The act empowered the New York delegates in Congress to draw the western boundaries of the state in any manner they should judge expedient.[5] Whatever the validity of New York's claim, or the motives behind the cession, it was an important step in the direction of confederation. Other states must now assume the responsibility for obstruction if they failed to follow her example.

* * *

During the early part of 1780 the South was falling under the control of the British forces. Southern representatives were desperately trying to stay the northward-moving tide; no measure that might prove effective could be neglected. Members of Congress felt that completion of the Confederation would at least be a step in the right direction, and hence a good deal of activity was directed toward that end. In May, 1780, James Duane reported that he was busily engaged in an attempt to complete the Articles of Confederation and that the Virginia delegates were "warmly disposed to give it all the Aid in their Power." [6] In June, Joseph Jones of the Virginia delegation wrote Governor Thomas Jefferson that the present was the time for completion of the Articles of Confederation. He cited the New York cession as worthy of imitation. Virginia, he wrote, was too large for vigorous government. She should cede her territory beyond the Ohio River, although conditions should be attached to such a cession.

[4] Philip Schuyler to the Lieutenant-Governor and Speaker of the Assembly of New York, Albany, January 29, 1780, in Burnett, *Letters*, 5:21–22.

[5] *Report of the Regents of the University on the Boundaries of the State of New York* (Albany, 1874), 141–155; Cochran, *New York in the Confederation*, 76–78.

[6] To George Washington, May 4, in Burnett, *Letters*, 5:125.

He reported that the New York cession, the Maryland instructions, and the Virginia remonstrance were before a committee of Congress and that he expected the committee to recommend cessions by the claimant states.[7]

Jones wrote also to George Mason and requested his opinion on the subject of a land cession and on the conditions which ought to be attached to a cession by Virginia. In a lengthy reply Mason said that Virginia had done nothing since presenting its remonstrance to Congress, in which Congress had been invited to make some proposal for settling the question at issue, and that it would do nothing until Congress made some reply. If Congress would agree, he said, to guarantee the Mason and Dixon line as far as the Ohio and thence down the Ohio to the northern boundary of North Carolina, Virginia would be willing to cede both the right to the soil and sovereignty over the region northwest of the Ohio.

If such a cession were made, Virginia would attach certain conditions to it which must be accepted by Congress before it became final. In brief these were (1) that the territory to be ceded be laid out into no fewer than two separate states; (2) that Virginia be paid for George Rogers Clark's expedition and for other expenses in the Ohio Valley; (3) that the French inhabitants of the region, who had become citizens of Virginia, be guaranteed their privileges and possessions and be protected from the British at Detroit; (4) that Clark and his men be given the 150,000 acres which had been promised them northwest of the Ohio; (5) that Clark be confirmed in the grant of land promised him at the Falls of the Ohio; (6) that if the lands southeast of the Ohio should prove insufficient for Virginia soldiers, the deficiency would be made up north of the Ohio; and (7) that all the lands thus ceded be considered a common fund for the Confederation, and all purchases from Indians or deeds from Indian nations for any lands in the region be declared void.

Mason attached a series of explanations to the conditions which he felt Virginia should insist upon. With reference to the seventh condition requiring the voidance of all deeds and titles from the

[7] June 30, *ibid.*, 5:245. See also Ezekiel Cornell to Governor Greene of Rhode Island, June 18, *ibid.*, 225. ". . . the once patriotick state of Virginia weighs but littel at present in the scale of Defence, Or furnishing of men or Supplies, her whole attention is ingrosed in making sale of her out lands."

Indians, he said it was notorious that various men in neighboring
states had purchased from twenty to thirty million acres for a
mere trifle; and that two companies, the Illinois and the Wabash,
had united and had strengthened themselves by giving shares to
members of Congress. Anyone who read the Maryland Declaration, he wrote, could see that it was calculated to save those purchases, and if accepted by Congress the most valuable territory
ceded would go to private individuals.[8]

By the autumn of 1780 the members of Congress were more
than ever convinced of the necessity of completing the Confederation.[9] Maryland had long since refused to confederate unless
Virginia would cede her Western claims. George Mason had
made it plain that the next move was up to Congress. Furthermore, it was necessary for Congress to act soon, for with the close
of Governor Jefferson's ill-fated administration, which was not
far off, many of those sympathetic to the idea of a cession would
be retiring from the Assembly. Richard Henry Lee wrote Sam
Adams that it would be wise for Congress to approach Virginia
with a proposal for a land cession, since further delay might result
in failure. If approached by Congress, the Assembly would make
a cession at its next meeting. If Congress delayed, there would be
little hope for the success of such action in the future.[10]

Congress had not been inactive, however. In response to the
growing desire for the completion of the Confederation, a committee had been appointed in June, 1780, to which had been referred the instructions of the Maryland Assembly to its delegates,
the Virginia remonstrance, and the New York cession. This new
committee was quite unlike the committee which had shown so
much sympathetic regard for the petitions of the land companies
in the fall of 1779. It was composed of James Duane, John Henry,
Joseph Jones, Roger Sherman, and Willie Jones. At least a majority of these men favored compromise and confederation, and,
what is more, the majority represented the interests of the landed
states.[11]

[8] Rowland, *George Mason*, 1:359–367.
[9] Ezekiel Cornell to Governor William Greene of Rhode Island, September
2, in Burnett, *Letters*, 5:355.
[10] September 10, in Lee, *Letters*, 2:201.
[11] *Journals*, 17:559–560.

The report of the committee, submitted in July, 1780, was not taken up until September, when it was agreed to. It represented something of a compromise between the extreme positions taken by Maryland and Virginia, although it tended to favor the landed states. The committee neatly evaded the central problem by declaring that it was unnecessary to examine the merits of either the Maryland instructions or the Virginia remonstrance, since both of them involved questions which Congress had declined to discuss when the Articles of Confederation had been up for debate and which it was therefore useless to revive now. The vital thing was to complete the federal union. The New York cession had been a start in the direction of impartial consideration of the matter. Therefore the committee proposed that Congress send a general recommendation to the land-claiming states asking them to pass such laws as would remove the obstacle to final ratification of the Articles of Confederation.[12]

Congress accepted the report. The Virginia delegates at once took the offensive by moving that Congress provide certain guarantees as to the disposal of any land ceded to it; it was suggested that the land ceded be laid out into separate states of specific proportions; that the remaining territory of the ceding states be guaranteed to them; that the ceding states be reimbursed for expenses in the West; that all lands so ceded and not disposed of in bounties for the American army should be a common fund; and that Congress should declare null and void all deeds or purchases from the Indians of lands in the regions to be ceded.[13] In general these were the guarantees which George Mason had set forth in his letter to Joseph Jones on July 27, 1780.

Immediately after making this proposal Joseph Jones left for Virginia to promote a cession by the Virginia Assembly.[14] James Madison stayed behind to watch matters in Congress, where a committee was appointed to consider the guarantees proposed by the Virginia delegates. The committee's report was favorable, and Congress agreed to all the proposed guarantees except the crucial one voiding land purchases from Indians. On September 19 Madi-

[12] *Ibid.*, 580, 586, 806–807. The report was agreed to on September 6.
[13] *Ibid.*, 808.
[14] Joseph Jones to George Washington, September 6, in Burnett, *Letters*, 5:364.

son wrote to Jones that consideration of that condition had been postponed by Congress without any intention of resuming it. Some members argued that it was unnecessary, others that it was improper, since it implied that without previous guarantees to the ceding states Congress would have the right to surrender lands to private claimants. The arguments were specious, as Madison well knew, for he wrote that these motives prevailed "with more than the real view of gratifying private interest at the public expense." However, Virginia had not yet ceded and she might attach whatever conditions she pleased to an act of cession.[15]

The land companies were distinctly alarmed over this move of Virginia's and once more began petitioning Congress for support. On September 26 the Illinois-Wabash Company presented an appeal, and the next day the Indiana-Vandalia Company presented a memorial.[16] George Morgan of the Indiana Company was impatient that Congress had done nothing and was very bitter against the "Nabobs" of Virginia. Their enmity for him, he declared, was the result of his "steady Attention to the Interest of the United States, in preference to the partial views of One." [17] An Indiana Company memorial signed by William Trent stated that the memorialists had seen a copy of the report on the guarantees demanded by the Virginians and that they had observed in it the words nullifying all deeds and purchases within the territory to be ceded. They were "struck with Apprehension" lest Congress might decide the matter hastily and agree to the report. They therefore requested to be heard by Congress as soon as possible.[18] Two weeks later Trent sent another memorial to Congress on behalf of the Indiana Company, and this time he was even more specific. The company had been informed, he stated, that Virginia had denied the jurisdiction of Congress in the matter of the petitions of the Indiana and Vandalia companies. "Your Memorialists

[15] *Journals*, 18:815–816, 828, 836; President of Congress to the Several States, September 10, in Burnett, *Letters*, 5:366–367; Madison to Edmund Pendleton, September 12, and to Joseph Jones, September 19, *ibid.*, 1:67–68, 68–70; James Lovell to Samuel Holton, September 19, in Burnett, *Letters*, 5:380.

[16] *Journals*, 18:862, 868.

[17] George Morgan to [William] Trent, Princeton, September 12, in the Draper MSS., 46J59, in the Wisconsin Historical Society.

[18] Memorial by William Trent for the Indiana and Vandalia Proprietors, Philadelphia, September 27, in the Papers of the Continental Congress, No. 77, ff. 217–221.

humbly conceive," said Trent, "that this Question of the Jurisdiction of Congress, is of the very essence of their claims; that it is
of infinite Consequence to the American Union as well as to your
Memorialists; and that it ought to receive a speedy and solemn
Decision." [19] This memorial was probably the most naive and yet
most honest confusion of private interest with public good that
occurred during the whole controversy.

Not only did the land companies memorialize Congress, but
they sought public support through the issuance of a series of
pamphlets in which their case was set forth in the best possible
light. Samuel Wharton, who had written *View to the Title of
Indiana* in 1776, now elaborated it in a pamphlet called *Plain Facts*.
Benjamin Franklin outlined the history of the Vandalia project
in the "Passy Memorial," which was not published but which was
read to Congress.[20] Thomas Paine was hired by the Indiana Company to prepare a pamphlet called *Public Good*, an attack upon
Virginia's charter claims, which appeared on December 30, 1780,
just before the Virginia cession of the Old Northwest.[21]

While the land companies thus kept up their struggle, Congress
continued to wrangle over the knotty problems arising out of
Virginia's demand that she be given guarantees of congressional
honor before ceding her Western claims. Before Congress took
final action on the proposed guarantees, some members expressed
themselves in a manner dictated more by wishful thinking than
by foresight. Thus Jenifer wrote to Governor Lee of Maryland that the motions by Virginia had alarmed some members of
the "Eastern States" and that he hoped the effect would be to
make them more favorable to the Maryland claim.[22] Willie Jones
informed the governor of North Carolina that Maryland's claims
had merit, but that it would be wise for North Carolina to wait
a while before surrendering her claims to the West.[23] Joseph

[19] Papers of the Continental Congress, No. 77, ff. 230–233.

[20] *Ibid.*, ff. 167–201. This memorial was dated at Passy, February 26, 1780,
and endorsed as read in Congress on March 16, 1781.

[21] George Morgan to Captain John Dodge, Fort Jefferson, December 1,
1780, in the Draper MSS., 50J76 in the Wisconsin Historical Society. Volwiler,
in his *Croghan*, 317, says that Paine was soon listed as owning three hundred
shares of Indiana Company stock. The pamphlet is printed in Conway's edition of Paine's *Writings*, 2:33–66.

[22] September 26, in Burnett, *Letters*, 5:392.

[23] October 1, *ibid.*, 394.

Jones, who was convinced that Virginia was too large for "republican Government," wrote from Virginia that he felt sure the condition voiding land purchases from Indians would be attached to any cession by the state, "as there are jealousies entertained of certain Individuals greatly interested in that question." [24]

Finally, on October 10, 1780, Congress disposed of the committee report in accordance with Virginia's demands by agreeing to all except the one voiding purchases and deeds from Indians. This was once more postponed.[25] Madison at first determined to lay the whole matter before the Assembly but finally concluded to leave it entirely in the hands of Joseph Jones to do with as he saw fit. Madison thought that many members of Congress who had voted against voiding the land claims did not wish to encourage the land companies. Furthermore, he did not want to discourage the Assembly from making a cession.[26] This postponement by Congress is undeniable proof that the interest of the land companies was a predominant influence in the whole dispute. Their desperation would not have been lessened by the knowledge that their rivals, the Virginia speculators, were to be protected in both the regions to be ceded and the region to be guaranteed to Virginia.

George Morgan was not a man to surrender easily. Once more he approached the Virginia delegates, this time with an entirely new scheme for settling the Indiana claim to his satisfaction. He proposed that the dispute between the company and the state be submitted to arbitration according to the method laid down by the Confederation. To this the Virginia delegates haughtily replied that their state had finally decided the matter and that it was beneath the dignity of a sovereign state to submit to a foreign tribunal a case that involved only the claims of individuals.[27] In spite of this rebuff Morgan was jubilant over the defeat of the Virginia demand for the voiding of Indian purchases and over the congressional recommendation for land cessions. He prophesied that "all the Country, West of Allegheny Mountain will probably

[24] To James Madison, in Burnett, *Letters*, 5:399; Jones to George Washington, October [2?], *ibid.*, 396.

[25] *Journals*, 18:915–916.

[26] Madison to Joseph Jones, October 17, in *Writings*, 1:79–81.

[27] Burnett, *Letters*, vol. 5, p. 455, note 2; Madison to Joseph Jones, November 21, in *Writings*, 1:98–99.

be put under the Direction of the United States, & Virginia limited to the Waters which fall into the Atlantic from the West & North West." [28]

In sending Morgan's propositions to Governor Jefferson, Theodorick Bland remarked that "every art has been and tis probable may be used, by that Company to extend their influence and Support their pretensions, and we are Sorry to say that we have Suspicions founded upon more than mere Conjecture, that the land Jobbs, of this Comp'y, the Vandalia, and the Illinois Companies, have too great an influence in procrastinating that desirable and necessary event of Compleating the Confederation." [29] Madison was even more alarmed than he had been over the rejection of the condition voiding Indian purchases. He reiterated the necessity of attaching conditions to any cession that might be made. While expressing his belief that Congress would not satisfy the cupidity of the "land mongers," he made it plain that he believed "the best security for their [*Congress'*] virtue, in this respect, will be to keep it out of their power." [30]

With such warnings and advice to guide it, and with the conviction among a majority that a grant should be made, the Virginia Assembly took up the matter of ceding her claims. On January 2, 1781, an act was passed by which all Virginia's claims northwest of the Ohio River — "The Old Northwest" — were ceded to Congress, providing the conditions were met. These conditions were the same which George Mason had suggested in his letter to Joseph Jones in July, 1780, including the guarantee which Congress had refused to give: that all purchases and deeds from Indians within the territory ceded be declared null and void.[31] Title to the land could not pass to Congress until these conditions were met.

[28] George Morgan to Captain John Dodge, Fort Jefferson, December 1, 1780, in the Draper MSS., 50J76, in the Wisconsin Historical Society.

[29] November 22, in Burnett, *Letters*, 5:455-456. See also Ezekiel Cornell to Governor William Greene, October 24, *ibid.*, 425-426. "The Indiana affair is a matter of great consequence. the state of Virginia hath undertaken to vacate the title made to the grantees and take the land to themselves, which proceedings gives much uneasiness to the original proprietors as it is a Country of immense value and they have made applications to Congress for relief who in my opinion, have little to do in the affair."

[30] November 21, in *Writings*, 1:98, 99.

[31] *Journal, House of Delegates, 1777-1780*, 80.

While Virginia was moving in the direction of a cession, Maryland was facing difficulties which caused many of her politicians to change their views with respect to ratification of the Articles of Confederation. When the Maryland Assembly met in October, 1780, a series of documents from Congress were laid before it, including copies of the Maryland instructions of 1779, the Virginia remonstrance, the request from Congress to the land-claiming states for a cession of their claims, and a request for the completion of the Confederation. But the Assembly refused to take up the question of ratification, for more important and immediate matters occupied its attention. Many Marylanders were terrified by the success of the British to the south of them. Appeals to Congress had brought no aid, and the state was apparently without resources to defend itself against an anticipated British invasion. The Assembly therefore appealed to La Luzerne, the French envoy, to order two French war vessels to cruise near Maryland waters for the protection of the state.

In accordance with this decision Daniel of St. Thomas Jenifer appealed to La Luzerne for help. In a letter of January 5, 1781, he pointed out the ever-growing danger of invasion and the effect it would have on the food supply of the American and French armies. La Luzerne at once saw an opportunity to further what he considered to be the interests of France. He recognized the possibility of bringing about a union of the colonies, which union he believed would best serve French interests. It was obviously to the British interest to keep the colonies in a weak and disunited state. Congress would be strengthened, the alliance would be safeguarded, the individual states would not need to ratify the alliance. Finally, La Luzerne seemed convinced that if the king of France would help Congress establish itself on a firm foundation, it would owe him a debt of gratitude which could not be expected from the separate states. For these various reasons La Luzerne decided to urge upon the distrait Marylanders the necessity of ratifying the Confederation. He wrote to Jenifer, president of the Maryland senate, and to William Bruff, speaker of the house, urging them to act at once. He refused to make any promises with regard to ships, while at the same time he deftly pointed out that completion of the Confederation would strengthen the states and disabuse the British of any hopes to be derived from the continued disunion of the thirteen states.[32]

La Luzerne's polite blackmail was effective; on January 20, 1781, the Maryland house passed a resolution in favor of ratifying the Confederation, for which La Luzerne properly took credit, since it was based upon his letter to Jenifer and Bruff. On January 27, 1781, Thomas Johnson of the Illinois-Wabash Company brought in a bill empowering the Maryland delegates in Congress to ratify the Confederation. The next day the Maryland senate refused to pass the bill, although it gave no official reason for its refusal. The house promptly sent a communication to the senate, in which it pointed out that the senate's refusal to authorize ratification was no doubt due to the fact that the matter of Western lands had not yet been settled. But, the house urged, Maryland's refusal to confederate would no longer be of service in the Western land question, and she might secure greater justice at the hands of the confederated states than otherwise. Furthermore, the good will of Maryland's neighbors, the improvement of the executive, and the gratification of France were desirable ends which would result from agreeing to the Confederation.

The Maryland senate was at last persuaded to agree to ratification, since the bill "in your opinion, cannot alter or injure our claim to the western country, but that claim may be as fully ascertained and as firmly secured after as before the confederation." [33] It returned an illuminating reply to the house, in which it was quite frankly stated that "it has been generally supposed, and in our opinion upon good grounds, that the claim of this state to a proportionable part of the western country can be better sup-

[32] This account is derived from Kathryn Sullivan, *Maryland and France*, 97–100, and St. George L. Sioussat, "The Chevalier de la Luzerne and the Ratification of the Articles of Confederation by Maryland," in the *Pennsylvania Magazine of History and Biography*, 60:393–394 (October, 1936).

[33] Sioussat, in the *Pennsylvania Magazine of History*, 60:416. Professor Sioussat argues rather convincingly that Johnson, Carroll, and Chase were not motivated merely by their interest in the Illinois-Wabash Company. *Ibid.*, p. 406, note 32. However, the history of the subsequent three years was to show very definitely that the land companies had by no means given up the struggle, for their fight against the obnoxious conditions attached to the Virginia cession of 1781 delayed the creation of the national domain until March, 1784. On this point see Merrill Jensen, "The Creation of the National Domain, 1781–1784," in the *Mississippi Valley Historical Review*, 26:323–342 (December, 1939).

ported under the present form of union, than that of the confederation; influenced by this opinion, we put our negative on the
bill." [34] This admission of the senate rather effectually disproves
the arguments which the Marylanders made at the time, and their
apologists ever since, that the concern of Maryland was entirely
for the "national welfare." Maryland, according to its senate, was
interested only in a *share* of the public domain, not in the creation
of a "national" domain. If the Virginia cession four weeks earlier
had any influence upon the deliberations of the Maryland Assembly, the official records do not reveal it. [35] The instructions
empowering the Maryland delegates in Congress to ratify the
Confederation made it perfectly plain that Maryland was not surrendering her claim to a share in the Western lands. [36]

The country had not heard the last of the dispute over Western
lands, but the completion of the first constitution of the United
States was at last made possible. After the Maryland delegates had
presented their instructions, Congress set March 1, 1781, as the
day for formal completion of the Confederation. On that day the
New York cession was delivered to Congress by the state's delegates. The Maryland delegates then signed the Articles of Confederation. [37] Thus three years after the date set by Congress for
ratification, the thirteen states were united in a constitutional
union which was to last for eight years. It was an occasion for
great jubilation, as contemporary diaries, letters, and newspapers
testify. "Collations," receptions, dinners, fireworks, salutes from
John Paul Jones' ship the *Ariel*, all demonstrated the joy of Congress over the establishment of the first constitution of the United
States. [38]

[34] Sioussat, "The Chevalier de la Luzerne and the Ratification of the Articles
of Confederation by Maryland," in the *Pennsylvania Magazine of History*,
60:401–403, 415–416.

[35] *Ibid.*, 406–407. Professor Sioussat says that "the last push, the influence
which determined the action of Maryland *at this time*, came from the minister
plenipotentiary of Louis XVI," although he thinks that the "really determining forces" were the solicitations of Congress and the evidences of yielding on
the subject of Western lands, particularly on the part of Virginia.

[36] *Ibid.*, 416–417.

[37] *Journals*, 19:138–139, 186, 208–214.

[38] Burnett, *Letters*, 5:552; 6:1–4.

XIII

Conclusions

THE ARTICLES of Confederation were the constitution of the United States from 1781 to 1789, when the Confederation Congress held its last session and turned over the government of the thirteen states to the new national government. The fact that the Articles of Confederation were supplanted by another constitution is no proof either of their success or of their failure. Any valid opinion as to the merits of the Articles must be based on a detailed and unbiased study of the confederation period. Though no such comprehensive study has yet been made, it is possible to draw certain tentative conclusions by approaching the history of the period from the point of view of the American Revolution within the American states rather than from the point of view that the Constitution of 1787 was a necessity, the only alternative to chaos.

An analysis of the disputes over the Articles of Confederation makes it plain that they were not the result of either ignorance or inexperience. On the contrary, they were a natural outcome of the revolutionary movement within the American colonies. The radical leaders of the opposition to Great Britain after 1765 had consistently denied the authority of any government superior to the legislatures of the several colonies. From 1774 on, the radicals continued to deny the authority of a superior legislature whether located across the seas or within the American states. The reiteration of the idea of the supremacy of the local legislatures, coupled with the social and psychological forces which led men to look upon "state sovereignty" as necessary to the attainment of the goals of the internal revolution, militated against the creation of such a centralized government as the conservative elements in American society desired. It can be said that the constitution which the radicals created, the Articles of Confederation, was a constitutional expression of the philosophy of the Declaration of Independence.

Today "states' rights" and "decentralization" are the war cries of the conservative element, which is not wielding the influence in national affairs it once did and still longs to do. But in the eighteenth century decentralization and states' rights meant local self-government, and local self-government meant a form of agrarian democracy. The mass of the population was composed of small farmers, who in the long run could control the politics of their individual states. Since this was the belief of the fathers of the constitution of 1787, who were thus in substantial agreement with the radical leaders of 1776, the testimony might very well be regarded as conclusive.

The writing of the Articles of Confederation brought to the fore political issues that were to be of vast significance in the history of the United States. Many a debate in later years was merely a reiteration or an elaboration of arguments used in 1776 and 1777. Those ideas upon which it is necessary to place the inadequate but necessary label of "conservative" were as well expressed in 1776 as in 1787, and often by the same men: John Dickinson and James Wilson, for instance. The vital change which took place between 1776 and 1787 was not in ideas nor in attitudes but in the balance of political power. The radical organization which had brought about the Revolution disintegrated with success, for the radicals had won their real goal, local self-government. Radical leaders returned to their states to enjoy the results of their efforts unhampered by a central government of extensive power. The conservatives, on the other hand, made only occasional gains in the states, as in Massachusetts, where their rule was met by open rebellion in 1786. In other states the attack upon their position was a slow but sure process, as in Virginia. Some of them had realized in 1776 that centralization was their protection: a central government to suppress internal rebellions, to regulate trade, and to control the actions of the state governments as the British government had controlled the colonial governments.

The fight for centralization did not stop with the completion of the Articles of Confederation. Discontent with the document was expressed in the private correspondence of such conservative leaders as Washington, Dickinson, Charles Carroll, Robert Morris, Gouverneur Morris, James Wilson, and Alexander Hamilton. Even before they were finally ratified Hamilton proposed a revolutionary convention to create the kind of government the conservatives wanted. Once the Articles had been ratified, many serious attempts were made to amend them in such a way as to strengthen the central organization. These attempts at amendment failed, as did efforts to "interpret" into the Articles certain "nationalistic" ideas foreign to both the purpose and character of the document. Even if such amendments had been adopted, the constitution would not have been satisfactory to the conservative element, for it was impossible to change its nature by mere amendment. From the conservative point of view it was the wrong *kind* of government. Even if Congress had been given a limited income, as was proposed in various amendments, the central government would still have been a federal government and therefore inadequate in conservative opinion. The alterations proposed during the Confederation period were not fundamental, for they did not touch the vital question of the distribution of power between the states and the central government. The vast field of undefined and unenumerated powers lay with the states. Congress could function only within an area of precisely delegated and carefully limited authority. It was the creature of the state governments and thus, ultimately, of the electorate of the states.

Centralized government with a legal veto on state laws, the power to enact general and uniform legislation, and the power to use arms to subdue rebellious social groups within the states, had disappeared with the Declaration of Independence. The Articles of Confederation were designed to prevent its reappearance, and for this reason were not, and never could be, adequate from the point of view of the conservatives, who wanted the essence of the British imperial system restored in the American states.

John Dickinson and his conservative committee had sought to lay the legal foundation of such a system in their first draft of articles of confederation. The document was involved and legalistic to the point of obscurity, but it was an obscurity which would lend itself readily to multiple interpretation. Legally, ultimate authority lay with the central government, for only one conditional guarantee was given to the states, and only one specific restraint was placed on Congress. The states were guaranteed the control of their "internal police" in matters where such control did not interfere with the Articles of Confederation. Congress was restrained only from levying taxes other than those for support of the post office. This was a great but not insurmountable obstacle in the way of centralization. The important point is that the vital area of undefined and unenumerated powers fell within the domain of the central government, as Thomas Burke demonstrated to Congress in 1777.

The final draft of the Articles of Confederation was, as James Wilson said in the convention of 1787, "how different." Certain powers and no others were delegated to Congress. No phrase in the document could be construed as making the central government supreme over the states. Nothing remotely resembling such phrases as "obligation of contract," "supremacy of the laws," "necessary and proper," or "general welfare" were to be found in it. The control of war and foreign affairs was expressly granted to Congress, as was the power to regulate the trade with Indians who were not members of any of the states, but Congress might not infringe upon the right of any state to legislate upon matters within its own limits. Congress was given the power to regulate the value of both its coinage and that of the states, but no control over the emission of paper money by the states. Congress was a court of last appeal, or rather a board of arbitration, in disputes between one state and another, and between private individuals claiming lands under different grants. Congress was given charge of the post office and the regulation of weights and measures. These were its "sole and exclusive" powers. In addition, it was given the authority to appoint a committee of the states to sit during the recesses of Congress and the power to control its own organization and sessions.

Eighteenth-century radicals looked upon the desire for office as a disease which fed upon office-holding. Hence they were careful to provide that Congress should never become an association of office-holders. No one could be a member of Congress for more than three out of any six years. No one could be president of Congress for more than one year out of any three; thus no individual would be likely to acquire much prestige as head of the central government. The delegates were subject to recall at any time by the state governments which had selected them, and hence were usually responsive to the will of their electorates as expressed in the state legislatures. This serves to explain why so many votes in Congress were often inconsistent with a given delegate's political and economic views.

The Articles of Confederation placed few restraints upon the states, and even these tended to be qualified out of existence. No state could receive or send embassies or enter into alliances or treaties without the consent of Congress. No two or more states could enter into a confederation without the consent of Congress. No state could levy imposts or duties which might interfere with stipulations in treaties made by Congress. No treaty made by Congress, on the other hand, could interfere with the right of a state to subject foreigners to the same imposts and duties as were levied on its own citizens. The states were not to keep vessels of war in peacetime unless Congress deemed it to be necessary for purposes of defense. Neither could a state maintain troops unless Congress considered them necessary to garrison forts. States were forbidden to declare war without the consent of Congress except where sudden invasion would permit of no delay. Letters of marque and reprisal were to be granted only after a declaration of war by Congress and under conditions laid down by it. None of these restraints was a serious check upon the sovereignty of the states.

Between the states there was complete equality. Every state was required to have at least two representatives in Congress, and it might have as many as seven, though each delegation was to have only one vote. When more than two delegates from a state were present, the state's vote was decided by the majority of the delegation. If the vote was a tie, the state had no vote. Citizens of any state were allowed to emigrate freely to another. Extradition of criminals was provided for. The Articles declared that each state should give full faith to the judicial proceedings of every other state. Except in these things the states were not responsible to one another. The union that had been created was a federal union of equal states in which the central organization was carefully subordinated to the members of it.

The Articles of Confederation were designed to prevent the central government from infringing upon the rights of the states, whereas the Constitution of 1787 was designed as a check upon the power of the states and the democracy that found expression within their bounds. The character of the Articles of Confederation was the result of two realities: the reality of the psychological and legal independence of the states, and the reality of the belief that democracy was possible only within fairly small political units whose electorate had a direct check upon the officers of government. Such a check was impossible where the central government was far removed from the control of the people by distance and by law. The independence of the states was a product of colonial history. The distrust of centralization, of government spread over a great area, was the product of both political theory and practical experience. The rise of radicalism had been checked often enough to teach the radicals that central governments, however democratic in form, were fundamentally undemocratic in action.

This government, the product of the forces which brought about the American Revolution, failed not because it was inadequate but because the radicals failed to maintain the organization they had created to bring about the American Revolution. The radical movement was essentially a movement of parties within states, and their political and social aims were to a great extent local. To achieve their purpose, local independence, unity of all the states had been necessary. What the radicals failed to see was that they must continue their union if they were to maintain their local independence under the Articles of Confederation. Thomas Burke of North Carolina expressed the radical view admirably. Congress, he said, was a general council instituted for the purpose of opposing the usurpations of Great Britain and of conducting a war against her, of forming necessary foreign alliances, directing the army and navy, and making binding treaties. Since this was the nature of Congress and its powers, it eliminated "all pretence for continuance of a Congress after the war is concluded, or of assuming a power to any other purposes."

Thus when the radicals had won their war, most of them were well content to go home and continue with the program of action they had started long before the war began. The thwarting of that program by the local conservatives and the British government had been one of the major causes of the Revolution. Needless to say, the motives of the radicals were not always the highest or the most disinterested, but their program was essentially democratic in tendency, for it widened the bases of political power and it declared that men should be bound only by those laws to which they had given their consent. Above all, when that program was idealized, as in the Declaration of Independence, it declared that the purpose of government was the protection of the life, liberty, and happiness of the individual, and when it did not fulfill this ideal it should be overthrown. Such a revolution was a practical possibility in a state unchecked by an outside and superior authority. Such an authority was rendered impossible by the Articles of Confederation.

What the radicals did not see was that the conservative elements in American society had learned a bitter lesson at the hands of the radicals. They too could call conventions. They too could paint dark pictures of the times and blame the supposed woes of the country on the Articles of Confederation, as the radicals had blamed the British government before 1776. They too could, and did, adopt the radical theory of the sovereignty of the people; in the name of the people they engineered a conservative counter-revolution and erected a nationalistic government whose purpose in part was to thwart the will of "the people" in whose name they acted. They too could use one name while pursuing a goal that was the opposite in fact. Thus, although the purpose of the conservatives was "nationalistic," they adopted the name "Federalist," for it served to disguise the extent of the changes they desired. True, the government they created had a good many "federal" features, but this was so because the conservatives were political realists and had to compromise with the political reality of actual state sovereignty.

What the conservatives in their turn failed to see was that the government they created might be captured by the radicals united on a national scale. Madison in *The Federalist* wrote that such a union was impossible, though he shortly helped to bring it about when faced with the workings of the government under the Constitution of 1787.

Wise old John Adams probably had the last word. Writing in 1808, he declared, "I have always called our Constitution a game at leapfrog."

APPENDIX

Progress of the Articles through Congress

ON JUNE 7, 1776, Richard Henry Lee moved that "a plan of confederation be prepared and transmitted to the respective Colonies for their consideration and approbation," as the second part of his motion that "these United Colonies are, and of right ought to be, free and independent States."[1] On June 12, 1776, a committee consisting of one member from each of the thirteen colonies was appointed to draw up a plan of confederation for the consideration of Congress.[2] The Committee leaned decidedly to the side of the conservatives, for three of its members, John Dickinson, Robert R. Livingston, and Edward Rutledge, were the outstanding opponents of a declaration of independence. Samuel Adams and Stephen Hopkins were the only prominent radicals appointed.

The outstanding man on the committee was John Dickinson. Presumably because of that prominence, and because of his fame as a penman, he was given the task of drafting articles of confederation,[3] and a draft in his handwriting was presented to Congress on July 12. Eighty copies of this draft were ordered printed under injunctions of strictest secrecy.[4]

On July 22 Congress resolved itself into a committee of the whole and proceeded to debate the Articles as submitted to them by the committee of thirteen. They were debated each day that Congress was in session from that date until August 2, and on August 6, 7, 8, and 20. Then a new draft was ordered printed,

[1] *Journals*, 5:425.

[2] *Ibid.*, 433. The committee consisted of Josiah Bartlett, New Hampshire; Sam Adams, Massachusetts; Stephen Hopkins, Rhode Island; Roger Sherman, Connecticut; Robert R. Livingston, New York; John Dickinson, Pennsylvania; Francis Hopkinson, New Jersey; Thomas McKean, Delaware; Thomas Stone, Maryland; Thomas Nelson, Virginia; Joseph Hewes, North Carolina; Edward Rutledge, South Carolina; and Button Gwinnet, Georgia. Francis Hopkinson did not become a member of the committee until June 28. See the *Journals*, 5:491.

[3] Edward Rutledge to John Jay, June 29, 1776, in Burnett, *Letters*, 1:517.

[4] *Journals*, 5:555.

embodying the elisions and amendments made by Congress during the course of the debates.[5]

After the first few days of debate the major issues were clearly defined and the lines of cleavage sharply, though variously, drawn. So bitter was the dispute that one delegate wrote that "what we shall make of it God only knows. I am inclined to think we shall never modell it so as to be agreed to by all the Colonies."[6] John Adams wrote Mrs. Adams that since she loved to pick a political bone, he would throw her one: "If a confederation should take place, one great question is, how we shall vote. Whether each colony shall count one? or whether each shall have a weight in proportion to its wealth, or number, or exports and imports, or a compound ratio of all? Another is, whether Congress shall have authority to limit the dimensions of each colony, to prevent those, which claim by charter, or proclamation, or commission, to the south sea, from growing too great and powerful, so as to be dangerous to the rest."[7] A third dispute was over the basis of apportioning taxation. The Dickinson draft proposed that it should be according to total population. The South was against the inclusion of slaves.[8]

Samuel Chase reported that the great difficulties were "Representation, the mode of voting, and the claims to the South Sea," the whole of which he thought might be settled "if candour, justice, and the real interests of America were attended to. We do not all see the importance, nay, the necessity, of a Confederacy." Chase, in common with other members from the middle states, felt that without a confederacy, "we shall remain weak, distracted, divided in our councils; our strength will decrease; we shall be open to all the arts of the insidious Court of Britain, and no foreign Court will attend to our applications for assistance before we are confederated. What contract will a foreign State make with us, when we cannot agree among ourselves?"[9] On the other hand,

[5] Charles Thomson, "History of the Confederation," p. 19, in Papers of the Continental Congress, No. 9. Thomson summarizes the action of Congress on the Articles in this short "History," which is really a record of the action of Congress on the Confederation rather than an analysis thereof. See also the *Journals*, 5:600, 603–604, 608, 609, 611, 612, 615, 621–622, 624, 624–625, 628, 635, 636, 639–640, 674, 689.

[6] Joseph Hewes to Samuel Johnston, July 28, in Burnett, *Letters*, 2:28.

[7] John Adams to Mrs. Adams, July 29, *ibid.*, 28–29.

[8] Thomas Jefferson, Notes on Debates, in *Writings*, 1:39–42; John Adams, Notes on Debates, in *Works*, 2:496–498.

[9] Samuel Chase to Richard Henry Lee, July 30, in Burnett, *Letters*, 2:32; Chase to Philip Schuyler, August 9, *ibid.*, 44.

men like Jefferson and John Adams, outstanding leaders of the revolution, were not so much interested in the problem of confederation, but seemed anxious to return home.[10]

About a week later another delegate wrote that slow progress was being made, "as every Inch of Ground is disputed, and very jarring Claims and Interests are to be adjusted among us, and then all to be agreed to by the sev[era]l Legislatures, so that between both, I almost Despair of seeing it accomplished."[11] The seriousness of the situation is indicated in a letter of Edward Rutledge to Robert R. Livingston saying that Congress had made "such a Devil of it already that the Colonies can never agree to it" and suggesting that a special Congress be appointed for the sole purpose of constructing a confederation.[12]

On August 20 the Articles as amended by the committee of the whole were ordered printed a second time.[13] The second printed draft was dropped from consideration, partly because some of the states were unrepresented, and partly because of the tremendous demands that the conduct of the war made upon every member of Congress.[14] Still another reason was that a good many delegates were simply not interested in a confederation, now that the revolution was going on. Not until April 8, 1777, was it agreed by Congress to take up the problem of Confederation again. At that time it was decided to spend two days a week on it until it was completed.[15] It was debated from time to time from then until June 26, interruptions occurring as a result of the bitter Vermont controversy and the Schuyler controversy. Various motions were

[10] Thomas Jefferson to Richard Henry Lee, July 29, in Burnett, *Letters*, 2:28.

[11] William Williams to Joseph Trumbull, August 7, *ibid.*, 41.

[12] [August 19 (?), 1776] *ibid.*, 56. This suggestion of a convention, according to Burnett, is one of the earliest. See *ibid.*, p. 56, note 8. Jefferson had the idea some months previously. See his *Writings*, 2:7–9.

[13] *Journals*, 5:674, 689.

[14] Edward Rutledge to Robert R. Livingston, October 2, in Burnett, *Letters*, 2:113. The burdens of the war imposed on the members of Congress were a constant factor in the delay. In discussions of the Congress these added responsibilities are often overlooked. Another factor was the changing personnel of Congress. John Adams wrote to James Warren in February, 1777, that few of the faces he had seen in the first Congress were present. He named only Sam Adams, Roger Sherman, Richard Henry Lee, Samuel Chase, and William Paca. "The rest are dead, resigned, deserted or cutt up into Governors, etc. at home." *Warren-Adams Letters*, 1:293.

[15] *Journals*, 7:240; James Sykes to George Read, April 10, 1777, in Burnett, *Letters*, 2:323.

made for its consideration, but nothing seems to have been done.[16]
By the middle of August "almost every member of Congress is
anxious for a Confederacy, being sensible, that a Confederacy
formed on a rational plan will certainly add much weight and
consequence to the united States collectively and give great Security to each individually, and a credit also to our paper money." [17]
On the other hand, the business went but slowly, "occasioned by
the immensity of the business created by the war." [18]

By September it had been reported that "Confederation and
financies [sic] are now the great objects but ten thousand necessaries are dayly Crouding in," all being agreed on the end, however, and differing only as to the proportion of representation and
taxation.[19] On October 7 Congress took up seriously the task of
completing the Confederation, spurred on by the belief of many
"that the very Salvation of these States depend upon it; and that
none of the European powers will publicly acknowledge them
free and independent, until they are confederated." [20] Another
spur to action was the steady rise in prices and the depreciation
of currency; the states being unable to enforce price-fixing measures, and the Congress having "no practicable way to remedy the
great and growing [evil] but a firm Union to establish the Credit
of the [currency] which the Tribe of Speculators and other [gen-
try] begin to pick Flaws in." [21]

On the other hand, men of strongly democratic views, like
Thomas Burke of North Carolina, considered the plan unsuited
for the states and declared that a time of peace and tranquillity was
the time for deciding upon so important a matter.[22] Disputed
issues were settled rapidly and at last, on November 13, Cornelius
Harnett was able to write to Burke that "the child Congress has

---

[16] *Journals*, 7:287, 300, 328, 351; 8:490, 492, 497, 501, 525, 648; Introduction
in Burnett, *Letters*, 1:xviii–xix; Sam Adams to Richard Henry Lee, June 26,
1777, in *Writings*, 3:378.

[17] Charles Carroll to Benjamin Franklin, Douhoregan Ann Arundel County
[Md.], August 12, 1777, in Burnett, *Letters*, 2:450–451.

[18] Richard Henry Lee to Thomas Jefferson, August 25, 1777, in Lee, *Letters*,
1:319–320.

[19] Eliphalet Dyer to Joseph Trumbull, September 7, 1777, in Burnett, *Letters*, 2:485.

[20] Cornelius Harnett to Gov. Richard Caswell, Yorktown, Pa., October
10, 1777, *ibid.*, 514; *Journals*, 8:704.

[21] William Williams to Jabez Huntington, York, October 22, 1777, in Burnett, *Letters*, 2:529. For action of Congress see the *Journals*, 8:760.

[22] Thomas Burke to Gov. Richard Caswell, Tyaguin, November 4, 1777, in
Burnett, *Letters*, 2:542.

been big with, these two years past, is at last brought forth . . .
I fear it will by several Legislatures be thought a little deformed, —
you will think it a Monster." [23]

A committee was appointed to suggest further amendments to
the Articles.[24] Several amendments were submitted and some of
them were adopted. Then another committee was appointed to
arrange the Articles in their final form. Three hundred copies
were ordered printed.[25] On November 17 the Articles of Confederation in their final form were sent to the states for their action,
with the request that powers of ratification be given to each state
delegation by the tenth of March, 1778.[26]

[23] Cornelius Harnett to Thomas Burke, York, November 13, 1777, in Burnett, *Letters*, 2:547–548; also Pennsylvania Delegates to the President of Pennsylvania, *ibid.*, 550.
[24] *Journals*, 9:885. Richard Law, Richard Henry Lee, and James Duane were
the committee.
[25] *Ibid.*, 887–890, 893–896, 899, 900, 907, 928.
[26] *Ibid.*, 932–935.

The Dickinson Draft of the Confederation[*]

ARTICLES OF CONFEDERATION AND PERPETUAL UNION, BETWEEN
THE COLONIES OF NEW HAMPSHIRE, MASSACHUSETTS BAY, RHODE
ISLAND, CONNECTICUT, NEW YORK, NEW JERSEY, PENNSYLVANIA,
THE COUNTIES OF NEW CASTLE, KENT AND SUSSEX ON DELAWARE,
MARYLAND, VIRGINIA, NORTH CAROLINA,
SOUTH CAROLINA, AND GEORGIA.

ART. I. THE Name of this Confederacy shall be "THE
UNITED STATES OF AMERICA."

ART. II. The said Colonies unite themselves so as never to be
divided by any Act whatever, and hereby severally enter into a
firm League of Friendship with each other, for their common
Defence, the Security of their Liberties, and their mutual and
general Welfare, binding the said Colonies to assist one another
against all Force offered to or attacks made upon them or any of
them, on Account of Religion, Sovereignty, Trade, or any other
Pretence whatever.

ART. III. Each Colony shall retain and enjoy as much of its
present Laws, Rights and Customs, as it may think fit, and reserves
to itself the sole and exclusive Regulation and Government of its
internal police, in all matters that shall not interfere with the
Articles of this Confederation.[1]

---

[*] This copy of the Dickinson draft is taken from the *Journals*, 5:546–554,
July 12, 1776. The editor of the *Journals* says (p. 546, note 1), "I have sought
to give in this place the Articles as they were prepared by Dickinson, with
the few changes he made while writing them, and with the queries which he
noted on the margin." In reprinting the Dickinson draft here, the stylistic
changes indicated in the *Journals* have not been reproduced. Two significant
deletions, however, have been placed in brackets.

[1] "Q. Should not the first Article provide for a Toleration and ag^t. Es-
tablishments hereafter to be made?" J. D.

"Quaere. The Propriety of the Union's garranteeing to every colony their
respective Constitution and form of Government?" J. D.

ART. IV. No Colony or Colonies, without the Consent of the United States assembled, shall send any Embassy to or receive any Embassy from, or enter into any Treaty, Convention or Conference with the King or Kingdom of Great-Britain, or any foreign Prince or State; nor shall any Colony or Colonies, nor any Servant or Servants of the United States, or of any Colony or Colonies, accept of any Present, Emolument, Office, or Title of any Kind whatever, from the King or Kingdom of Great-Britain, or any foreign Prince or State; nor shall the United States assembled, or any Colony grant any Title of Nobility.

ART. V. No two or more Colonies shall enter into any Treaty, Confederation or Alliance whatever between them, without the previous and free Consent and Allowance of the United States assembled, specifying accurately the Purposes for which the same is to be entered into, and how long it shall continue.

ART. VI. The Inhabitants of each Colony shall henceforth always have the same Rights, Liberties, Privileges, Immunities and Advantages, in the other Colonies, which the said Inhabitants now have, in all Cases whatever, except in those provided for by the next following Article.

ART. VII. The Inhabitants of each Colony shall enjoy all the Rights, Liberties, Privileges, Immunities, and Advantages, in Trade, Navigation, and Commerce, in any other Colony, and in going to and from the same from and to any Part of the World, which the Natives of such Colony [or any Commercial Society, established by its Authority shall] enjoy.

ART. VIII. Each Colony may assess or lay such Imposts or Duties as it thinks proper, on Importations or Exportations, provided such Imposts or Duties do not interfere with any Stipulations in Treaties hereafter entered into by the United States assembled, with the King or Kingdom of Great Britain, or any foreign Prince or State.

ART. IX. No standing Army or Body of Forces shall be kept up by any Colony or Colonies in Times of Peace, except such a Number only as may be requisite to garrison the Forts necessary for the Defence of such Colony or Colonies: But every Colony shall always keep up a well regulated and disciplined Militia, sufficiently armed and accoutred; and shall provide and constantly have ready for Use in public Stores, a due Number of Field Pieces and Tents, and a proper Quantity of Ammunition, and Camp Equipage.[1]

ART. X. When Troops are raised in any of the Colonies for the common Defence, the Commission Officers proper for the Troops raised in each Colony, except the General Officers, shall be appointed by the Legislature of each Colony respectively, or in such manner as shall by them be directed.

ART. XI. All Charges of Wars and all other Expences that shall be incurred for the common Defence, or general Welfare, and allowed by the United States assembled, shall be defrayed out of a common Treasury, which shall be supplied by the several Colonies in Proportion to the Number of Inhabitants of every Age, Sex and Quality, except Indians not paying Taxes, in each Colony, a true Account of which, distinguishing the white [2] Inhabitants, shall be triennially taken and transmitted to the Assembly of the United States. The Taxes for paying that Proportion shall be laid and levied by the Authority and Direction of the Legislatures of the several Colonies, within the Time agreed upon by United States assembled.[3]

ART. XII. Every Colony shall abide by the Determinations of the United States assembled, concerning the Services performed and Losses or Expences incurred by every Colony for the common Defence or general Welfare, and no Colony or Colonies shall in any Case whatever endeavor by Force to procure Redress of any Injury or Injustice supposed to be done by the United States to such Colony or Colonies in not granting such Satisfactions, Indemnifications, Compensations, Retributions, Exemptions, or Benefits of any Kind, as such Colony or Colonies may think just or reasonable.

ART. XIII. No Colony or Colonies shall engage in any War without the previous Consent of the United States assembled, unless such Colony or Colonies be actually invaded by Enemies, or shall have received certain Advice of a Resolution being formed by some Nations of Indians to invade such Colony or Colonies, and the Danger is so imminent, as not to admit of a Delay, till the other Colonies can be consulted: Nor shall any Colony or Col-

---

[1] "Q. Should not this Article specify the Particulars, as to Age, Arms, Field pieces, &c." J. D.

[2] This word was inserted on striking out "who are not slaves."

[3] "Q. If no Notice should be taken of the Bills already emitted, and if there should not be a Contract to contribute in due Proportion towards sinking them?" J. D.

onies grant Commissions to any Ships or Vessels of War, nor Letters of Marque or Reprisal, except it be after a Declaration of War by the United States assembled, and then only against the Kingdom or State and the Subjects thereof, against which War has been so declared, and under such Regulations as shall be established by the United States assembled.[1]

ART. XIV. A perpetual Alliance, offensive and defensive, is to be entered into by the United States assembled as soon as may be, with the Six Nations, and all other neighbouring Nations of Indians; their Limits to be ascertained, their Lands to be secured to them, and not encroached on;[2] no Purchases of Lands, hereafter to be made of the Indians by Colonies or private Persons before the Limits of the Colonies are ascertained, to be valid: All Purchases of Lands not included within those Limits, where ascertained, to be made by Contracts between the United States assembled, or by Persons for that Purpose authorized by them, and the great Councils of the Indians, for the general Benefit of all the United Colonies.[3]

ART. XV. When the Boundaries of any Colony shall be ascertained by Agreement, or in the Manner herein after directed, all the other Colonies shall guarantee to such Colony the full and peaceable Possession of, and the free and entire Jurisdiction in and over the Territory included within such Boundaries.[4]

ART. XVI. For the more convenient Management of the general Interests of the United States, Delegates should be annually appointed in such Manner as the Legislature of each Colony shall direct [or such Branche thereof as the Colony shall authorize for that purpose], to meet at the City of Philadelphia, in the Colony of Pennsylvania, until otherwise ordered by the United States assembled; which Meeting shall be on the first Monday of November in every Year, with a Power reserved to those who appointed the said Delegates, respectively to recal them or any of them at any time within the Year, and to send new Delegates in their stead for

[1] "Q. How far the Expence of any War is to be defrayed by the Union?" J. D.

[2] "Q. How far a Colony may interfere in Indian Affairs?" J. D. To this point this paragraph was omitted in the printed version.

[3] "This Article is submitted to Congress." J. D.

[4] "This Article is submitted to Congress.

"Q. Should there not be an Article to prevent those who are hereafter brought into these Colonies, from being held in Slavery within the Colonies?" J. D.

the Remainder of the Year. Each Colony shall support its own Delegates in a Meeting of the States, and while they act as Members of the Council of State, herein after mentioned.[1]

ART. XVII. In determining Questions each Colony shall have one Vote.

ART. XVIII.[2] The United States assembled shall have the sole and exclusive Right and Power of determining on Peace and War, except in the Cases mentioned in the thirteenth Article – Of establishing Rules for deciding in all Cases, what Captures on Land or Water shall be legal – In what Manner Prizes taken by land or naval Forces in the Service of the United States shall be divided or appropriated – Granting Letters of Marque and Reprisal in Times of Peace – Appointing Courts for the Trial of all Crimes, Frauds and Piracies committed on the High Seas, or on any navigable River, not within the Body of a County or Parish – Establishing Courts for receiving and determining finally Appeals in all Cases of Captures – Sending and receiving Ambassadors under any Character – Entering into Treaties and Alliances – Settling all Disputes and Differences now subsisting, or that hereafter may arise between two or more Colonies concerning Boundaries, Jurisdictions, or any other Cause whatever – Coining Money and regulating the Value thereof – Regulating the Trade, and managing all Affairs with the Indians – Limiting the Bounds of those Colonies, which by Charter or Proclamation, or under any Pretence, are said to extend to the South Sea, and ascertaining those Bounds of any other Colony that appear to be indeterminate – Assigning Territories for new Colonies, either in Lands to be thus separated from Colonies and heretofore purchased or obtained by the Crown of Great-Britain from the Indians, or hereafter to be purchased or obtained from them – Disposing of all such Lands for

---

[1] "Q. If there should not be an Oath or Affirmation prescrib'd for every Delegate to take? See 31st. Vol. of Mod. Univ'l Hist.

"Q. If a Delegate should be permitted to vote by Proxy or by Writing, when absent by Reason of Sickness, &c.?" J. D.

[2] "Q. How the power is to be describ'd, if any is to be given to the United States assembled, of erecting Forts and keeping Garrisons, *in any Colony*, for the genl. Defence? Should it be done, if the Colony objects?

"Q. The power of arresting and trying persons in the Service of the United States, *in any Colony*, without applying to the Government *of such Colony?* A Dispute on this Head occasioned great Confusion in Holland.

"Q. The power of laying Embargos?" J. D.

the general Benefit of all the United Colonies — Ascertaining Boundaries to such new Colonies, within which Forms of Government are to be established on the Principles of Liberty [1] — Establishing and regulating Post-Offices throughout all the United Colonies, on the Lines of Communication from one Colony to another — Appointing General Officers of the Land Forces in the Service of the United States — Commissioning such other Officers of the said Forces as shall be appointed by Virtue of the tenth Article — Appointing all the Officers of the Naval Forces in the Service of the United States — Making Rules for the Government and Regulation of the Said Land and Naval Forces, and directing the operations — Appointing a Council of State, and such Committees and civil Officers as may be necessary for managing the general Affairs of the United States, under their Direction while assembled, and in their Recess, of the Council of State — Appointing one of their number to preside, and a suitable Person for Secretary — And adjourning to any Time within the Year.

The United States assembled shall have Authority for the Defence and Welfare of the United Colonies and every of them, to agree upon and fix the necessary Sums and Expences — To emit Bills, or to borrow Money on the Credit of the United Colonies — To raise Naval Forces — To agree upon the Number of Land Forces to be raised, and to make Requisitions from the Legislature of each Colony, or the Persons therein authorized by the Legislature to execute such Requisitions, for the Quota of each Colony, which is to be in Proportion to the Number of white Inhabitants in that Colony, which Requisitions shall be binding, and thereupon the Legislature of each Colony or the Persons authorized as aforesaid, shall appoint the Regimental Officers, raise the Men, and arm and equip them in a soldier-like Manner; and the Officers and Men so armed and equipped, shall march to the Place appointed, and within the Time agreed on by the United States assembled.

But if the United States assembled shall on Consideration of Circumstances judge proper, that any Colony or Colonies should not raise Men, or should raise a smaller Number than the Quota or Quotas of such Colony or Colonies, and that any other Colony or Colonies should raise a greater number of men than the Quota or

[1] "These clauses [from Limiting the Bounds, &c.] are submitted to Congress." J. D.

Quotas thereof, such extra-numbers shall be raised, officered, armed and equipped in the same Manner as the Quota or Quotas of such Colony or Colonies, unless the Legislature of such Colony or Colonies respectively, shall judge, that such extra-numbers cannot be safely spared out of the same, in which Case they shall raise, officer, arm and equip as many of such extra-numbers as they judge can be safely spared; and the Officers and Men so armed and equip[p]ed shall march to the Place appointed, and within the Time agreed on by the United States assembled.

To establish the same Weights and Measures throughout the United Colonies.

But the United States assembled shall never impose or levy any Taxes or Duties, except in managing the Post-Office, nor interfere in the internal Police of any Colony, any further than such Police may be affected by the Articles of this Confederation. The United States assembled shall never engage the United Colonies in a War, nor grant Letters of Marque and Reprisal in Time of Peace, nor enter into Treaties or Alliances, nor coin Money nor regulate the Value thereof, nor agree upon nor fix the Sums and Expences necessary for the Defence and Welfare of the United Colonies, or any of them, nor emit Bills, nor borrow Money on the Credit of the United Colonies, nor raise Naval Forces, nor agree upon the Number of Land Forces to be raised, unless the Delegates of nine Colonies freely assent to the same: [1] Nor shall a Question on any other Point, except for adjourning, be determined, unless the Delegates of seven Colonies vote in the affirmative.

No Person shall be capable of being a Delegate for more than three Years in any Term of six Years.

No Person holding any Office under the United States, for which he, or another for his Benefit, receives any Salary, Fees, or Emolument of any Kind, shall be capable of being a Delegate.

The Assembly of the United States to publish the Journal of their Proceedings monthly, except such Parts thereof relating to Treaties, Alliances, or military Operations, as in their Judgment require Secrecy – The Yeas and Nays of the Delegates of each Colony on any Question to be entered on the Journal, where it is desired by any Delegate; and the Delegates of a Colony, or any of them, at his or their Request, to be furnished with a Transcript

[1] "Q. If so large a Majority is necessary in concluding a Treaty of Peace?" J. D.

of the said Journal, except such Parts as are above excepted, to lay before the Legislatures of the several Colonies.[1]

ART. XIX. The Council of State shall consist of one Delegate from each C[o]lony, to be named annually by the Delegates of each Colony, and where they cannot agree, by the United States assembled.[2]

This Council shall have Power to receive and open all Letters directed to the United States, and to return proper Answers; but not to make any Engagements that shall be binding on the United States — To correspond with the Legislature of each Colony, and all Persons acting under the Authority of the United States, or of the said Legislatures — To apply to such Legislatures, or to the Officers in the several Colonies who are entrusted with the executive Powers of Government, for occasional Aid whenever and wherever necessary — To give Counsel to the Commanding Officers, and to direct military Operations by Sea and Land, not changing any Objects or Expeditions determined on by the United States assembled, unless an Alteration of Circumstances which shall come to the Knowledge of the Council after the Recess of the States, shall make such Change absolutely necessary — To attend to the Defence and Preservation of Forts and strong Posts, and to prevent the Enemy from acquiring new Holds — To procure Intelligence of the Condition and Designs of the Enemy — To expedite the Execution of such Measures as may be resolved on by the United States assembled, in Pursuance of the Powers hereby given to them — To draw upon the Treasurers for such Sums as may be appropriated by the United States assembled, and for the Payment of such Contracts as the said Council may make in Pursuance of the Powers hereby given to them — To superintend and controul or suspend all Officers civil and military, acting under the Authority of the United States — In Case of the Death or Removal of any Officer within the Appointment of the United States assembled, to employ a Person to fulfill the Duties of such Office until the Assembly of the States meet — To publish

[1] "Q. Whether the proceedings of the Assembly of the States should not be published weekly, except such Matters as relate to Alliances, military Operations, &c, which require Secrecy? If this is not proper, yet, should not every Delegate have a Right to enter his Protest, and assign his Reasons, and even publish them, if he thinks fit?" J. D.

[2] "Q. The Oath of a Councillor?" J. D.

and disperse authentic Accounts of military Operations — To summon an Assembly of the States at an earlier Day than that appointed for their next Meeting, if any great and unexpected Emergency should render it necessary for the Safety or Welfare of the United Colonies or any of them — To prepare Matters for the Consideration of the United States, and to lay before them at their next Meeting all Letters and Advices received by the Council, with a Report of their Proceedings — To appoint a proper Person for their Clerk, who shall take an Oath of Secrecy and Fidelity, before he enters on the Exercise of his Office — Seven Members shall have Power to act — In Case of the Death of any Member, the Council shall immediately apply to his surviving Colleagues to appoint some one of themselves to be a Member thereof till the Meeting of the States, and if only one survives, they shall give him [1] immediate Notice, that he may take his Seat as a Councilor till such Meeting.[2]

ART. XX. Canada acceding to this Confederation, and entirely joining in the measures of the United Colonies, shall be admitted into and entitled to all the Advantages of this Union: But no other Colony shall be admitted into the same, unless such Admission be agreed to by the Delegates of nine Colonies.

These Articles shall be proposed to the Legislatures of all the United Colonies, to be by them considered, and if approved by them, they are advised to authorize their Delegates to ratify the same in the Assembly of the United States, which being done, the Articles of this Confederation shall inviolably be observed by every Colony, and the Union is to be perpetual: Nor shall any Alteration be at any Time hereafter made in these Articles or any of them, unless such Alteration be agreed to in an Assembly of the United States, and be afterwards confirmed by the Legislatures of every Colony.[3]

---

[1] This word omitted in the printed version.

[2] "Q. If the Secretary of the Congress should not be Secretary to the Council of States to prevent unnecessary Expence and the Discovery of Secrets — It would also promote the Despatch of Business." J. D.

[3] "Q. If there should not be a solemn Oath taken by every Colony, or its Delegates, authorized for that Purpose, by the respective Legislatures, to observe and abide by all and similar the Articles of this Confederation?" J. D.

The Articles of Confederation and Perpetual Union

BETWEEN THE STATES OF NEW HAMPSHIRE, MASSACHUSETTS BAY, RHODE ISLAND AND PROVIDENCE PLANTATIONS, CONNECTICUT, NEW YORK, NEW JERSEY, PENNSYLVANIA, DELAWARE, MARYLAND, VIRGINIA, NORTH CAROLINA, SOUTH CAROLINA, GEORGIA.*

ARTICLE 1. The stile of this confederacy shall be "The United States of America."

ART. 2. Each State retains its sovereignty, freedom and independence, and every power, jurisdiction, and right, which is not by this confederation expressly delegated to the United States, in Congress assembled.

ART. 3. The said states hereby severally enter into a firm league of friendship with each other for their common defence, the security of their liberties and their mutual and general welfare; binding themselves to assist each other against all force offered to, or attacks made upon them, or any of them, on account of religion, sovereignty, trade, or any other pretence whatever.

ART. 4. The better to secure and perpetuate mutual friendship and intercourse among the people of the different states in this union, the free inhabitants of each of these states, paupers, vagabonds, and fugitives from justice excepted, shall be entitled to all privileges and immunities of free citizens in the several states; and the people of each State shall have free ingress and regress to and from any other State, and shall enjoy therein all the privileges of trade and commerce, subject to the same duties, impositions, and restrictions, as the inhabitants thereof respectively; provided, that such restrictions shall not extend so far as to prevent the removal of property, imported into any State, to any other State of which the owner is an inhabitant; provided also, that no imposition,

* This copy of the final draft of the Articles of Confederation is taken from the *Journals*, 9:907–925, November 15, 1777.

duties, or restriction, shall be laid by any State on the property of the United States, or either of them.

If any person guilty of, or charged with treason, felony, or other high misdemeanor in any State, shall flee from justice and be found in any of the United States, he shall, upon demand of the governor or executive power of the State from which he fled, be delivered up and removed to the State having jurisdiction of his offence.

Full faith and credit shall be given in each of these states to the records, acts, and judicial proceedings of the courts and magistrates of every other State.

ART. 5. For the more convenient management of the general interests of the United States, delegates shall be annually appointed, in such manner as the legislature of each State shall direct, to meet in Congress, on the 1st Monday in November in every year, with a power reserved to each State to recal its delegates, or any of them, at any time within the year, and to send others in their stead for the remainder of the year.

No State shall be represented in Congress by less than two, nor by more than seven members; and no person shall be capable of being a delegate for more than three years in any term of six years; nor shall any person, being a delegate, be capable of holding any office under the United States, for which he, or any other for his benefit, receives any salary, fees, or emolument of any kind.

Each State shall maintain its own delegates in a meeting of the states, and while they act as members of the committee of the states.

In determining questions in the United States, in Congress assembled, each State shall have one vote.

Freedom of speech and debate in Congress shall not be impeached or questioned in any court or place out of Congress: and the members of Congress shall be protected in their persons from arrests and imprisonments, during the time of their going to and from, and attendance on Congress, *except for treason*, felony, or breach of the peace.

ART. 6. No State, without the consent of the United States, in Congress assembled, shall send any embassay to, or receive any embassy from, or enter into any conference, agreement, alliance, or treaty with any king, prince, or state; nor shall any person, holding any office of profit or trust under the United States, or any of them, accept of any present, emolument, office or title, of any kind whatever, from any king, prince, or foreign state; nor shall the United States, in Congress assembled, or any of them, grant any title of nobility.

No two or more states shall enter into any treaty, confederation, or alliance, whatever, between them, without the consent of the United States, in Congress assembled, specifying accurately the purposes for which the same is to be entered into, and how long it shall continue.

No state shall lay any imposts or duties which may interfere with any stipulations in treaties entered into by the United States, in Congress assembled, with any king, prince, or state, in pursuance of any treaties already proposed by Congress to the courts of France and Spain.

No vessels of war shall be kept up in time of peace by any State, except such number only as shall be deemed necessary by the United States, in Congress assembled, for the defence of such State or its trade; nor shall any body of forces be kept up by any State, in time of peace, except such number only as, in the judgment of the United States, in Congress assembled, shall be deemed requisite to garrison the forts necessary for the defence of such State; but every State shall always keep up a well regulated and disciplined militia, sufficiently armed and accoutred, and shall provide, and constantly have ready for use, in public stores, a due number of field pieces and tents, and a proper quantity of arms, ammunition and camp equipage.

No State shall engage in any war without the consent of the United States, in Congress assembled, unless such State be actually invaded by enemies, or shall have received certain advice of a resolution being formed by some nation of Indians to invade such State, and the danger is so imminent as not to admit of a delay till the United States, in Congress assembled, can be consulted; nor shall any State grant commissions to any ships or vessels of war, nor letters of marque or reprisal, except it be after a declaration of war by the United States, in Congress assembled, and then only against the kingdom or state, and the subjects thereof, against which war has been so declared, and under such regulations as shall be established by the United States, in Congress assembled, unless such State be infested by pirates, in which case vessels of war may be fitted out for that occasion, and kept so long as the danger shall continue, or until the United States, in Congress assembled, shall determine otherwise.

ART. 7. When land forces are raised by any State for the common defence, all officers of or under the rank of colonel, shall be appointed by the legislature of each State respectively, by whom such forces shall be raised, or in such manner as such State shall direct; and all vacancies shall be filled up by the State which first made the appointment.

ART. 8. All charges of war and all other expences, that shall be incurred for the common defence or general welfare, and allowed by the United States, in Congress assembled, shall be defrayed out of a common treasury, which shall be supplied by the several states, in proportion to the value of all land within each State, granted to or surveyed for any person, as such land and the buildings and improvements thereon shall be estimated according to such mode as the United States, in Congress assembled, shall, from time to time, direct and appoint.

The taxes for paying that proportion shall be laid and levied by the authority and direction of the legislatures of the several states, within the time agreed upon by the United States, in Congress assembled.

ART. 9. The United States, in Congress assembled, shall have the sole and exclusive right and power of determining on peace and war, except in the cases mentioned in the 6th article; of sending and receiving ambassadors; entering into treaties and alliances, provided that no treaty of commerce shall be made, whereby the legislative power of the respective states shall be restrained from imposing such imposts and duties on foreigners as their own people are subjected to, or from prohibiting the exportation or importation of any species of goods or commodities whatsoever; of establishing rules for deciding, in all cases, what captures on land or water shall be legal, and in what manner prizes, taken by land or naval forces in the service of the United States, shall be divided or appropriated; of granting letters of marque and reprisal in times of peace; appointing courts for the trial of piracies and felonies committed on the high seas, and establishing courts for receiving and determining, finally, appeals in all cases of captures; provided, that no member of Congress shall be appointed a judge of any of the said courts.

The United States, in Congress assembled, shall also be the last resort on appeal in all disputes and differences now subsisting, or that hereafter may arise between two or more states concerning boundary, jurisdiction or any other cause whatever; which authority shall always be exercised in the manner following: whenever the legislative or executive authority, or lawful agent of any

State, in controversy with another, shall present a petition to Congress, stating the matter in question, and praying for a hearing, notice thereof shall be given, by order of Congress, to the legislative or executive authority of the other State in controversy, and a day assigned for the appearance of the parties by their lawful agents, who shall then be directed to appoint, by joint consent, commissioners or judges to constitute a court for hearing and determining the matter in question; but, if they cannot agree, Congress shall name three persons out of each of the United States, and from the list of such persons each party shall alternately strike out one, the petitioners beginning, until the number shall be reduced to thirteen; and from that number not less than seven, nor more than nine names, as Congress shall direct, shall, in the presence of Congress, be drawn out by lot; and the persons whose names shall be so drawn, or any five of them, shall be commissioners or judges to hear and finally determine the controversy, so always as a major part of the judges who shall hear the cause shall agree in the determination; and if either party shall neglect to attend at the day appointed, without shewing reasons which Congress shall judge sufficient, or, being present, shall refuse to strike, the Congress shall proceed to nominate three persons out of each State, and the secretary of Congress shall strike in behalf of such party absent or refusing; and the judgment and sentence of the court to be appointed, in the manner before prescribed, shall be final and conclusive; and if any of the parties shall refuse to submit to the authority of such court, or to appear or defend their claim or cause, the court shall nevertheless proceed to pronounce sentence or judgment, which shall, in like manner, be final and decisive, the judgment or sentence and other proceedings being, in either case, transmitted to Congress, and lodged among the acts of Congress for the security of the parties concerned: provided, that every commissioner, before he sits in judgment, shall take an oath, to be administered by one of the judges of the supreme or superior court of the State where the cause shall be tried, "well and truly to hear and determine the matter in question, according to the best of his judgment, without favour, affection, or hope of reward:" provided, also, that no State shall be deprived of territory for the benefit of the United States.

All controversies concerning the private right of soil, claimed under different grants of two or more states, whose jurisdictions, as they may respect such lands and the states which passed such grants, are adjusted, the said grants, or either of them, being at the same time claimed to have originated antecedent to such settlement of jurisdiction, shall, on the petition of either party to the Congress of the United States, be finally determined, as near as may be, in the same manner as is before prescribed for deciding disputes respecting territorial jurisdiction between different states.

The United States, in Congress assembled, shall also have the sole and exclusive right and power of regulating the alloy and value of coin struck by their own authority, or by that of the respective states; fixing the standard of weights and measures throughout the United States; regulating the trade and managing all affairs with the Indians not members of any of the states; provided that the legislative right of any State within its own limits be not infringed or violated; establishing and regulating post offices from one State to another throughout all the United States, and exacting such postage on the papers passing through the same as may be requisite to defray the expences of the said office; appointing all officers of the land forces in the service of the United States, excepting regimental officers; appointing all the officers of the naval forces, and commissioning all officers whatever in the service of the United States; making rules for the government and regulation of the said land and naval forces, and directing their operations.

The United States, in Congress assembled, shall have authority to appoint a committee to sit in the recess of Congress, to be denominated "a Committee of the States," and to consist of one delegate from each State, and to appoint such other committees and civil officers as may be necessary for managing the general affairs of the United States, under their direction; to appoint one of their number to preside; provided that no person be allowed to serve in the office of president more than one year in any term of three years; to ascertain the necessary sums of money to be raised for the service of the United States, and to appropriate and apply the same for defraying the public expences; to borrow money or emit bills on the credit of the United States, transmitting, every half year, to the respective states, an account of the sums of money so borrowed or emitted; to build and equip a navy; to agree upon the number of land forces, and to make requisitions from each State for its quota, in proportion to the number of white inhabitants in such State; which requisitions shall be binding; and, thereupon, the legislature of each State shall appoint the regimental officers, raise the men, and cloathe, arm, and equip them in a soldier-like manner, at the expence of the United States;

and the officers and men so cloathed, armed, and equipped, shall march to the place appointed and within the time agreed on by the United States, in Congress assembled; but if the United States, in Congress assembled, shall, on consideration of circumstances, judge proper that any State should not raise men, or should raise a smaller number than its quota, and that any other State should raise a greater number of men than the quota thereof, such extra number shall be raised, officered, cloathed, armed, and equipped in the same manner as the quota of such State, unless the legislature of such State shall judge that such extra number cannot be safely spared out of the same, in which case they shall raise, officer, cloathe, arm, and equip as many of such extra number as they judge can be safely spared. And the officers and men so cloathed, armed, and equipped, shall march to the place appointed and within the time agreed on by the United States, in Congress assembled.

The United States, in Congress assembled, shall never engage in a war, nor grant letters of marque and reprisal in time of peace, nor enter into any treaties or alliances, nor coin money, nor regulate the value thereof, nor ascertain the sums and expences necessary for the defence and welfare of the United States, or any of them: nor emit bills, nor borrow money on the credit of the United States, nor appropriate money, nor agree upon the number of vessels of war to be built or purchased, or the number of land or sea forces to be raised, nor appoint a commander in chief of the army or navy, unless nine states assent to the same; nor shall a question on any other point, except for adjourning from day to day, be determined, unless by the votes of a majority of the United States, in Congress assembled.

The Congress of the United States shall have power to adjourn to any time within the year, and to any place within the United States, so that no period of adjournment be for a longer duration than the space of six months, and shall publish the journal of their proceedings monthly, except such parts thereof, relating to treaties, alliances or military operations, as, in their judgment, require secrecy; and the yeas and nays of the delegates of each State on any question shall be entered on the journal, when it is desired by any delegate; and the delegates of a State, or any of them, at his, or their request, shall be furnished with a transcript of the said journal, except such parts as are above excepted, to lay before the legislatures of the several states.

ART. 10. The committee of the states, or any nine of them, shall be authorized to execute, in the recess of Congress, such of the powers of Congress as the United States, in Congress assembled, by the consent of nine states, shall, from time to time, think expedient to vest them with; provided, that no power be delegated to the said committee, for the exercise of which, by the articles of confederation, the voice of nine states, in the Congress of the United States assembled, is requisite.

ART. 11. Canada acceding to this confederation, and joining in the measures of the United States, shall be admitted into and entitled to all the advantages of this union; but no other colony shall be admitted into the same, unless such admission be agreed to by nine states.

ART. 12. All bills of credit emitted, monies borrowed and debts contracted by, or under the authority of Congress before the assembling of the United States, in pursuance of the present confederation, shall be deemed and considered as a charge against the United States, for payment and satisfaction whereof the said United States and the public faith are hereby solemnly pledged.

ART. 13. Every State shall abide by the determinations of the United States, in Congress assembled, on all questions which, by this confederation, are submitted to them. And the articles of this confederation shall be inviolably observed by every State, and the union shall be perpetual; nor shall any alteration at any time hereafter be made in any of them, unless such alteration be agreed to in a Congress of the United States, and be afterwards confirmed by the legislatures of every State.

These articles shall be proposed to the legislatures of all the United States, to be considered, and if approved of by them, they are advised to authorize their delegates to ratify the same in the Congress of the United States; which being done, the same shall become conclusive.

INDEX

Index

Reference to works cited in the footnotes is to the page on which complete bibliographical information appears. Entry is made under author or editor except in the case of anonymous works, which are entered under title. Personal names appearing as author or editor entries are distinguished by the use of small capitals.